Praise for *Love, Loss and Lifelines*

"Self-effacing and revelatory, *Love* ▮▮▮ memoir, part-travelogue, and part-group chat, a young widow's account of her journey across the globe with two small children in search of solace, strength, and self. Heart-wrenching and hilarious, this book will change you."

—Lee Murray, USA Today Bestselling Author

"Through heartache and humor Dawn takes you around the world with two young children as the family works through the overwhelming grief of losing a husband and father. I shed so many tears and laughed out loud. A must read."

—Leanne Suter, ABC7 LA reporter

"Dawn's writing is a gift. It was hard for me to put the book down. This story is a deeply-felt reminder to anyone who has lost a loved one that the journey of grief never dies."

—Debra Gore, MD Specialist in Family Medicine, Spokane, Washington

"I felt so immediate and with Dawn and her children as I read *Love, Loss and Lifelines*. It's sad and funny and real all at once. I know it will be the kind of book that will help so many people living through grief. I'm amazed how Dawn was able to process loss while turning the tale into an adventure as she traveled and mourned."

—Vanessa Gorman, Producer, Australian Story, ABC TV

"*Love, Loss and Lifelines* is an incredible story of resilience, courage and strength. Dawn pulls you through the messiness of shouldering unimaginable grief in a beautiful, compelling way. This work is truly inspiring and will undoubtedly help so many people who wrestle with hardship and loss."

-Ilana Gold, former CBS New York reporter

photo credit: Fine Art Photography by Barbara Chase

Love, Loss and Lifelines

My Year of Grief on the Run

Dawn Picken

Paperback: 978-0-473-63751-4
Print on demand: 978-0-473-63752-1
Ebook: 978-0-473-63753-8
Kindle: 978-0-473-63754-5
Library of Congress Number: 9780473637514
First paperback edition November, 2022.

Edited by Christie Stratos, Proof Positive
Cover art by David Schembri
Layout by Grace Bridges

Title:
Love, Loss and Lifelines: My Year of Grief on the Run / by Dawn Picken

Subject: BISAC:
Nonfiction/Memoir/United States/Illness/Family/Travel
Nonfiction/Autobiography/New Zealand/Illness/Anecdotes/Travel

CAMHAOIR
PRESS
Printed by Camhaoir Press
New Zealand and USA
dawnpicken.com

For Fiona and Finley, and in memory of Sean.
My love for you is eternal.

Contents

Introduction

This book partly answers the question of how I survived catastrophe and hop-scotched the globe to inhabit an island near the bottom of the world. It may not answer why I would revisit the past, why I've sat with these stories for hours, days, and years when the main event—Sean's death—happened long ago, in 2010. Why write a whole book about it? And why send it into the world?

I revisit conversations with Sean often, whether I write about them or not. His absence is palpable each day that his children grow up without him. Sean has left a husband/father-sized hole in our lives that no one can fill. I write to remember. I write because our children have forgotten their father's voice. I write so they will always know the person he was. I write because I still love him and I want to inhabit his universe, if only in my mind through the sweet, small details that surface when I tell Sean's stories.

Our experience is something I share because many of you can relate. You have lost a loved one, and whether it happened months ago or decades ago, it still hurts. For those of us who are missing our person, there is no moving past death. We scooch forward in our own way, playing the hand that grief has dealt us. I am not here to judge your journey but to bear witness. Some who mourn will retreat, while others like me will launch themselves into the world, trying to ensure we live before we die. A formula for grief does not exist.

Writing has always been my balm. I kept journals from an early age and saw the pen — and later, a keyboard — as an extension of my brain. Putting words onto a page or screen helps me unravel emotions and discern what is important and who matters most. Writing is an isolating experience, but sharing phrases and paragraphs with other people forges connection and healing.

I started this memoir shortly after the kids and I arrived in New Zealand, thinking I would slam it out within a year of Sean's death. Life and doubt interceded, and I wondered whether I would ever share this time capsule. More than a decade after I started, I was unable to relinquish the project. I hope it helps another person or two, and I'm grateful to have spent extra time with Sean during an infinite number of revisions.

This story is filtered through the lens of memory and my own biases and perceptions. I reconstructed the narrative via many pages of social media posts, collected by friends in the year following Sean's death. I always had a notebook and pen with me while Sean was in the hospital, and I continued to write and blog.

This memoir is the result of a collective effort of friends and family who encouraged me to tell this tale. People identified in the story have graciously allowed me to repurpose their social media musings for this book. I have changed some names and details to protect privacy, brushing aside Anne Lamott's admonition that if people wanted to be written about warmly, they should have behaved better. I have replaced names with initials for most Facebook posts to avoid confusing readers with an unwieldy cast of characters. Posts have been edited for clarity, but their meaning has not been altered.

I hope you take some comfort in this story. I want you to get a sense that you have traveled with us, not only through hospital corridors, but through the streets of Paris, the hills of Ireland, the tip of South Africa, and the beaches of New Zealand. Most of all, I hope you tell your loved ones today and every day how much they mean to you.

Dawn Picken
July 2022
Tauranga, New Zealand

Part 1

Before

*"Hope begins in the dark,
the stubborn hope that
if you just show up and
try to do the right thing,
the dawn will come.
You wait and watch and work:
you don't give up."*

– Anne Lamott

Chapter 1

In Sickness and in Hell

September, 2009

I thought it was the worst case of man-flu ever. I'm no doctor, but I'd already diagnosed my husband, Sean, as another victim of the swine flu pandemic sweeping North America. Influenza A (H1N1) took hold in the United States and was spreading worldwide. The advice was to stay home and not bring the virus into a doctor's office unless things were grim.

I kept Sean home for four days, spooning soup into his mouth and blending smoothies while trying to keep our two young children from screaming through the house like Dr. Seuss's Thing One and Thing Two. In normal times, we would laugh (I'd snort if things got really funny) as our preschoolers danced, wrestled, or bounced down the stairs. But Sean needed quiet to rest, to fight whatever had knocked him off his feet into bed with fever and chills.

One night, frazzled by the constant need to disinfect every surface in the house while shushing the kids, I packed a bag for the

7

kids and me and decamped to the Coeur d'Alene Resort thirty minutes down the road. Sean encouraged us to go: "I'm a full-grown man. I'll be fine."

Sean had been fine until he suddenly spiked a fever of 102 degrees Fahrenheit the day after we returned from Camp Cross on the shores of Lake Coeur d'Alene. He returned early from a job videotaping a wedding, his sickness surging and flattening him with fatigue. Sean told me he felt terrible the first couple of days but insisted on staying home to ride out the flu instead of going to the doctor. Even then, he would ask how the kids and I were doing. We were okay.

We were living in Spokane, Washington, a city of about 200,000 people near the state's eastern edge punctuated by pine trees and pickup trucks. We had left the big city, Seattle, in 1999 for jobs at KARM-TV. Sean was a photographer, and I was a reporter. In Seattle, he had been an overnight editor, and I had freelanced as an anchor, which provided an unpredictable schedule and spotty income.

We expected to spend a couple of years in Spokane, a town with a waterfall at its heart west of the Rocky Mountain foothills. We would return to Seattle once we had a surer footing in local news. But we became Velcroed by friends, outdoor activities, and the fact that we could afford to buy a home in Spokane. Then we had two children. Work, run, play, raise kids, repeat…Two years became ten.

At the end of his four-day quarantine, Sean's legs turned leaden and numb. Over just a few days, the bedroom in our two-story home had become a sick bay, its plum feature wall a backdrop for suffering. This house had been our refuge, a place we were proud of. Now, the fourteen carpeted steps leading to our bedroom might as well have been the steep scree slope at Mount Si, a peak Sean and I had summited in healthier times. "I'm having a hard time feeling my legs," Sean said, when I told him it was time to see a doctor. His breathing sounded labored, like he was trying to suck air through a straw. He couldn't keep food or even water in his system without throwing up. I called our GP, who said to bring him in.

Like a tugboat, I guided, slid, and pulled him down the stairs from the second floor to the first. I was fifty-five pounds lighter than my husband and bore his full weight as he draped a clammy arm across my shoulders. I maneuvered Sean into our minivan before returning to the house for three-year-old Finley. He'd stay with my friend Cheryl and her chickens. Our five-year-old daughter, Fiona, was in morning kindergarten. Calling an ambulance was out of the question. They were for old or dying people. And a ride in one might set us back thousands of dollars.

Cheryl lived less than a mile from the hospital in a bungalow near Manito Park. Once there, Finley clambered from the van, ready to lay hands on some urban hens. Cheryl peeked at Sean, slumped in the passenger seat. "He looks really white," she said. "Like a ghost."

We parked at the hospital, where our family doctor practiced on the sixth floor. Unlike other appointments, he saw us immediately. No staring at the fish tank or thumbing old copies of *Woman's Day*.

Dr. S couldn't find Sean's pulse or determine why he was so sick. "You're not going to order a bunch of expensive tests, are you?" asked Sean. Even with insurance, our co-pays might ratchet up a raft of bloodwork and scans costing hundreds of dollars.

We would need to visit another hospital just blocks away, the one our insurance covered. "I'll let you drive him to the emergency room," said Dr. S. "But go right away. I'll call to say you're coming."

In the ER, a nurse took our insurance information and led us to a small cubicle off the main corridor. In the intervals between staff shuffling in and out, metal ball bearings on the curtain holders gliding to and fro, blood pressure and oxygen saturation checks, we talked about what we would do after Sean recovered from this mystery illness. He viewed this sickness as only a bad flu — nothing fluids and meds couldn't solve. "I'm definitely going to start eating better, and maybe get a trainer at the gym," he said between pulls on a Tootsie Pop. His mouth was dry, so he had asked if I had any candy stashed in my purse (I usually did). Worry lodged in his gray-blue eyes, but he didn't seem alarmed. He looked miffed when a nurse told him to ditch the lollipop in case staff needed to perform a procedure, like surgery. That set off alarm bells for me. I reached into my bag for one of my security blankets — my phone.

My smartphone was an IV drip, a constant source of sustenance. If I kept it charged to report Sean's condition and receive encouragement from others, I'd survive. Drip: Update Facebook. Drip: Receive text messages. Drip: Read friends' Facebook posts. "Distracted from distraction by distraction," wrote T.S. Eliot.

> **Facebook:** What's on your mind, Dawn Picken?
> **September 14, 2009 at 10:11 p.m.**
> **Dawn Picken:** Sean has been moved to ICU, as of tonight. He is in getting another scan. We still don't know why his kidneys are failing. No flu, no connection to it. More CT scans, blood tests, trying to keep him stable. I'm camped out here. Fiona wanted to know why Mommy gets to sleep in the hospital. Just lucky, I guess.

Who knew how long Sean would need to stay in the hospital? One night? Maybe two? I brought Fiona and Finley to my friend Janelle's down the street from our house.

"Daddy's really sick," I told the kids. "The doctors and nurses are trying to make him better." No promises. This would be their first overnight at a friend's house. Thank God they saw adventure instead of crisis. No tears, just excitement about bunking with neighbor kids.

Back home, I stuffed a duffle bag with a change of clothes, plus running gear. If I stayed at the hospital tonight, maybe I could run in the morning. Just like I'd run five miles around the Cleveland Clinic during Mom's breast cancer surgery. Just like I'd run a marathon less than a year after being diagnosed with life-threatening liver disease (Columbus, Ohio, 1996 in three hours, forty-one minutes, thank you very much). Run away. Runaway. That was me. I embraced the Chinese proverb, *Do not fear going forward slowly. Fear only to stand still.*

Standing still was never my game. I had left my hometown, Ashtabula, in Northeast Ohio, at age seventeen to live as an exchange student in Luxembourg for a year. I improved upon my high school French, learned Luxembourgish, and rode the rails throughout Europe, traveling solo to Prague, Budapest, and Oslo. I moved to the southwest corner of Ohio to attend Miami University in 1998 and later moved to Illinois, Michigan, and Washington for school, work, and eventually, for Sean. And now I found myself haunting the ICU waiting room of Providence Sacred Heart Medical Center in Spokane, Washington.

At four in the morning, a doctor from the intensive care team found me curled under blankets, lying across two blue armchairs. He thrust a clipboard and pen into my hands, along with a form that would give permission for Sean to be placed on a ventilator.

Ventilator? I struggled to understand what that meant. I had seen breathing machines in TV hospital dramas. I once used the theme music from *ER* in a series about kidney transplants I produced and reported for local TV news. It was the closest I had gotten to qualifying as a pulmonary technician. In the purgatory of the ICU waiting room, ventilator equaled terror, a last resort reserved for the sickest of the sick. Already emotionally exhausted, a cataclysm of terms provoked a cosmic mind crash: breathing/machine/death/respiratory failure/risk. Even the horror movies I watched as a teenager could not have prepared me for the news Sean needed a machine to breathe, to live. But I didn't have time to cry, scream, or dial a shrink. I had to decide my husband's path — now.

I read the disclaimer about potential complications like death. I signed because doctors said Sean needed a breathing machine to survive. That single sheet of paper affirmed I was not only Sean's partner but also the person making legal decisions that would impact his life forever. And mine.

I suddenly felt hopelessly and helplessly alone.

Facebook Post: September 15 at 4:46 a.m.
Dawn Picken: *Medical staff just now intubating Sean. He's working too hard to breathe. They think the cause of all this is some kind of bacterial infection. Still don't know exactly what it is or how it started. Sean will remain sedated while on the ventilator. We don't know how long he'll need the machine.*

The first person I phoned after signing the intubation paper was Leanne. She was a TV news reporter in California used to waking at odd hours. She had been where I was now. Leanne had paced hospital corridors after her husband's helicopter crash on September 11, 2007. Mark had been flying a chopper off the coast of Florida when it plummeted into the sea. He survived. His two passengers did not. Mark shattered bones and spent two weeks in intensive care.

Leanne listened to my thousand-miles-away sobs and said, "I understand. I am so sorry for what you're going through. Get your family in. They'll know what to do when they get there."

Another waiting room on the second floor offered a change of scenery. I needed to move my numb ass, if only down the hall. There, I met Paul, whose wife needed a heart transplant. We weren't whiling away time, we were thumb wrestling it. We pretended to skim *Reader's Digest* and stared at stained, nubby dark blue carpeting. I sat beside a square side table with a gray Formica top where I'd stacked a half dozen paperbacks and periodicals. It was the sixth hour of waiting on Day Two and I had yet to touch a single volume.

Stand, stretch, inventory the counter's contents: pot of coffee, Styrofoam cups, packets of coffee whitener. I sat again and grabbed my phone, my IV drip to the world.

Down the hall, Sean was tethered to real IVs that trickled survival liquids into his body: saline, morphine, penicillin, plus eleven other drugs. Medicine hung from bags above his head. Staff flowed through his room like starlings in murmurations, rustling thousands of pairs of wings. Doctors circled burgeoning purplish blotches on Sean's arms and legs in black marker. Nurses monitored oxygen levels, blood pressure, heart rate, and temperature inside an alternate universe of white-coated workers, medicines, and machines orbiting Planet Sean.

A seventeen-year-old boy named Drew, tackled and head-knocked during a high school football game, was admitted around the same time as Sean. I'll never forget the sobs, the wailing of teenagers after he died from concussion. Until that moment, I thought keening was something African tribal women did. Adolescent agony roared, an uncontrolled wail from deep in the gut. The sound made me want to double over, made my lips quiver. I was enveloped in one of Dante's nine circles of suffering, where the gates of hell bear the inscription: *"Lasciate ogne speranza, voi ch'intrate."*

Abandon all hope, ye who enter here.

Facebook Post: September 15 at 3:41 p.m.
Dawn Picken: *Sean is in surgery right now to try to clear infection. Vitals okay but still critical. Identified as strep infection. He has toxic shock. Please understand if I can't call*

or return your e-mail messages. But we do appreciate your thoughts and prayers and all the help you've given. We love you.

Sean's surgeon, Dr. B, found me in the waiting room. He was thin with close-cropped light brown hair and a white three-quarter length lab coat, name embroidered in black thread. He looked around my age — late thirties. Weird. My doctors to this point had been older than me. They weren't getting younger. I was getting older.

I scribbled on a reporter notepad (one of many gifts from friends at my old TV station), trying to digest new information and pretend I was working on a story about someone other than my husband. Paper and notes had always been more than a repository for thoughts; writing had been a way of understanding the world, a stab at untangling the jumble in my head and, as Anaïs Nin wrote, to "taste life twice." This description felt more apt for my teenaged diaries and adult travel journals than writing at my husband's hospital bedside, where step by step, I chronicled how Sean's body was failing him.

Ray Bradbury said, "You must stay drunk on writing so reality cannot destroy you." I felt closer to disintegration as each new diagnosis was revealed. Opening that fresh notebook, I was using a familiar tool in a new, awful way, writing words like "dialysis" and "ventilator." I tried to let my reporter persona offer a sense of detachment, but my stomach knotted each time a doctor entered the room. I couldn't say I got wasted on words, but I was shielding myself with a notebook and phone. When I ran out of thoughts, I scribbled in the margins. Anything to keep my hands moving, my mind distracted inking flowers and birds.

Dr. B told me Sean had necrotizing fasciitis (NF for short), otherwise known as flesh-eating bacteria. It's a misnomer. Bacteria don't eat tissue. Instead, they destroy skin and muscle by releasing toxins.

Between doctor visits and status updates, I had a fathomless canyon of time to drop inside and reminisce. To remember how Sean and I had fallen in love. We'd met at a WOOD-TV employee picnic in August, 1996, the week before I started my new reporting job in Grand Rapids, Michigan. Standing beside me on a picnic table, Sean had turned and asked, "Who are you?"

I was about to turn twenty-six. I had dark shoulder-length hair, stood around five feet five inches tall (with shoes, which I counted) and weighed what I reported on my driver's license — 125 pounds. But my girl-next-door appearance belied a fondness for black humor and penis jokes. People often told me they thought I was reserved, even aloof — until we had eaten a meal or taken a road trip together.

Sean was not a potential match for two reasons: we worked together, and I had a serious long-distance boyfriend, Matt. I thought Matt and I would find our ever after, as soon as one of us was able or willing to uproot. It was also a convenient way to hang with other guys without worrying about dating and sex. Except Sean wanted to date me. At first, I brushed off his overtures — until he told me he couldn't stand Michigan anymore and was moving back home to Seattle.

After he moved two thousand miles away, I missed Sean horribly. I broke up with Matt.

Sean wrote long letters and sent me a plane ticket to visit him in Seattle. As I deplaned and walked into the airport terminal, he was waiting in a striped polo shirt and jeans, grinning like a lottery winner. He wrapped his arms around me, the clean scent of a manly cologne wafting to my nose.

We feasted on wild Alaskan salmon in Ballard, watched fishmongers fling cod, rockfish, and steelhead at the Pike Place Market, and hiked near the base of Mount Rainier, which towered 14,000 feet above the valley floor. Seattle was a film set, its skyline immortalized in the screen credits of the TV show *Frasier*. On a clear day, you could see not only Rainier, but also the peaks of Mount Adams and Mount Baker, offset by the sparkling waters of Lake Washington. The Olympic range towered to the west. To the east rose the Cascades, where one day Sean and I would climb 1,476-foot Mt. Si, made famous by a starring role in the Twin Peaks credit sequence.

Despite the adventure, natural beauty, and food that induced a belly-led sense of joy, I couldn't decide whether Sean was boyfriend material. He was nine years older than me and, at five feet, nine inches, on the short side. Was I physically attracted? What if he wanted to kiss me? What if he wanted more? "Don't overthink this," said Leanne. "Follow your heart."

How do you follow an organ beating within your chest? What the hell does that trite phrase mean? It meant do whatever I felt like doing.

Sean's kisses were soft, yet urgent, setting that cardiac muscle aflutter. I shouldn't have worried.

Facebook Post: September 15 at 5:12 p.m.
Dawn Picken: *For everyone who knows Sean: please share your stories and thoughts about what you like most. I'll read them to him. Even if he can't hear, he can still feel your love.*
MS: *Please remind him about our "Gold Bond" party and how much we all loved the "cool breeze flowing through our pants"!!! Laughter is good medicine.*

MS had remembered a party in my apartment in Grand Rapids. A gaggle of beer-fueled women crowded into the bathroom, taking turns shaking Gold Bond powder down the fronts of our underwear. The stuff had menthol, which created a cool, tingly sensation on the skin. At that moment, we weren't twenty-six — we were six-year-old giggling school girls. We emerged from Gold-Bonding and told Sean what we'd done. He laughed, then shook his head when we offered the canister.

"No thanks," he said. "I don't want to burn my junk."

My friend, neighbor, and running mate, Janelle, wrote a post on behalf of my daughter, Fiona:

Dear Daddy, I hope you feel better, Daddy. So get well soon. I learned the letter F in school. I played with Rachael and Libby at the playground at school. We got Space Buddies at the library and Hannah Montana. I like cats. I got a splinter in my foot, Dada. I had pizza and little beans for dinner. I had fun at the sleepover, Dad, at Rachael's.
KD: My favorite Sean story: we were all working on a Sunday morning. We were doing a huge live show and were told we all had to wear our KARM 5 polo shirts. Sean walks in wearing his polo and it was so tight and tiny, I kept wondering if he had gained weight. Turns out, he had gotten dressed quickly and put your KARM 5 polo on instead.

I read the stories to Sean in his ICU room. His eyes were closed, body bloated from heart medication and IV fluids. He rested on an air mattress, which competed with the respirator to see which machine could create more noise. The mattress hummed. The respirator whooshed, orchestrating Sean's breathing: hah-whoo, hah-whoo, hah-whoo. A heart monitor beeped in rhythm. An electronic survival symphony. I inhaled scents of clean sheets and sterility, of rubbing alcohol and floor cleaner. Aromas of hospital, hope and healing, plus heartbreak and pain.

I stood beside Sean's bed, laughing at stories our friends had dredged from the riverbed of carefree days before children and a mortgage. But when I saw Janelle's note from Fiona, my throat was suddenly packed with cotton. Fat tears pooled in my eyes. My kids. His kids. They'd be terrified to see Daddy this way.

Dr. B entered the room. I tossed the phone in my bag and fished out my notepad. The doctor told me he'd found necrotizing fasciitis on the back of Sean's right thigh and in his right forearm.

"If we don't cut out all the infection, he'll die," he said. I had read patients with necrotizing fasciitis have a 30-70 percent mortality rate. Infection spreads rapidly. People often die within hours of diagnosis.

"How did Sean get this?" I asked.

"We don't know," Dr. B said. "In about half these cases, we never find the cause."

The kids and I had visited the same places as Sean, slept in the same house, eaten the same food. Why had he gotten so sick when the rest of us were fine?

Facebook Post: September 15 at 6:25 p.m.
Dawn Picken: *Sean just got out of surgery that sliced away infected skin. Doc says one thigh looks like it got a shark bite. Hoping that will stop infection from spreading. Dialysis tonight to clear toxins from his blood. We're told to prepare for a "long night."*
MO: *It may be a long night, but you're not alone. Tell your hubby he is one hot topic on FB. :)*
LK: *So is this different from the flu thing? Cause now, I'm worried.*

I tried to pray silently in the hospital but couldn't find words beyond, "God help Sean. Help me. Help us."

Chapter 2

The Woods

The intensive care unit was like a dense forest Sean and I had gotten lost in. We had been on our way somewhere else, laughing and joking on a flat gravel path until it narrowed to a single track and spiked upward like a snapped twig. Tree roots clutched our ankles, toppling us face-first to the forest floor. These woods never let us pass without extracting a price. We couldn't leave, but others could join us.

Sean's mother, his youngest sister, Rochele, her husband, and five-month-old baby had arrived from across the state. Dr. B insisted I call them to the hospital. Fast. They slept at a motel nearby. I was too scattered to contemplate hosting three adults and a baby. Besides, we weren't close. Sean and I saw them a few times a year when we would pile the kids into the van and road-trip to the west side.

We had grown our own small family, planting roots hours from Sean's relatives near Seattle and states away from my folks in Ohio. Sean and I didn't have nearby grandparents who could swoop in on short notice and watch Fiona and Finley. We forfeited perks that came with extended family down the road — the ability to pop out for dinner or a weekend away while Grandma and Grandpa watched the kids. But we built a family of friends we turned to for advice, play dates, and commiseration. We hung with other families at the neighborhood sandpit, met with friends for walks and runs on tree-lined paths, and drank countless cups of coffee in each other's kitchens.

We marveled over our children's rapid growth and delighted in where we lived. Even in suburbia, we saw elements of Western wilderness — a mama moose would wander into our yards with her calves; the howl of coyotes in summertime pierced the midnight air like a battalion of ambulance sirens.

In this crisis, we had help in the hood. Sean's oldest sister, Stephanie (Steph for short), drove six hours from Olympia to stay with us. I valued her company, the steady way she laid out plans and encouraged me to find the next right thing — and do it. She was upbeat and sweet without the saccharin aftertaste. "Whatever you need, I'm here," she said. Steph was staying in Finley's room with its cerulean blue walls lined with tropical fish decals. Beyond buoying my spirits, she would help with the kids when I was at the hospital.

Stephanie was an artist and mother of two sons, plus a stepdaughter. She stood nearly six feet tall, with natural blonde hair and cornflower-blue eyes. She created paintings instead of drama, depicting a girl with duct tape across her mouth in one, a woman with wings in another.

The morning after Steph's arrival, I drove seven miles to Sacred Heart Hospital, traveling north on I-195 and east on I-90 before taking the Division Street exit and heading up the steep hill. The waning days of summer were warm, the landscape dotted with the green lawns of people who watered and the brown scrub of those who didn't. I pulled into the parking garage, a place that would become too familiar, crammed with cars and empty reserved spaces. How many times would I pull the ticket from the machine before winding up, up, and up five stories to find a space?

I took an elevator to the ground floor, then walked across to the main building, where I quickstepped the gauntlet of corridors, zigging and zagging left, right, left, past people pushing wheelchairs and walls lined with photos of nuns—the Sisters of Providence who founded the hospital. Another elevator whisked me to the second floor—the ICU, where a large steel door swung open to another hallway—this one containing patients with one foot in the world and the other on the edge of a grave.

I entered Sean's bright, air-conditioned room, where the scene was the same as the day before. He lay beneath a tangle of wires with a tube in his throat as a ventilator pumped oxygen into his body.

We had been transported into some weird space-time continuum where seconds stretched and hours bled into each other. Time is endless—and short. It's like water through a sieve. Reading a book seemed doable, yet between looking at and talking to an unconscious Sean, asking questions of medical staff, and fielding messages, I had yet to crack the first page of a novel someone gave me. I was pretty sure it was afternoon (maybe it was already evening?) when our priest, Father Bill, from St. John's Episcopal Cathedral on the next block arrived. We were talking when my friend Melissa appeared at the door. I let her in and the three of us studied Sean, trying to discern progress, any difference from yesterday. "His color is better," said Melissa. He still looked sallow to me, like a pale butternut squash.

I thought about what Dr. B had said earlier—that Sean might die. Suddenly, I was burning up. My shirt was too hot. My shoes were too hot. Even my watch's thin leather strap created a ring of sweat around my wrist. I was certain the world could hear my veins pulsing, "Ba-boom, ba-boom, ba-boom." My knees buckled, and I felt arms grab my elbows on each side, holding me like twin

21

cranes. Father Bill and Melissa propped me up, keeping my knees and face from whacking the hospital's cold tiled floor.

I cried, blew snot, and dried my tears with a tissue. A wave of guilt crashed over me. If I had been a better partner my husband wouldn't be lying in the ICU. A better caregiver would not have assumed it was man-flu. A better wife would've known to deliver her husband to the doctor much sooner.

But this time, fatigue trumped guilt. Fatigue prescribed a night at home instead of another sleepless night at the hospital. Anne Lamott wrote, "Almost everything will work again if you unplug it for a few minutes, including you." I must unplug.

I drew the back of my hand across my face to wipe it dry, left the ICU, and drove home. I tucked the kids in bed, pressing needy, anxious lips against Fiona's and Finley's smooth, chubby cheeks. Then I closed the door to my bedroom—mine and Sean's.

I remember telling our realtor while standing outside the double doors of the master bedroom that we were expecting a second child. We moved here the year Finley was born, leaving behind a craftsman bungalow near the manicured gardens of Manito Park for a bedroom community with a waterfall entrance and a 1996 Colonial that had once been a show home. We had plenty of space—around 3,000 square feet, including a large basement, which we remodeled to include a rumpus room, bathroom, and extra bedroom. From upstairs, we could see the South Hill cliffs facing the front of the house. At the back, grass and gray paving stones lined the tiny terraced backyard. This had always been a happy place, and now it was a temporary respite from a reality that was hard to face.

I looked at the bed my husband and I should have been sharing that night, and another flood of memories bashed me like a tidal wave. The first time Sean and I slept together, we had nestled in separate sleeping bags, as friends. I'd just arrived in Michigan in 1996 and Sean had organized a weekend trip for a couple dozen colleagues from WOOD-TV. He and I shared a canoe, then snoozed, side by side, zipped into separate insulated sleep sacks. We tented with two other people. One of them got so drunk he peed in someone else's tent before crawling into ours.

Letter from Sean, March 17, 1997

I wish you were here; it would be nice to have you beside me. I remember our camping/canoe trip. Funny, we didn't even know each other, yet we wanted to be close to each other even then. See, I told you it was meant to be. I think about you every day, and at night you are in my dreams — no kinky stuff, don't worry. Well, not that kinky, anyway.

Facebook Post: September 16, 2009 at 9:41 a.m.
Dawn Picken: *Surgeon is checking Sean's leg wound. May go in again and remove some skin on his arms. Sean's eyes (closed) look better. Not as puffy and yellow as last night. Our family doc was in this morning. One of the few medical folks who doesn't keep repeating how sick Sean is. We get it. We know.*

Dr. S, our family physician, checked Sean daily during those first few weeks in the hospital. He'd look at me and say, "It's not easy being the spouse. You're doing a good job. Hang in there. Call me any time." Dr. S surveyed the universe of my husband's care, assessing not just Planet Sean, but the many moons in his orbit: wife, children, extended family, medical team.

After Dr. S left, Dr. B entered the ICU. He examined my husband's bloated arms and legs, the graffiti of black marker indicating infection. He said it was difficult to tell which tissues were dead and which were only damaged. That was why they had done exploratory surgery as well as an operation to remove flesh the bacteria killed.

"I think we got all the necrotizing fasciitis," said Dr. B. "But

Sean still has strep bacteria in his body. High doses of penicillin should clear that. I don't anticipate more skin surgeries."

This sounded *somewhat* positive. My husband was on life support; doctors had removed a chunk from his thigh and another from his arm and he was battling a strep infection, a notorious killer resistant to antibiotics. The good news: Sean was alive and, so far, still had his limbs. Although, as my nurse friend, Jennifer, had said, "A one-legged husband is better than no husband at all."

I had laughed at that, blowing oxygen into the coal fires of black humor. Maybe my attempts to mock illness and death were a result of what Freud said was the ego, refusing to be distressed by the "provocations of reality." Maybe it was a result of my own hospitalization and misdiagnosis more than a decade earlier.

In 1996, I was shuffling and shivering around my new workplace in a trench coat, doffing it a minute later because a sudden heat wave had emerged. My doctor tested for everything from pneumonia to HIV. My white blood cell count plunged, triggering admission to the hospital.

That's where a specialist told me I had a liver disease that could kill me.

I was young and unmarried with no children, sharing a room divided by a sheet with an old lady with stovepipe ankles. She told a nurse she'd been as skinny as me when she was my age. My weight had dropped from 125 to 114 pounds in a month. I was still fighting a fever. I hung one leg outside the thin white sheet that smelled of bleach while a young Indian doctor delivered the name of an idiopathic disease: primary sclerosing cholangitis. PSC would scar my liver, rendering it useless, like rancid roast. My body would fill with toxins; I'd turn sickly yellow and eventually lapse into a coma. Median life expectancy from diagnosis to death was nine to twelve years, according to Medscape online. Without a transplant, I could die.

Despite the pathetic predictions, I didn't get sick again until shortly after Finley was born in 2005. The fevers returned. I lost weight and needed antibiotics. This time, I escaped the hospital, recovering at home.

My Spokane specialist, a short, bearded man who favored tweed jackets with suede elbow patches, sent me for yearly blood tests. I had nicknamed him Dr. Death, as his bedside manner rivaled Hannibal Lecter's and his doomsday health predictions gave Nostradamus a run for his *livres* (gold coins). Even though I was running thirty miles per week and was rarely sick, Dr. Death was certain my liver was kaput.

In 2007, I refused to check myself into a Seattle hospital to be evaluated for transplant. I wanted treatment instead at Cleveland Clinic, near family. Dr. Death had summoned me to his office, where he said, "I don't give a damn where you go. Just get some treatment. Go to Mayo Clinic. It's the only place investigating your disease." I held back tears until I fled his office. I sobbed in the hallway and never returned. I did, however, make an appointment to see a specialist at Mayo.

That's where the eighth or ninth specialist I'd seen declared my initial diagnosis a mistake. Instead of PSC, he told me I had Caroli's Syndrome, a double-recessive inherited disease requiring monitoring whose prognosis may not be as dire as PSC. I emerged from Dr. K's office and called Sean, who'd stayed home in Spokane with the kids. "Honey," I said, "great news. I get to see our kids grow up!"

"Sweetie." Sean's voice vibrated solid and tender in my ear. "You were always going to see the kids grow up."

I wanted to say that to Sean in the hospital in Spokane. I sat, willing him to survive. I made one-legged husband jokes and tried to think of any place but here.

Humor is our best diversion against mortality. Laugh until you die. Because you will. The Reaper comes for all of us. Wouldn't He be more agreeable if He looked like Jerry Garcia? Jerry would say something like, "Dude/Babe. It's been a long, strange trip. Time to get truckin'. Uh-huh."

Jerry would then hand you a fat joint before bringing you into The Woods to meet your maker.

The Woods. The dreaded freakin' Woods. Medical professionals often metaphorically wheel a patient in or out of "the woods." "He's not out of the woods" is a euphemism for, "Your husband is still in danger," or even, "This poor guy could die soon."

The Woods reminded me of WOOD-TV, where Sean and I met. A coworker, Mike, used to joke we should call the morning show "Morning WOOD." Our slogan could be "Wake up with WOOD."

Facebook Post: September 16, 2009 at 10:53 a.m.
Dawn Picken: *Doc says he is "cautiously optimistic," but Sean's "not out of the woods yet." Still on vent and getting dialysis. Will need skin graft for the "shark bite" wound on his leg. No work for six months. Physical therapy for one year or longer. Goodbye soccer career (attempt at humor).*
JM: *Gives me chills and tears at the same time!*
KL: *No more leg modeling either. :)*

My friends and neighbors provided more help than I knew to ask for. Family cycled in and out, sitting with me by Sean's bedside. But no one helped more than his sister, Steph. That first day in the Emergency Room, when Sean was still coherent and a specialist told us his kidneys had failed, I asked him to name the family member he'd most want by his side.

"Call Steph," he said. "I want Steph here."

We'd already named Steph and her husband, John, guardians for Fiona and Finley, should anything happen to us. And something *was* happening, an epic, existential threat. We had entered the Mirkwood of Norse mythology, a dangerous forest that heroes and even gods traversed with difficulty. We were lost outside normal human existence. We would be destroyed if I didn't summon help.

This last line is bullshit. I would soon hear more platitudes from well-meaning family, friends, and acquaintances than I could count. "Everything happens for a reason." "God never gives us more than we can bear." "It's all part of God's plan." Clichés meant to comfort pissed me off.

Rabbi Harold Kushner, author of *When Bad Things Happen to Good People*, lost his son to a rare degenerative disease. After that tragedy, he wrote that God is not a puppet master causing disease, famine, and war. Instead, random, inscrutable chaos in the universe and humans' God-given free will intertwine to create bad things. Kushner argued if God never gave us more than we could handle, no one would commit suicide, get divorced, or kill (although you could argue those are all methods of "handling" a problem).

I couldn't prove or disprove the rabbi's theories. But his concept makes me feel less lonely, less lost in the woods. Our family was not divinely tapped for torture. There existed no cosmic reason my children were missing their father. I was, back then, a Christian who believed in the coexistence of Jesus Christ and unholy crap.

Facebook Post: September 16, 2009 at 10:29 p.m.
Dawn Picken: Doing the evening stint at the hospital for at least another hour. Sean's about the same, which is good. Still needs all the machines and meds, but at least it's not getting worse. I got to enjoy a little slice of normal earlier this evening during Fi's soccer practice. Hearing "Go Silver Princesses!" did my heart good. New game Steph invented: kids are meat and we roll them up in a tortilla blanket [a rug].
CM: Dawn, I can read the difference in your posts. You sound much more relaxed. I'm so happy about Sean's progress. Try to rest. Tell Steph I said hello!

During those first endless days of vigil, supporters from around the world found me on Facebook. Former newsroom colleagues, university friends, sorority sisters, family friends, friends of friends, and people we didn't know emerged in cyberspace, offering hopeful messages and real help, as opposed to the nebulous, "If there's anything I can do to help, let me know." I fielded dozens of Facebook friend requests each day. Our online circle doubled from about 500 to 1,000 within the first few weeks of Sean's hospitalization. I didn't care whether I knew these people; Sean was critically ill, and it was my duty as The Wife to report his condition. The responses provided nuggets of encouragement; maybe I wasn't as alone as I'd thought.

DR: We are thinking of you and Sean and the kids and keeping you in our prayers. I have passed the word on to some of the old KARM-TV people so that they know as well.
CL: We kept your profile "open" on the laptop at the anchor

desk. Thank you for the updates and we are all keeping positive about this.

MM: Joey and I are thinking of you from Springfield, Illinois at the University of Illinois soccer fields where we are at two soccer practices.

RK: Hi Dawn, just read about Sean's illness. Your friends from Luxembourg are all praying for Sean and your family. We're all thinking of you and send our love and best healing wishes over the ocean to your beloved man. If there's something we can do from Luxembourg, just let me know.

JF: I just found out about Sean's illness. I wish I had some profound or witty thing to say, but I don't. It just sucks. Wish I was there to help, so I'll just pray from here and continue checking in for updates. If you need to rant or cry or scream you can call.

KW: Praying, hoping, sending positive vibes and strength your way. You're certainly earning that Italian bottle of wine. Red or white, my Zeta sister?

While I read messages, a doctor shepherded a team of medical students through Sean's room, saying, "We're all excited he's still alive."

I imagined the chatter between them once they left: *He's a train wreck. Very critical condition. Rare case. Lucky to be alive. So young — only forty-eight years old. Unknown cause. Unknown prognosis. We're all rooting for him, though.*

I know why so many people were pulling for Sean. With his dry sense of humor and kindness, he was easy to love. He was the neighbor who spent an hour shoveling snow from his own driveway, then cleared yours; the guy who always had an extra beer for friends at a picnic; the father who'd gladly look after an extra child or two so you can run to the store. When he worked in TV news, he was often paired with young reporters new to the business. Sean would remind them to check the spelling of subjects' names, coach the rookies before the camera, and help them find the right word to complete a sentence.

I had started out as one of Sean's greenies: the first winter we'd worked together at the TV station, Grand Rapids was slammed with typical Michigan snowstorms. I had helped Sean lug video cables until my teeth chattered and my lips stuck together. "Go warm up in the truck," he'd said. "Otherwise, you won't be able to talk during your live shot." I didn't know Sean well back then, in 1996, but I liked that he laughed a lot. He never made me feel rushed or nervous. Being with Sean was easy. Uncomplicated.

After my contract ended at WOOD-TV, Sean and I decided we'd move in together (my first shack-up). He sent me a letter a couple of weeks before our June 1998 reunion:

Just thinking about you here seems like a miracle. Sometimes I think to myself she is still not here and may change her mind. But I hope that doesn't happen. There is so much to look forward to and I can't wait to get started.

We loaded a fifteen-foot rental truck with my childhood double bed, the rest of my second-hand furniture, and my teal 1992 Pontiac Grand Am. Sean and I spent a week driving from Michigan to Seattle, visiting great American attractions and tourist traps Mount Rushmore, Wall Drug, and Yellowstone National Park. We cooled off at a water park in Kansas City and I sang "Seasons of Love" from *Rent* somewhere in South Dakota. We recorded our drive, possibly the world's most boring home video: miles and miles of highway that I narrated with gems like, "Wow! Look at those mountains!" I also kept a travel journal.

June 23, 1998 — South of Springfield, Illinois
Funny how everyone keeps referring to Sean as my fiancé. Guess they figure no woman in her right mind would leave a good job and move cross-country without a commitment. Am I in my

right mind? I think so.

Watching my husband unconscious in a hospital bed made me feel helpless. Fate was holding a magnifying glass to my impatience. My strong partner had been replaced by a wired and tubed, bloated man-shell. All I could do was sit, stand, take notes, and send and receive messages on my phone. When your other half is critically ill, you question why *you're* not in the bed instead of them. I am *not* worthier of health and wholeness. Sean was the better angel of my nature. He was the person who'd prevented me from tearing an advertisement for a psychiatrist from the yellow pages and sticking it under the door of the crazy woman who lived upstairs from our rented condo when we lived near Seattle. He listened to my angst so other people didn't have to.

I fantasized about a wormhole, a shortcut from this hell to the other side of the universe. Even a plane ticket out of Spokane would do. Or a bus. A handful of pills would end the siege. I did not, however, seriously consider suicide, because a) my children needed me, b) a little voice whispered life would not always be this way, c) if I was dead, who'd update Sean's condition on Facebook?

despite my wifely roar, he didn't rouse. And I'm kicked out of his room for shift change. That's okay. I'll have lots of time to yell at Sean.

PC: I think I heard your wifely roar all the way downtown. Here's more warm thoughts and good wishes. Stay strong.

Meanwhile, friends helped me connect with people I wanted to tell about Sean—a distant auntie in Canada, a former au pair in Switzerland, a friend in Luxembourg, and Sean's brother in Australia. They followed my Facebook posts like a trail of crumbs through the wilderness.

A [Switzerland]: Dawn, I've just read all your posts. Can't believe what you're going through—it is so scary to hear! Sean just has to get better. I'm sending all my love to you and your family and hope you'll stay strong to get over this nightmare.

A.S. was our "practice kid" in 2002—a seventeen-year-old exchange student. Her father had moved to Argentina shortly after divorcing her mother when A.S. was a toddler. She told me her stay with Sean and me was the first time she could remember living with a happily married couple.

Sean's skin grew more blistered each day, thanks in part to the enormous volume of fluids pumped into him. Blisters appeared where blood flow was compromised: arms, legs, hands, and feet. He looked like a burn victim. He looked like hell. I wondered what he'd think when he saw himself for the first time.

Facebook Post: September 19, 2009 at 11:12 a.m.
Dawn Picken: *Ran three miles this a.m. before coming to see Sean. Surprisingly hard for someone used to eight and ten-mile training runs (was planning to run a half-marathon Oct. 3, but not anymore). I know it's supposed to be a metaphor, but my heart weighed me down. And I kept thinking, "This. is not. happening. to me. To us."*

I had started crying during the run. I stopped. The sobbing, not the running, because I couldn't do both at once. I needed that run. I could cry later.

> **TM:** *I'm so sorry, Dawn. None of us can believe this is happening to your family. Keep running. It's important for you to have some time to recharge. We're all ready to help in any small way. Please don't be afraid to ask for anything.*
> **JL:** *Call me if you want to run again! My heavy breathing while trying to keep up with you may distract your mind.*

Sean was still unconscious, so I took cues from staff, interpreting not only what they said, but how they said it. A new nurse entered Sean's ICU room, surveyed his purplish puffer fish body and said, "Poor guy," with such pity, I felt my cheeks suck in.

> **Facebook Post: September 20, 2009 at 3:02 p.m.**
> **Dawn Picken:** *Snuck into St. John's to get the kids and communion. Comforting to smell the familiar scents of incense and wood polish. Organist asked about Sean; my eyes started leaking. Fiona: "Mommy, I don't want you to cry." Then Fi started bawling 'cause Finn took her paper.*

> **Facebook Post: September 20, 2009 at 3:59 p.m.**
> **Dawn Picken:** *Sister-in-law headed back to Olympia today, but only after finishing a large color-coded chart with names of our helpers. She also noticed our Tupperware was crap and bought new stuff. Each container actually has a lid! Plus, she got the kids each a doctor kit, Band-Aids, and a bear so they can nurse it to health. I like the kids' kits much better than what I see in the hospital, but I bet they don't work nearly as well.*

Stephanie's departure deflated me. She had become like a blood sister during these early days at the hospital, much the same as her brother, my husband, had become my supporter and champion more than a decade ago. As she drove away in her giant navy Nissan Armada, I could almost hear the "phhtt" emanating from my flattened heart.

Leaving was tough on Steph, too. Her eyes watered as she coerced a smile. "Next time I come," she said, "Sean will be awake and talking. He'll be out of the woods."

Chapter 3

Fiona, Finley, and Frankie Too

Between condition updates, trips to the hospital cafeteria, and naps in the waiting room, I shoehorned time with the kids at their schools and sports practices, pretending to be a parent whose sanity wasn't hanging by a spidery thread in a world blasted by a series of cyclones.

Fiona had started kindergarten and Finley had entered his first preschool. Their primary caregiver, Dada, was himself getting care around the clock. "When is Dada coming home?" they would ask. Looking back, I see how I played hide-and-seek with that question, not dismissing it, but not able to answer it either. *Shield, don't sugarcoat.* Don't lie about the danger Sean is in, but spare the kids details about surgeries, medications, and multiple tubes delivering life-sustaining fluids and removing waste.

The two of them recorded a get-well message to Sean, which I showed him on my camera—or rather, held in front of his inscrutable face. His eyes remained sealed to the outside world, as if hidden by a permanent Halloween mask. Amid sounds of, "We love you, Daddy! Get better soon and come home to us," breathed the constant *hah-huh, hah-huh* of the respirator and whir of the air mattress. My little ones were telling their story, just like I was. And if Sean couldn't hear it, I could. I would.

Sean's surgeon said he may need a skin graft on his right foot, in addition to one on his leg wound. He wanted to extract a piece of dead muscle from Sean's leg where he'd removed necrotizing fasciitis. Dr. B called my husband's case "phenomenal bad luck," saying, "I see it in about one patient every three years. It's like being hit by lightning."

Sean still hadn't moved on his own, but a slim blonde occupational therapist with high cheekbones and wide eyes was stretching and moving his hands. While she did this, I wrote in (and read) an old faux-leather journal of Sean's, half the pages still blank. He had started it when I was pregnant, a missive to his unborn child that he would give her when she turned sixteen.

Sean's journal, written for Fiona: July 14, 2003
(date of first prenatal ultrasound)
I had a premonition about you even before we found out your mom was pregnant. I see a big head of dark hair like your mother. Your mom has gone into overdrive. She is probably thinking what college you will attend. Your mom is a planner. Both of us are lucky; she is the best thing that ever happened to me. Ask to see some pictures. I'm sure there will be thousands. Dawn loves to document all our travels. We have been so many places. Hopefully you will see them also. Today is the beginning. I

already love you. See you soon.

Sean's journal for Fiona: July 28, 2003

We got a call from my sister, Steph, today — she is pregnant! It's kind of funny because she recently mentioned that she was trying. We tried for you for nine months — Steph seems to have taken about a week. She recently got remarried and this will be their first child together. She and John each have one kid from previous marriages, both are around ten. You should arrive about a month before your cousin. Maybe you will be friends as you both grow up together.

Facebook Post: September 22, 2009 at 1:05 p.m.

Dawn Picken: *May get to see a friend's baby who's in the NICU here. Babies are very life-affirming. Need that. Fiona spent two weeks in NICU. Back then, worst day of my life was when the doc told me she wasn't coming home. Seems like another lifetime ago.*

Fiona had been born five weeks early — January 27, 2004 — in the same hospital where Sean now lay unconscious, supported by machines. I had presented the first half of the morning news before shooting lower back and leg pains forced me to flee the anchor desk. My waters broke at home. By noon, my contractions were still weak. I had napped and was eating lunch — soup and ice cream — when the obstetrician's office rang. They told me to put down the spoon and haul my pregnant ass into the hospital (they said it more politely). Sean drove me there, then left. I told him he had plenty of time to drop off a videotape (he was freelancing as a court videographer) because I was still in early labor.

Forty-five minutes later, Sean raced, breathless, to the birth as the doctor performed an emergency caesarean section. A fetal monitor strapped around my beluga-sized belly showed Fiona's heart rate had been dipping and climbing like the Magnum roller coaster at Cedar Point. One crisis followed another: my first-born had scarcely drawn her first breath when the medical team discovered a kidney mass. At two days old, weighing four pounds, twelve ounces, she endured a six-hour operation to remove the tumor and the kidney. She spent two weeks in neonatal intensive care, sleeping in a baby box with plexiglass sides. She was a relative brute among the twenty-four-week-old creatures the size of butter blocks. Until now, those two weeks had been the longest of my life.

Sean's journal for Fiona: January 28, 2004

For about two days you did not move after the operation. You were on a ventilator that breathed for you. Then you came off oxygen and started to move a bit. Then you were allowed to be held for a moment while we touched your soft skin. The tubes and wires were still attached to your tiny body. We want to be able to hold you in our arms in our own house. Both of us love you so much. We hate to see you having to go through all this, but we know you are a strong one – just like your mother.

On Day Nine of Sean's ICU stay, he still couldn't breathe on his own. The ventilator forced the air in and out of his lungs. And his blistered, bloated body continued to fight necrotizing fasciitis. Contrary to what the surgeon had said earlier, Sean did, in fact, need another operation.

At 1:50 p.m., I walked beside nurses as they pushed Sean, still unconscious, on a green inflatable air mattress, down the ICU's muted beige corridor. We passed a door with a sign that said "Blood Gas Room" and another marked "Supply Room." I saw a pregnant nurse and marveled at gestation, the epitome of optimism. The other side of intensive care revealed a queue of chambers where patients sat up in bed, seemingly awake and lucid.

Some were even *eating*. Compared to Sean, they were cruising.

> **Facebook Post: September 22, 2009 at 2:05 p.m.**
> **Dawn Picken:** *Nurses just wheeled Sean into surgery. I was sitting in the bowels of the hospital waiting for his surgeon. The anesthesiologist said, "This really hits home. He's my age. And he was healthy otherwise?" Yes. Was.*
> **MW:** *Dawn, thank you for taking the time to find me. Sean and you guys are my first thought every day, every hour. Prayers and LOVE, LOVE, LOVE from here. I'll get this to Leanne and get her on here. "COURAGE is being scared to death, but saddling up anyway." —John Wayne ("Doesn't mean you can't cry and throw a fit." —Me)*
>
> **Facebook Post: September 22, 2009 at 4:40 p.m.**
> **Dawn Picken:** *Dr. B says Sean's surgery went well. Lasted about one hour. Doc took the rest of Sean's hamstring muscle out (because it was dead), leaving him with three hamstrings. God willing, someday he should be able to walk again. Dr. says no signs of necrotizing fasciitis or other infection. I'm exhaling.*
> **CM:** *We're all exhaling!*
> **LK:** *Exhaling and crying.*
> **TD:** *Dawn, I had two hamstrings removed from one leg to rebuild my MCL, leaving me with two. He should do fine with three.*
> **KC:** *He will walk again. He will run!*

Sean lost just one ounce of blood during the operation. His surgeon also debrided, or scraped, dead skin from my husband's arms. Dr. B said, "There's no question he's getting better."

Afterward, I escaped to the playground behind our home, where a neighbor twisted the cap off a bottle of Normal, a beer, which I accepted and downed like water after a five-mile run in the Arizona desert.

In the hospital, a friend revealed she was pregnant. Another woman, a former coworker, invited me to visit with her preterm baby in neonatal intensive care. The hospital played recorded chimes each time a baby was born. Reminders of life were everywhere. Reminders of death, too.

I asked Fiona and Finley what new messages they had for Daddy.

Fiona said, "Tell Daddy I love him. Don't forget."

Finely said, "Tell Daddy I want a motorcycle."

As a toddler, Finley would scoot around the family room saying, "Vroom, vroom," while propelling a toy motorcycle. When he was three, he got a toy Vespa-style motor scooter for his birthday. Finn was hell on wheels until he pulled too hard on the handlebars, which broke. He then spent hours crashing Hot Wheels cars into each other on the kitchen floor. Sean taught Finley to ride a bike with training wheels shortly before he got sick. I can still picture the scene on our tree-lined sidewalk in the morning, before the sun started sizzling. I can still hear Sean saying, "Keep pedaling, Finley. You've got it. Keep going."

We adored our son, but he was also our challenge child. The child-who-came-second-so-you-wouldn't-have-another child. He's a ball of boy-on-fire, Curious George, Ben Ten, and Bart Simpson in one. He's destined for lawyerdom. The negotiator.

"Finley!" I'd yell. "Don't put your feet on the table." This prompts Finley to rat-a-tat-tat a series of questions, as if firing a BB gun: "Can I put them here? What about here? How about here?" Finley's the child who removes your brain, chucks it into a fragile glass bowl (the one you shipped from Italy at great cost), and pinches your best hair brush to scramble your cerebellum. That child. He's also smart, funny, and devilishly cute with saucer-sized blue eyes, thick brown hair, and apple cheeks. Charm and good looks are powerful life supports. So is GOING TO SLEEP so your parents can have peace.

Sean developed tachycardia overnight—his heart rate spiked while his blood pressure plummeted. Staff stabilized him and increased his morphine dosage. Over the phone, my Aunt Leslie asked, "What other fucking thing can go wrong?"

Sean's journal for Fiona: September 24, 2003
We found out that we are having a girl! A nurse called. She told Dawn first, then me. Dawn cried and I just beamed. I knew you were a girl since the beginning, so I was not terribly surprised. We practiced saying "Fiona." Your mom pointed out that we no longer needed to worry about circumcision.

Facebook Post: September 24, 2009 at 9:43 a.m.
Dawn Picken: *Dr. B suggested I consider bringing Fi and Finn to see Sean so they can see where and how sick their dad is. I've resisted, since I'm having such a tough time coping, and seeing Sean upsets me. How would it be for a five- and almost four-year-old? Dr. said, "A five-year-old can understand more than you think." We could have them meet with the hospital's Child Life Specialists; they can get a feel for how my kids might handle seeing Sean.*
LK: *Children understand and often cope better than adults;*

they believe, they have unquestionable faith, they generate joy. It's hard to be a kid and feel worried but not have a visual to go with it. It makes it worse, you know? Then it's like a monster under the bed.

HW: *What a decision to have to make. Sometimes it's better to let them see what's going on.*

MD: *Hey Dawn, my dad was telling me they generally don't think this is a good idea (doctors included). They likely won't remember it except for the fear, especially since Sean is out. It would probably be a lot less scary when he is no longer sedated.*

I talked with the hospital's Child Life Specialist. She argued against the kids seeing Sean until he was conscious and would know who they were. She said, "I've only seen bringing kids in at this stage go badly. Especially where a dad is concerned. Kids see their Dad as a hero, and seeing him lying there unconscious on a vent can really scare them." She recommended I start taking pictures of the staff home instead, so Fiona and Finley could see who was caring for Daddy.

It was only much later that I realized why the surgeon had pressed for the kids to see Sean: he feared Sean would die. Though he was improving, my husband was still one of the sickest, if not the most debilitated patient in the hospital. What if Fiona and Finley never got a chance to see their father again, even if it meant witnessing him prone, tubed, purplish, puffy, and unconscious? I couldn't accept the idea our children might never hear their dad's voice again.

Facebook Post: September 25, 2009 at 6:46 p.m.
Dawn Picken: *Not a moment's rest when I'm home with kids. They're just as needy as always. Guess that's good; they may be oblivious to my extreme stress! "Mommy's tired" doesn't mean anything.*

On the plus side, I got to sing 12 choruses of "Little Bunny Foo-Foo," complete with hand motions. They liked that.

Facebook Post: September 26, 2009 at 3:20 p.m.
Dawn Picken: *Kids with friend, Frankie, at Mobius. They hadn't met her before, but thankfully, they're independent souls who usually get on well with people I trust. Fiona said, "I thought Frankie was a boy's name." "Well," I said, "sometimes girls are called Frankie." "Oh," said Fiona, "then my name's Frankie, too." "I'm Frankie, too," said Finley.*

I wanted to be Frankie, too. I wanted to be a child or an adult who could play with friends, who didn't have to make life or death decisions, or even understand what was happening to Sean.

But I couldn't be Frankie.

I had to be Dawn.

Chapter 4

Hope Breathes

Good news arrived the next morning. After two weeks on a ventilator, Sean's doc proposed easing sedation to prepare for removing the breathing tube. This was a relief for more reasons than one. Breathing is so fundamental, part of our independence we take for granted. We breathe on our own from the moment we're born, from that first great gasp. But anyone who has birthed a baby has tiptoed into the tiny bundle's room at night to make sure she's still breathing. My kids had the respiration of a plant; I had to lean in close. At least with Sean, I could see his belly rise and fall. But that was the ventilator's handiwork. If he could breathe on his own, I could hope to regain a well version of my husband.

I'd also started stressing about Sean's mental health. Lying sedated for this long in the ICU could result in a menu of mental disorders. A nurse told me prolonged sedation carried risk of brain damage. Dr. B said many patients in intensive care developed serious psychiatric symptoms of ICU psychosis. "You could take a healthy seventy-year-old and make him nuts. The days and nights get confused."

I was confused, and I was conscious and walking. The ICU did that to you.

Darcey, the occupational therapist, measured Sean's swollen fingers and arms. She told me her last patient with necrotizing fasciitis recovered full use of his fingers. Sean got an extra hit of morphine before physical therapy, where Darcey would bend his digits and limbs. Even in his unconscious state, it hurt, and he winced. I watched his face for signs of pain. I watched his face like I never had before. For signs of anything.

Another nurse arrived and took Sean's temperature. It had been 103 last night. Down to 101 today. She explained that they couldn't take Sean off the vent until his temperature reduced. Patients with a fever worked harder to breathe.

I could see his belly quivering, he was shivering so much. The nurse gave him Tylenol to try to reduce his fever.

Facebook Post: September 23, 2009 at 5:21 p.m.
Dawn Picken: *Breanne (RN) says I'm freaking out all the nurses because I write everything down. "Don't all families take notes?" I asked. "Uh, no, not usually." Writing stuff down is the only way I can remember anything, since I'm in a fog. Plus, I've always found a notebook to be a handy shield. Finally, Sean needs a record of time spent down the rabbit hole.*
KK: *The reporter in you. I'd be doing the same thing.*
RW: *That's OK. Keep writing. You're just exporting from the hard drive in your head. You need to make room for all the love and good thoughts coming your way!!!*
AH: *When families take notes, we worry it's for a lawsuit.*
JM: *Make sure you tell them that Sean is a medical attorney. That will REALLY freak the nurses out!*

The next day, Dr. B noticed that Sean was starting to lose some of the fluid they'd pumped into him. He said it was a good sign. Now the forty-six pounds Sean had gained at the hospital would start to go away. I could already tell his face didn't look as puffy, and his hands looked less sausage-like, too.

What Sean's color lacked in normalcy, it made up for in variety. Half the skin on his arms and legs was purplish-maroon. Patchy bits shone and oozed yellow pus. Other bits were rough and blistered. The rest of it bore a yellow tinge. Even Sean's eyes were rimmed in sickly yellow, like a Yukon Gold potato left in the pantry too long.

Clear plastic circles were stuck to the skin on either side of his mouth. They held straps attached to a breathing tube from which three more plastic tubes sprouted like eyes on a potato. The ventilator setup was so grotesque, I forced myself to focus instead on the rise and fall of his stomach. His belly was a void of splotches and black marker outlines, wires and tubes. His navel was slightly herniated — half "inny," half "outy." It was the only part of my husband that appeared remotely normal. *Hello, belly. Keep rising. Keep falling. Keep moving. You look great.*

I wrote notes to Sean in his Fiona journal. He would read them when this whole ordeal was over, laughing about my commentary.

September 24, 2009

Sean,

*I miss you. I sit by your bed each day, writing, updating Facebook, waiting. Everyone thinks I'm the strong, devoted wife, but let me tell you — **you** are much stronger and devoted than I'd ever be. I write because it's all I can think to do. I simply muddle through each day — kiss kiddos goodbye, go to the hospital, talk to doctors, nurses, update our friends, eat, drink, pee, and wait for you to get better. Am I scared? Hell yes. I'm also still numb. In a fog. Not sure what to do or think. I tell you I love you at least a dozen times a day. I love you.*

September 25, they started weaning Sean from narcotics, so he could regain consciousness. He opened his eyes halfway when I spoke. I felt his chest shudder and saw his shoulders tremble, almost like he was trying to cry. I told him, "Relax and breathe. Just breathe."

Then he opened his eyes wide when he heard our friend Greg's voice. I couldn't see anything behind those yellowish-white orbs but fear.

Facebook Post: September 25, 2009 at 3:06 p.m.
Dawn Picken: *Just met with my boss in the visitor's lounge. After the Sean update, talked a little "shop." It's a good thing: reassuring to know the entire world has not imploded; just mine and everyone else with loved ones in the ICU. I welcome the diversion. Just don't ask me to watch any PowerPoint presentations. You know who you are!*

The boss I had met was the head of the local chamber of commerce. I no longer worked for a newsroom. In 2007, after nearly fifteen years of reporting and anchoring, my contract had not been renewed and no reason was given. I suspected my salary, likely higher than other morning show anchors, made me a target.

Whatever the reason, I was humiliated, deeply ashamed the job I had invested in and loved for years was being yanked away.

I called a mentor I had met at a workshop who told me this was normal, that for many on-air people in TV news, not getting renewed wasn't an *if* but a *when*. It still sucked. I had wanted to work in television since I was fourteen years old. I wriggled my way from intern to anchor, covering stories along the way ranging from an execution of a death row prisoner, to a fire training exercise where I suited up to stand inside a burning house, to a series of consumer investigations that had won money back for my subjects and an award for me.

Thanks to wise counsel from a former news director, I had a clause in my contract requiring a six-month notice period for nonrenewal — they couldn't fire me right away. Still, I felt as if I'd been flattened by a garbage truck, unsure of my worth, and what the fuck was I meant to do now? I had a noncompete proviso in my contract, meaning I could not jump to another TV station in Spokane for six months. The clause had helped squash my career (the law changed in 2020, nullifying noncompete agreements for any employee earning $100,000 or less per year, which would have been me). We couldn't live without my salary for half a year, and we also didn't want to move.

After declining offers for TV gigs in other parts of the country, I landed a job as marketing and communications director for the Spokane chamber of commerce and economic development council. For the first time, I worked at a place that closed on nights, weekends, and holidays. I had a small staff, a better salary, more autonomy than I'd ever seen in news, and much to learn about how businesses and nonprofits worked. My boss became a mentor as well as a leader. I watched him greet the night custodial staff with the same warmth and respect he gave his board members. It was a great relief to know my job was secure, despite what I was navigating with Sean.

Sean's temperature persisted, fluctuating between 101 to 102. In his semiconscious state, he looked scared, confused. Staff ordered lab tests to see if Sean had pneumonia, the most common and deadly healthcare-associated infection, which affects nearly a third of ventilated patients.

I so craved normalcy, I convinced myself it was okay to leave my feverish husband. I had to eat, right? I escaped the ICU to dine at our friends Matt and Mindy's house. My thoughts ran parallel tracks of fear and denial. I was terrified of losing Sean but wouldn't let myself believe he could die. *Too young; kept alive by machines; improving*. I needed backup at the hospital. I texted my friend Paul, asking if he could be on standby in case Sean's condition got worse.

His message: "I'll just come down to the ICU and sit with you tonight."

After the impromptu ICU anointment, Paul stuck around and we talked. He had been a family friend since the kids were toddlers. An Episcopal priest, he didn't fit the man-of-the-cloth stereotype:

he was in his mid-thirties, married with two boys, drank beer, and sported tattoos (on his calves). He laughed at raunchy comedians like Dave Chappelle and once told me he wanted AC/DC's "Hell's Bells" played at his funeral. He was a scholar and neighbor/philosopher who was just as comfortable with addicts and crazy people as with suburban yuppies. While I placed myself in the sub-yup camp, I didn't discount the possibility of Sean's hospitalization plunging me into the addict/crazy camp.

"Sean was always my rock," I told Paul.

"How does it feel to be the rock, now?" he asked.

"Awful. I'm just — showing up."

"Ninety percent of life is showing up," Paul countered. "Sometimes, part of being the rock is knowing when to be justifiably alarmed and alert others. That means you understand the gravity of the situation, and you're not in denial. This is what you signed on to when you said those wedding vows."

"I know," I said. "But I'm so scared."

Paul's boys, Isaac and Owen, were similar in age to Fiona and Finley. Our children had played together at the Oregon Coast and at Camp Cross, scaling sand dunes and skipping rocks. I wondered aloud why I was still breaking up fights over toys and scraps of paper and washing out sippy cups when Sean was struggling to survive. Paul's theory was that children ground us. "Maybe they give us manageable problems to solve."

One thing I couldn't solve was aggravation over the recurring theme of pernicious positivity. One friend told the story of a woman diagnosed with stage four breast cancer who heard someone quip about how lucky the cancer patient was: "Oh, you get to meet Jesus before I do!" This kind of dimwittery makes me want to shove the Jesus freak in front of a train. Figuratively speaking, of course.

Paul said the non-Catholic, non-Calvin way of viewing God — the way espoused by Anglicans and Jews — is that God is in everything but doesn't cause everything. We are not chosen to undergo some divine test. "We are creatures of free will and God is not controlling every single thing in the universe. In the midst of this, there's death and resurrection. Faithfulness is saying yes when there's every good reason to say no. We don't deny God's presence when things are great, and we don't deny it on the other end, either."

Facebook Post: September 27, 2009 at 2:30 p.m.
Dawn Picken: *Just had a few moments of lucidity with Sean. He's able to raise his right arm a bit and can move his head around. I followed his eyes as he took in his surroundings, with all the tubes, wires, and machines. His eyes seemed to say, "What the hell happened to me?" The nurses and I continue to remind him where he is and why he's here, and I keep repeating, "You're strong, and you're getting better."*

Facebook Post: September 27, 2009 at 9:15 p.m.
Dawn Picken: *Kids have been up giggling in bed for 1.5 hours while I'm downstairs paying bills and catching up in cyberspace. Oh well. I always think Fiona's going to ask me something serious about Sean right before bed, and then she says something like, "Mommy, what would your hair look like in a bun?" Tough questions, Fiona-style.*

After tucking the kids in bed, I called the ICU. A nurse told me Sean was more alert, but his fever had spiked again, to 101.5. He was being packed in ice. Pneumonia was still a possibility, though it hadn't shown on a chest x-ray.

Facebook Post: September 28, 2009 at 11:41 a.m.
Dawn Picken: *RN Marcy says if Sean fails breathing test during wound dressing change, they'll likely replace the breathing tube with a trach (throat) tube to prevent throat injury. She said, "At least he won't remember the vast majority of this." I will. I want Versed, the amnesiac sedative*

51

they've been giving him, too. Feels like I'm falling further down the rabbit hole...just falling.

MS: Hang in there, Dawn. I can hear the stress in this one. Just know that we are all praying for you and sending you, Sean, and the kids strength and love.

Aunt Leslie arrived from Michigan. Paul picked her up at the airport. She later asked me rhetorically, "How much do we love Paul?"

The answer was, "Lots."

Leslie, with her spiky blonde hair and purple-rimmed glasses, possessed a wicked sense of humor, coupled with passionate Presbyterianism and a gift for prayer-plus-gratitude. She didn't brook small talk and asked lots of questions. This made some people uncomfortable, but to me, she was interesting and interested.

I got to know my dad's brother, Bob, and his family when I worked in Grand Rapids, Michigan for two years in the mid-'90s. For the first time since starting my TV career, I lived just over an hour from relatives. Being so close was like a revelation—my own family, down the highway! I would drive to the Pickens' house in St. Joseph and hang out in the kitchen as my cousins Conor, Tyson, Dary, and Chelsea served themselves cereal after school from giant boxes of Chex, Cinnamon Toast Crunch, and Cheerios.

Leslie would roll her eyes as Bob and I engaged in a family obsession—discussing directions (just so you know, I usually took I-196 through Holland, then along the coast of Lake Michigan, past Saugatuck and South Haven). We Pickens will outline our travel route in minute detail. As a child, family road trips found me in the back seat of the car, studying auto club maps in my lap (on paper— this was the Mesozoic era, before satellite guided navigation systems). The TripTiks highlighted our route from Ohio to South Carolina or Florida.

Leslie laughed, recalling an instance where Uncle Bob and I indulged in road chat. "One time, you had to take a detour, and Bob's eyes lit up. I wanted to put my head in the oven."

She was an excellent observer, a student of human behavior. She told me, "You have people around you to help you bear this. Your legacy is such that you're beating people off with a stick who want to help."

I asked Leslie how I could ever hope to return a fraction of the favors friends and family had given us.

She said, "Say 'thank you.' Be mindful of the folks around you; pass it on. Be present in someone's life."

I was trying to be present in Sean's life because he couldn't be present in his own. But sometimes I couldn't even do that.

Facebook Post: September 28, 2009 at 2:48 p.m.
Dawn Picken: *Sean opened his eyes briefly just now, before the wound care nurses started doing their thing. He looked confused. They give him extra pain meds before any dressing change. I don't watch this part of the "Seventh Circle of Hell" show; I've seen enough. They should be done in about 40 minutes, at which point they'll know if Sean passed his breathing test so he can get off the vent.*
JF: *Sitting with you right now in prayer.*
LW: *Chanting: No vent! No vent! Come on, Sean! No vent!*

Sean passed his breathing test. They let him breathe on his own after the dressing change and he kept it up spontaneously, even tolerating passive physical therapy with few grimaces. The nurse said they'd restart the vent at night, so he could get some rest. He'd have another breathing test tomorrow after dialysis.

My heart fluttered like a bird in my chest. That's how hope feels sometimes.

The kidney doctor told me Sean's kidneys showed no signs of working, but he was stable enough to reduce dialysis from daily to three times per week. The doc said he'd seen function return after as long as nine months.

Sean also got regular transfusions of A-positive blood, because his body wasn't making enough. The bagged stuff was a deep scarlet color and made me think of the *Twilight* books I had read the summer before. Sean hadn't been able to understand why so many women, from age eleven to white-haired grannies, were raving about the book.

Even so, he had watched the first *Twilight* movie with me at home a couple weeks before he was hospitalized. Something about the dynamic between the high school female lead and her vampire beau got me steamed up. Sean succumbed to my mortal charms that night and let me seduce him. I think he appreciated the appeal of the books much more after that.

KL: When I was little I sucked a piece of popcorn up my nose. The paramedics had to get it out. So a pansy's not so bad. :)

Sean's respiratory system had more challenges than pansies and popcorn. Radiology removed a third of a liter of fluid from his left lung. They could only clear one lung at a time. He'd have another spontaneous breathing test later that day. Hopefully the tube would come out on Thursday? They didn't know for sure, but they call that extubation.

September 30, 2009 at 6:32 a.m.
Dawn Picken: A doctor told a mostly coherent Sean (and me), they planned to remove the breathing tube. Then, Sean started coughing into his tube, so the nurses suctioned him. It's frightening, and I'm powerless to help. I'm just a bystander, a witness to suffering. I pray each day that Sean won't remember any of this. It's harder to see him awake than asleep, and he's spending more and more time awake as they reduce his pain meds.
Susan Picken: Does Sean know you are there when he is awake?
Dawn Picken: Mom, he nods his head "yes" when I ask if he knows who I am.
DR: How could he not know it's you? Seeing you will definitely make him well! As Sean always says: "Look at what I landed...Dawn's hot!"

Facebook Post: September 30, 2009 at 3:01 p.m.
Dawn Picken: Tube is out!!! Sean's first raspy, barely audible words: "Jackin' me around." (His way of saying he's getting poked and prodded.) Then, he choked out, "Beer." I kid you not! Maybe his sense of humor has survived this sickness.
AJ: Dawn and Sean, I'm so happy for the progress!! Jeez, give the guy a beer!!!
DH: Next time I'm in town, I'll get him a case of whatever he wants!

I missed the actual extubation — the liberation of Sean from mechanical ventilation — by minutes. Where was I? Returning from dropping the kids at the children's museum. I was grateful Paul was there. The clerical collar was his all-access pass. Paul described the extubation as "the closest thing to Lazarus rising from the grave I've ever seen."

Like a kite, I was buoyed by the flood of messages from around the world at the news Sean was breathing on his own.

And I was so freakin' tired, I could barely stumble the hospital corridors to leave.

I drove home and leaned over Fiona's and Finley's beds to hear them breathe. In and out. In and out. In and out. The rhythm of hope.

Chapter 5

No Light, Only Tunnel

Yesterday, Sean was disconnected from the ventilator and his breathing tube was removed. Today, the first of October, I learned they might move him from the ICU soon. This felt like a light at the end of a very long tunnel. I wasn't sure if the light was sunshine or another train barreling down on us.

Yet the idea of Sean moving set my teeth on edge.

Sean hadn't moved for more than two weeks. He hadn't raised his arms, lifted a leg, or sat upright by himself. Under the fog of necrotizing fasciitis and heavy sedation, he could barely turn his head. Sean couldn't have performed a finger puppet show for Fiona or Finley. He would have to begin the long process of relearning to eat, drink, and finally, to move.

Facebook Post: October 1, 2009 at 11:47 a.m.
Dawn Picken: *Sean just finished a breathing treatment, woke up and looked sad. He looked down at his body and rasped, "Depressing." A nurse, Adrianne, says they'll probably start him on anti-depressants soon. Resident doc wants a*

psychiatric evaluation. Says 70% of ICU patients have post-traumatic stress disorder. My husband was whole when he entered the hospital seventeen days ago. And now he's not.
JR: I can't believe it's been that long. Then again, I bet it feels like an eternity!

It had been an eternity, but now, finally, I could talk with my husband. He was lucid, not unconscious. He was moving, not stationary. And he was trying to feed himself, gingerly inserting a nano-teaspoon of vanilla pudding between chapped lips and sipping two ounces of water, then throwing it up. He was as helpless as a baby, having to learn basic motor skills all over again.

Sean was incredulous when I mentioned the two weeks he spent on a ventilator. He remembered visiting our family doctor, but nothing about the ICU, aside from dreams or delusions — visions of being locked in a phone booth and getting stabbed. I shuddered and imagined that's how a wound dressing change felt: like someone slicing your flesh. Sean thought he was receiving last rites the time Paul the priest had dabbed him with oil.

Physical therapists flocked into the room like a mob of crows. They propped Sean up in a sitting position, his legs over the edge of the bed for the first time in weeks.

Even with the extra meds, his grimace told me this was painful.

"This is it," he said. "We gotta stop."

They asked him to raise his right arm — stiff and straight like the Tinman. He couldn't do it by himself. One of them had to help.

He sat up for nine minutes, a therapist on each side in case he fell over like a tower of blocks.

Then they let him lay back down. Mary, one of the therapists, said, "Great job. Because of that, you know what you get?"

"A new car?" Sean managed a grin.

"Nope," she smiled. "You get to see more of us more often."

I had struggled so much with the decision to bring the kids to the ICU to see Sean. Now they wouldn't have to see him lying unconscious, tubed, oozing, and bruised. Daddy was awake and (mostly) aware, and I would get to reunite my children with the father they adored. And it wasn't just for them. I wanted Sean to see the reasons he was fighting for his life.

I only brought Fiona that first visit, unsure what impact seeing her father weak and sick would have. We rode the elevator to the fifth floor, turned left, then right, entering Sean's white and green room. But he wasn't there. A nurse told us to try down the hall, in dialysis.

He lay between other dialysis patients, propped up in bed, white sheets draped over his purple legs and arms. I warned Fiona he'd be sleepy, confused, and tangled in tubes. As we entered the room, she took one look at him and thrust her body behind mine.

"Fiona, you don't need to be scared of Daddy. Why are you scared?" I asked her.

"Because he has all those tubes on him."

"Did you know when you were born, you were a baby bundle of plastic tubes and machines too?" I asked her. "You were born five weeks early, and you needed all those tubes to help you grow."

"Even though I'm scared of Daddy," she said bravely, "I still love him."

Fiona's second hospital visit was better, with Finley in tow. Sean was awake and alert, propped up in bed in his usual room. Fi held his hand. Finley ate his lemon-flavored pudding. Sean smiled. We decorated the room with drawings the kids had made at school, pictures of rainbows and lollipop people with arms and legs sticking out of their heads.

Facebook Post: October 5, 2009 at 4:45 p.m.
Dawn Picken: Fiona: "What if you get sick, Mommy? Who would take care of us?"
Me: "Someone will always be there to take care of you. Aunt Steph, for one, said you can stay with her, and play with cousin Sam anytime."
Fi: "Can I go now? I can pack my stuff."
Not so fast, kiddo!
Stephanie Stanelun Holttum: Tell her Sam is pretty excited to see her, and would love to have her come out!

I received my first hospital bill October 5: $4,000 for Sean's intubation anesthesia. It appeared the doctor had not been a preferred provider, which meant we had been billed at a higher rate. You're not supposed to think about money when your spouse is critically ill, you're supposed to wait until the storm has passed. But I wanted to inspect the damage before the next dump truck of bills. I knew intensive care would cost our insurer hundreds of thousands of dollars. I worried Sean would exceed his $2 million lifetime maximum, which most insurers had in place before the Affordable Care Act took effect in 2010.

Sean got dialysis at least three times a week. Specialists told me the longer he went without kidney function, the less likely his kidneys would ever recover. Meanwhile, Dr. B wanted to wait two weeks to graft skin onto Sean's right thigh. And like the parting gift you don't want from the world's worst game show, we had another problem. When he'd first been admitted to the emergency room, the doctors had found a mass on Sean's pancreas, an issue they had set aside while they worked to save his life. But now that had to be dealt with. Once he was 70 percent recovered (Sean was a pie chart now), doctors would remove the pancreas mass, which might or might not be cancerous.

One of the nurses said they called cases like Sean's a "train wreck" because even after they'd stopped the engine, the cars kept crashing off the track.

Facebook Post: October 6, 2009 at 5:23 p.m.
Dawn Picken: *For those who missed it: Pancreas issue: doctors found a fluid-filled mass on Sean's pancreas the night we brought him to the hospital. Said the finding was incidental to the massive bacterial infection that nearly killed him. Nonetheless, the mass needs to come out, along with possibly half his pancreas, maybe spleen, too. Hoping it's a cyst. Praying it's a cyst.*
KC: *Sigh! Missed this. Thanks for reposting. Geez, girl.*

Sean was getting better, so I should have been feeling better too. Instead, it all started to hit me: what he'd been through — the surgeries and intubation and wound dressing. And what I'd been through: endless days of worry and terror.

The night of October 6, I had a breakdown. For three weeks, I'd been spinning plates: the wife plate, the patient advocate plate, the mom plate, the town crier plate. Then, Sean's mother, Helen; sister Rochele; and her husband, Sam, visited again from Seattle. I crouched in a corner of Sean's room, taking notes while they fired questions at doctors and nurses like kids trying to win a snowball fight.

"What about a hyperbaric chamber? Can he take Heparin? How much Methadone is he on? What about anti-depressants?"

One of the nurses later asked me, privately, if Sean's family was stressing me out. I nearly hugged her. "Yes!" I said. "They're trying to take over his care. I've already asked and had all these questions answered. I'm the one who's been doing this all along."

Don't get me wrong. I *did* want help. But I didn't want a throng of people in Sean's room, second-guessing his treatment. Sean's blood pressure spiked when his mother was around. She had barked orders, even via Facebook, for breathing exercises; special foods like custard, warm fruit, milkshakes; assigned tasks for me like monitoring nurses, encouraging Sean to speak, placing cool cloths on his forehead, cajoling, encouraging — endless lists for an endless task.

Finally, I waved a white flag. When we got home that night (I'd invited them to the house for dinner), I trudged upstairs to the bedroom Sean and I shared. I sat on the beige carpet in my walk-in closet. Tears streamed down my cheeks. I was sobbing so hard I wheezed and gasped for air. *I can't do this anymore. I can't do this anymore. Having kids is the only thing keeping me going.*

Facebook Post: October 6, 2009 at 10:10 p.m.
Dawn Picken: *When it's just too much, what do you do?*

My Facebook cry for help resulted in twenty-three comments, mostly along the lines of "Hang in there" or "We're praying for you." Paul the priest delivered the most useful suggestion.

"Get some sleep," he'd said.

I took his advice, took some Ambien, and curled up in bed.

The next day, my dad flew in from Ohio. He put on Sean's red flannel shirt to protect his clothing while he went out to fix our back fence. As I stood at the kitchen sink, looking out the window into the yard at him, I almost came unglued again. It was like Sean was home, right there, healthy and normal.

Not since Fiona finally started using the toilet at age three was I so excited about urine. On October 8, Sean produced 100 cm³ of pee (equivalent to two shot glasses full of whiskey) after weeks of desert drought.

I cried at the news, which made Sean's nurse weep, too.

Later that day, Sean stood for ten seconds during physical therapy.

I told him, "You're the strongest man I know."

"I have a good team," he said. "Enough accolades. I want to brush my teeth."

My husband then brushed his own teeth. But hope was a mixed bag of dark chocolate and dog shit. Sean took two steps forward, then two steps back; an oncologist drained fluid from the orange-sized mass on his pancreas to check for cancer.

I registered for the Spokane half-marathon the same day Finley dog-paddled the width of the YMCA pool for the first time. Sean was missing our lives and his own, a prisoner of his mutinous body. In less of a medicated stupor, he began to realize how long he'd been in the hospital and what he had endured. He didn't remember the gory details, thanks to the drugs. But his body was telling him and so were the doctors and nurses. He asked, "How long will I have to stay here?"

They didn't have an answer.

Sean was also worried about his video jobs — his livelihood. His friends had stepped in to finish projects he'd started before getting sick — shooting a wedding, editing an anniversary. But I wondered how much of his business would remain by the time he was well.

When he started his company in 2004, Sean had sacrificed short snippets of time with his family to work. Mostly, this meant tinkering with equipment or editing videos after dinner. Because he stayed at home from the time Fiona was born, we were comfortable with him remaining in Spokane while I spent a few days with Fiona in Ohio. We believed our family would have many more chances to travel together.

"Are you sure you want to stay here while Fiona and I are gone?" I had asked.

"Yeah," he replied. "I need to figure out this new editing system. And we're going on a big trip next year." We were planning to take Fiona to Switzerland and Portugal to film an art project in the Alps and visit with my Luxembourgish friend Jean-Marie at his in-laws' home near Porto. Sean and I always traveled well together. I was the planner and he was a dependable companion, happy to drive while I navigated.

Sean's journal for Fiona: December 18, 2004
You and your mom are in Ohio visiting the family. I did not go this holiday because I had things to get done here. The biggest being getting my equipment to function. I plan on doing weddings soon and needed an editing setup that would be able to do that. So far, I got it plugged in and partially hooked up. I tried a few edits, but I still have some bugs to work out. It has been very quiet the past few days without you both here. I miss your screaming and big smile.

One month into Sean's hospitalization, I ran the hilly Spokane half-marathon in one hour, forty-seven minutes. I waited until crossing the finish line to collapse in the grass at Riverfront Park and cry. Big, wheezy, can't-catch-my-breath sobs. Runs are healing. They have a beginning and an end. Just like my first race, the

Columbus, Ohio marathon. I trained for months, up to twenty-two-mile runs, where I stashed water bottles along the route beforehand. Doofus that I was, I didn't know about water backpacks and had not investigated local running clubs. I thought running was lone wolf stuff. GPS watches were not yet sold, my race fuel was a Tootsie Roll (it was too cold and hard to eat), and I ran to my own rhythm, finishing 26.2 miles in three hours, forty-one minutes and change. I walked, stiff-legged, like Frankenstein's monster and groaned when squatting at the toilet for a week afterward.

When you cross the marathon line, the race is done. Where was Sean's finish chute? It kept moving.

Facebook Post: October 11, 2009 at 2:08 p.m.
Dawn Picken: *Sean ate four bites of tomato soup, three bites of apple Danish, drank half a carton of milk. I tried to make the Frosted Flakes sound appealing: "But honey, they'rrre great!" He didn't think that was funny. Told me I was "this close" to being on his bad side.*

We celebrated Finley's fourth birthday at the house with a Spiderman cake. Finley wore his sister's red satin dress with roses, which alarmed my father. "He's a boy. He shouldn't be wearing a dress." I told him bending gender rules was normal, especially at Finley's age. Still, Dad was relieved when my son got a green t-shirt with a truck on the front as a present and replaced the dress with his boy costume.

Back at the hospital, Sean told me he'd been having bad dreams. His description of nightmares reminded me of a poem he'd mailed me while we were apart in 1997. I could never figure out why he'd felt compelled to send it to me, sandwiched between pages of an otherwise romantic love note.

A dream by Sean Stanelun

A furious pounding of hoofs
cutting deeply into the wet sod
echoing whispers
gasping for breath
surrounded by wide-eyed black orbs
staring deeply, questioning
the scent of blood fills the lungs
life and death
but which one has it come for?
scraggled branches sway in the foggy haze
clacking out a song it has sung
a thousand times
I stand to face my fear
not knowing my fate
reluctantly willing to fight
the moment defines all that I am
sinewy muscle and bone
weathered with wisdom
weakened with wrongdoing
the blade heavy and dulled
whooshing through the air
only buying more time
a final question is asked but I refuse to hear
choosing instead to lash out
tiny rumble of hoofs, getting more distant
I look at the ground before me
my blood reddens the soil
I have lost once again

Sean's doctor cut his Methadone dosage in half. Yet he still fought nausea and fevers even as his blistered, oozing skin began to heal.

> **Facebook Post: October 13, 2009 at 1:31 p.m.**
> **Dawn Picken:** *This is a horrible sickness. When will it end? No light. Only tunnel.*
> **CM:** *Hold on, Dawn. Hold on.*
> **KC:** *Yes, hang in there, friend. You are deeply loved.*
> **RH:** *There IS light, Dawn, even though you can't see it. Keep looking for it and stepping into the darkness with faith and trust. Morning will come. Hope is generated by moving in faith. So many people are pulling and praying for you and Sean.*

October 13, a doctor called to say Sean might have a lung infection. The same doctor then told me a CT scan of the pancreas showed evidence of a "malignant process." I was driving home down West Third Avenue, past a phalanx of fast-food joints: Dick's Hamburgers, McDonald's, Arby's... Somewhere near Taco Bell, I pulled my minivan to the side of the street and held my cell phone with a trembling hand. Dr. K said, "Oh, sorry to tell you over the phone. I thought you knew."

She later called the house to backpedal, saying the consulting physician was *not* calling the pancreatic mass cancer. Another of Sean's doctors told me the mass was spongy, well-circumscribed, and very bloody. Dr. G said the topography of the mass, plus the fact it sat atop the pancreas, were good signs, markers that it was likely benign.

Sean continued dialysis three times a week, throwing up after each session.

At home, I punched holes through stacks of medical statements and placed them in a three-ring binder. Bills had hit the $500,000 mark in one month (full retail price, before the insurance adjustment). Black-and-blue-inked documents encased in clear-windowed envelopes were filled with indecipherable codes and procedures, an alien language for a product we never ordered. A train to financial ruin on a dark trip we didn't want to take.

Chapter 6

HelpSeanRecover.com

Our family has joined the ranks of causes célèbres: you could donate online to help the homeless, stray animals, and now — us. Friends Brad and Lucinda set up a website, "HelpSeanRecover.com," to solicit donations for all the bills that insurance might not cover.

When I told Sean, his eyes widened. "Really? I don't know what to say. That's very generous. But I'm also embarrassed. I don't want to be a charity case." At the moment, Sean needed company more than money. Now that he was aware of his shitty situation as prisoner in an institution for crimes his body had committed against him, he needed trusted humans at his side. He wanted me around, but I was also trying to see the kids. My Facebook plea for more visitors was answered when a couple of neighbors and guys Sean knew from work appeared in his room.

Sean had a new job as patient, marked by long hours, pain, and no pay. In a single day, he might endure four hours of dialysis, wound care involving the picking of large scabs from his arms, and a scope of his liver. He was still not eating enough, so his feeding tube was replaced with a new one.

I applied for disability benefits for Sean and started getting treatments at a massage school in hopes a therapist could relieve tension I felt from wearing my shoulders at ear level. Also, I'd have something to look forward to each week.

After the heart attack scare, Sean asked me to ensure our wills were in order. Considering life without him made my own heart shudder. He was my co-parent and confidante. He was my person, the one who had protected me during crises and helped celebrate wins. He saw who I was—my impatience, pathological need for busyness and order, a predilection for bargain shopping that had resulted in a closet stuffed with clothes. Sean saw my faults—liver disease and long second toe included—and loved me anyway. He kept his own much smaller wardrobe in Finley's room.

Sean was perfectly imperfect. He could sometimes retreat into himself, and he lacked close friends to lean on, meaning I was his ship and his anchor. Efforts at fitness were sporadic; his diet skewed toward potato chips rather than vegetables. But we split chores and childcare—actually, Sean had been doing most of the child rearing, allowing me to focus on work and extracurricular activities like board meetings and running.

downtown to do your whole back." Sean will go for another CT scan of abdominal area; checking to see if the pancreas mass ruptured.

JH: *Dawn, have they gotten pathology results back on that yet?*

Dawn Picken *Yes: pathology did NOT show cancer (of course, the docs say they can't completely rule it out for sure). Just a spongy mass of bloody cells. So, we know as much today about the mass as we did a month ago.*

The kids and I continued eating casseroles and other meals provided by friends from work, church, the neighborhood, and clubs I'd joined over the years.

I felt bad about it, like there was some sort of expiration date on how long you could ask people for help before you were just mooching. My friend Laura P had an answer for that. She said, "Your life is shitty right now. So if someone offers to treat you to lunch, take it. Might as well get a good meal out of all this. Heck, you might even want to put your shoe size out there."

I asked doctors to give Sean anti-nausea and anti-anxiety medications before each of his dialysis sessions. Sean proclaimed the first of these heavily-medicated treatments the "Best Dialysis Ever."

I returned to help in Fiona's kindergarten class. A neighbor, MaryAnn, offered to watch the kids for an entire week after school. Neighborhood business owners held a fundraiser, donating ten percent of the day's profits to Sean's fund.

Facebook Post: October 19, 2009 at 2:52 p.m.

Dawn Picken: *My kids will be obligated to perform many acts of kindness in their lives, because I'll never be able to repay all these good deeds in my lifetime.*

Stephanie Stanelun Holttum: *Honey, you're not due to repay. You have already put SO much into the karma bank, now you're just withdrawing some of your investments!*

I signed permission for Sean's skin graft with the same ease I signed my kids up for a school field trip. Signing off on bizarre medical procedures was my new normal.

A photographer, Colin, came to the interview with Pia. His pictures had won awards and brought the subject of the shot into your soul. His massive collection of photos spanned natural disasters, action shots of athletes, beautiful portraits, and now, the stark scene in the hospital with patient and wife. He, looking sad but composed in bed; she, looking lovingly at her train wreck of a partner. I didn't feel like the dutiful spouse — more like a fraud. I was not at Sean's bedside 24/7. I would flee the hospital at regular intervals to see Fiona, Finley, and even friends. At some point I would start working again part-time.

Sean got a first look in the mirror at his ashy face and the chicken-like crest of hair atop his head. He said, "I look petrified." He had been in the hospital five weeks. He started eating solid food in miniscule amounts, but he said it tasted like dog food and it often make him throw up. The feeding tube would stay, for now.

The graft went well. Dr. B harvested skin from the back of Sean's left leg and sewed it onto the back of his right thigh. The site was covered in white mesh like the kind around the base of young trees. I excused myself from yet another wound dressing change for a dose of retail therapy.

Sean tolerated my shopping habits because I had provided no evidence we would one day need to clear paths through our home thanks to the presence of too much junk. Also, I was incapable, on a cellular level, of buying shoes for anything but running that cost much more than $100. Jimmy Who and Manolo Blah-Blah? Not me. I did love dishes though. I scoured the shops in Portugal in 2005, amassing a set of heavy hand-painted terracotta plates and serving bowls painted in vibrant colors. We didn't have packing material like bubble wrap, so I encased each dish in clothing. It cost more to ship the set than to buy it in the first place, and a couple of the bowls broke in transit. "Just glue them back together and put them above the cabinets; you won't be able to tell they broke," said Sean. He was right.

At the hospital, a DJ Sean knew from the wedding business called to talk. He told Sean about the fundraiser their organization would be hosting for our family. Sean said he was grateful for the support.

"When you're this close to death, it puts things in perspective," Sean said. He had become unusually expressive since he'd woken up from the medication fog.

Sean's sister Steph created a calendar display of photos on the ceiling so Sean had something to stare at when he woke up at night. My dad left, having finished a double gate for our fence so we could store our travel trailer. Sean swapped war stories with another ICU survivor who told him he looked good. He quipped, "Yeah, good for someone who fell off a cliff and got stomped by elephants."

Dawn Picken: I was laughing and doing a dance in Sean's room tonight after visiting hours. One of the nurses said she nearly came to check on us, because they're not used to that much laughter on the floor. Sean had just told me he'd peed 400 mL into a plastic jug.
JM: That was her polite way of telling you to be quiet. Trust me, I know all the tricks!
PE: Sean would also like us to ask his doctor when he can start back on Guinness. Also, how soon is too soon to share a bag of Dick's burgers and fries?

Facebook Post: October 23, 2009 at 10:09 p.m.
Dawn Picken: Right before I left tonight, Sean said, "It means a lot to have you here. It makes me feel better when you're in the room. Even if you text the whole time (which I don't!), it's nice to have you here." I told him I'd been with him for six weeks and I wasn't going anywhere.

I registered Fiona for ballet and told Sean how much she loved it, scampering around a dance studio in pink tights with other sprightly five-year-olds. I opened a card from a prayer group in St. Maries, Idaho. The church ladies had done more than pray — they had also sent a hundred dollar check. Fiona's soccer team, the Silver Princesses, played their last game of the season. Sean hadn't seen a single one. His childhood friend, Jim, and wife, Kimm, visited to keep Sean company for several days.

Facebook Post: October 24, 2009 at 8:29 p.m.
Dawn Picken: I suggested Sean get into the reclining wheelchair so he could be more mobile and see something new.
"Why?" he said. "What's the point?"
"To get you out of the bed you've been in for 6 weeks," I said.
"What's the rush to get me up?"
Hmmm... I'm going to have to let the therapists be the bad cops.

Dr. B informed me that Sean's skin had to heal before he could endure more aggressive therapy. The insurance company wouldn't fund hospital care if there was a cheaper option available. Sean would be moved to a skilled nursing facility.

You don't know terror until you learn your forty-eight-year-old husband will be entering a nursing home. I wanted to throw myself on the hospital floor, kicking, sobbing, beating my fists. Instead, I toured a nearby facility and prayed Sean wouldn't get sent out of state or far from home.

I took the kids to church, to the stately, Gothic St. John's Cathedral. Ascending the stone steps to a massive set of wooden double doors always invoked awe. The sanctuary is lined with colorful stained glass windows depicting the gospel story. It also hosts an organ with more than 4,000 pipes. Inside this sacred space, Finley knelt beside me during communion. "Do I get to drink the wine after I eat this?" he asked. I laughed. Later, I felt my ears burn with recognition and agreement during Father Bill's sermon.

Real faith is what happens when our lives get shattered and we realize that even in the midst of great loss we live and love and hope and forgive and seek forgiveness. Real faith is what happens when we discover we are loved, not because things are going right, but precisely when we are faced with the fact that they are not going right at all.

It was true. Because of what had happened to Sean, our family had experienced a level of love and support we hadn't even known existed. It was more than website charity or online encouragement, a disability check or meals donated, volunteer childcare or a neighborhood fundraiser, a benefit concert or prayers and surprise checks. So much more than a list of deeds done for us. It was love in action when we needed it most.

Chapter 7

A Heavy Toll

You don't always get to choose your path in life, and some roads charge a heavy toll. Sean didn't choose to get sick. Nor did he do anything to deserve it. But he still had to pay the price for the road he was on. And sometimes, you don't understand how much crossing one bridge has cost you until you're on the other side looking back. And when you turn around to go forward, there's another bridge.

As Sean's body healed, slowly and incrementally, I began to see the toll his illness had taken on him mentally. The doctors saw it too. Finally, after I pestered them for weeks, they ordered a psychiatric evaluation.

The skin graft was healing well. When they did Sean's dressing changes though, I wanted to burst into his room and demand an end to the torture. One day, I was on the phone outside his room with the insurance company when I heard, "Arghhhh! Ugh! Arghhh!" It sounded as if the staff were stretching Sean on a rack. Dr. B later described this as an "exaggerated pain response." He said it was common in patients who've taken lots of morphine, and

Sean had taken enough to tranquilize a blue whale. I wondered if naming someone's reaction to pain made staff feel better about the torture they inflicted.

In ancient Greece, philosophers saw pain as an independent being that invades a subject to take it over. Aristotle described it like a spirit that enters through an injury. Pain was often seen as an act of the gods as punishment, or a test of faith. The word "pain" comes from the Latin "poena," meaning a fine, a penalty. Sean was paying the toll.

To sweeten the deal during this season of suffering, I was about to break a promise to Sean that I wasn't going anywhere. It would only be for two days, but still, it felt like a betrayal to leave his side.

Facebook Post: October 25, 2009 at 9:44 p.m.
Dawn Picken: *I'm flying out Tuesday morning to see my own doc in Minnesota. Yeah, it's a bit far to travel for an appointment. Yeah, the timing's lousy. Long story. For now, let's just say it's a routine appointment that's overdue. Routine. Routine. Routine. Sean's family and my mom are staying here, holding down the fort till I return Thursday night.*

I had told the kids I was visiting Aunt Nancy for a few days. It was technically true, because she was meeting me at the Mayo Clinic. But I knew my children thought that once someone went to the doctor, they never returned. That was the toll their young minds paid. If it could happen to Daddy, it could happen to anyone. I couldn't let them worry it would happen to me, too.

While tackling my own health demons in Minnesota, I got word that the hospital had decided to move Sean to a nursing home in Idaho *while I was gone*. Granted, out of state was a thirty-five-minute drive, so not a trip to the moon, but having Sean in town meant he was just fifteen minutes from our home. His doctor explained the Idaho hospital was the only skilled nursing facility around with in-house dialysis. I was flustered about the move and livid I wouldn't be there for the transfer. And it didn't help that Sean's psychological evaluation had come back diagnosing him as "massively depressed."

The bright spot was the specialist at Mayo, who said my liver disease was stable. This followed a battery of blood tests and a twenty-four-hour urine collection, where I got to carry a plastic bottle of pee with me everywhere. I threw a napkin over the jug when my aunt and I went out for dinner. I was not the only diner in that medical city slogging around her own urine. Restaurants in Rochester could have had a "wee" and "no wee" section.

At that point, I had no symptoms, just doctor's orders to get regular imaging and blood tests. There was also the nagging worry my health situation would one day implode. But not today. Praise the saints and pass the Pinot Gris. On second thought, skip it. Bad for the liver.

I returned home to Spokane, fuming about Sean's impending nursing home transfer, only to discover that the transfer had been delayed.

Sean's doctor said he expected Sean would soon walk and climb stairs again. The prediction lifted his mood, like fog rising above a valley floor. He began brushing his teeth and cleaning his ears without help. I coaxed small soap-like flakes from his scalp with a fine-tooth comb and baby oil. He had cradle cap—the same stuff I had teased from Fiona's head when she was a baby.

Trick-or-treating provided a welcome distraction. Fiona was a fairy. Finley was a Power Ranger. I arranged a phone call between Sean and another necrotizing fasciitis survivor who had e-mailed after seeing Sean's story in the paper. Bill reported living a normal life, working and playing golf. Sean asked the staff to remove his feeding tube after their talk.

Facebook Post: November 1, 2009 at 9:14 p.m.
Dawn Picken: *Fiona wanted to know how all the other people*

in the hospital with Daddy got sick. I said, "That's a good question, honey. I don't know. But sometimes, our bodies can't fight germs and other bad things."

Fiona said, "You mean fight, like this?" (throwing punches, kicking legs in the air). Uh, yeah, kind of like that. I didn't tell her our bodies often betray us.

Sean's urine output increased dramatically (file that under romantic questions for your spouse: "Honey, did you pee today?"). A doctor suspended dialysis indefinitely, though they left his port in, just in case. I relished returning to the office each Monday. At the Chamber of Commerce, no one measured pee, changed wound dressings, or moaned in pain.

Dr. B told me Sean's mental state had vastly improved from just a week before and added, "Congratulations, you're getting your man back."

Except they were moving him to Idaho. I got a call at work (where I took calls regularly from Sean's doctors, social workers, and physical therapists) saying Sean would be driven by ambulance to North Idaho Advanced Care Hospital at noon. When I talked to Sean, he tried to put a positive spin on it, saying, "We're gonna grow old together and watch the kids grow up."

Facebook Post: November 2, 2009 at 1:26 p.m.
Dawn Picken: *Just got to NIACH. Looks like a spiffed-up nursing home. Everything's new, except the patients. Average age appears to be around 80. Welcome to our new alternate universe.*
JS: *Just keep remembering that the hallway geezers were kids with dreams who fell in love and did crazy stuff. The important thing is how the staff touches the patients. No bruises allowed.*

Even Finley was beginning to grasp that no one knew when Daddy would come home. Finn told Sean over the phone, "Daddy, I want you to come home when you want to, and we'll play Hungry

Hippos." Our wide-eyed, pudgy-cheeked four-year-old asked often about Daddy. I could tell Finley wanted his guy back — the man who would swing him around or carry him on his shoulders. Out of all the other males in the universe, this was Finley's dude, the man who loved him best.

We rejoiced when Sean reported eating an entire hamburger for dinner.

Our last big family vacation, we had taken a ferry to Lopez Island north of Seattle and landed at the Love Dog Café, where Sean wolfed down a frisbee-sized burger. I snapped a picture of him stuffing it into his mouth, red onion and cheese dripping from the bun. That had only been three months ago.

November 2, 2009, I opened mail and found no bills. Only checks. I cried. I felt humbled, grateful, and guilty for all this help. Because somewhere, other people had it worse — I imagined a family where the parents were unemployed, sick, had six kids and few resources. Things could have been so much worse for us.

Sean was reclassified from "maximum assist" to "moderate assist," meaning he should be able to transfer himself to a wheelchair. A case manager at NIACH told me Sean's inability to move stemmed more from emotional pain than physical. I wondered how they knew. I also learned that children would soon be banned from all hospital and care facility areas except the entryway as a precaution against the H1N1 flu. If Sean couldn't get into a wheelchair and leave his room, he wouldn't get to see his kids. What kind of sadists were these people?

I briefly revisited the second floor ICU at Sacred Heart to leave the nurses a gift basket. Each time we left a floor, we deposited treats, leaving a trail of chocolate, nuts, and fruit. My heart thumped a wild syncopated rhythm when I emerged from the elevator onto that floor. My body remembered the ICU where my husband had nearly died. I dropped the basket at the nurse's station like it was a grenade about to blow and dashed out the door.

Our friend Shelby was visiting from Colorado. Sean insisted we leave his bedside to go to dinner. He barked orders at me but was sweet to Shelby, asking if she'd move into our basement. I chalked up Sean's anxiety to the demands of physical therapy. Lifting himself, standing, and relearning to walk was scary, exhausting, and painful. I was thankful he had a tough therapist who didn't suffer excuses. She encouraged Sean to lower himself into a wheelchair much the same as you'd insist a small child eat broccoli before dessert. Another therapist told me Sean likely had post-traumatic stress disorder because of wound dressing changes when he was sedated but conscious. It helped explain why Sean dreamt about people walking off with his legs.

My husband *looked* much less robust than he sounded. He had dropped twenty-six pounds (from his normal weight) since entering the hospital and was down to his high school weight of 160. His hair, already thinning, was sparser than ever. It looked like the bald patch in our front lawn, where several tufts of grass stood out to remind us that's where grass was *supposed* to grow.

Sean and I were interviewed by two local TV stations. One

team was made up of friends from our old workplace. They paused the shoot when Sean started crying. I felt odd, like I was on the wrong side of the camera. The wrong side of the story. I envied my former colleagues, who could leave this nursing-home-disguised-as-a-hospital to write and edit local history, while I was trapped inside the narrative.

We learned disability benefits were on hold because the government wanted to send its own doctor to examine Sean. Apparently catastrophic illness and a five-inch-thick medical file weren't enough to justify aid. Sean's professional group held a benefit that raised $10,000. More people attended the benefit, by several hundred, than attended our wedding. A half-dozen hospital staff showed up. Even strangers came, because they saw our story on the news. No longer a reporter/photographer team, Sean and I had become recipients of the community's generosity.

Facebook Post: November 8, 2009 at 6:57 p.m.
Dawn Picken: *Finally talked to Sean. First time he's answered his phone today. He said he slept for much of the day because he's been sick to his stomach, and the meds they gave him to counter nausea made him tired. He said he had planned to wheel himself around in a wheelchair but was too wiped for that. Hoping tomorrow is a better day.*

At home, Fiona stared at Sean's picture and sobbed. "I want Daddy back home! When is Daddy coming home?" Her long dark eyelashes beaded with tears. I told her Daddy needed to be stronger to come home, and people were helping him heal so he could do that. But I understood her agony. I was tired of sleeping alone, parenting alone, keeping the sky from falling down on our heads alone, just like millions of other single parents. But unlike most of them, my other half was desperately ill and longing to get home. It was hard for me not to pressure Sean to hurry up and get well. His life had stalled, while mine had amped up with more stress and responsibility than I'd ever had before. The man I loved existed beyond the borders of my daily life, and it sucked.

My visits to Sean became less frequent. He was thirty-three miles down the highway and I was working again. When he'd been in the hospital in Spokane, I'd dropped in several times a day, but now it was more like every other day.

One afternoon, I entered Sean's room and he wasn't there. An empty bed always filled me with panic and dread as I imagined Sean enduring some new medical crisis or procedure. My mind would reel with questions. *Where is he? Dialysis? Another CT? Please don't let it be ICU again.*

But at North Idaho Advanced Care Hospital, a vacant room often signaled that Sean was knuckling down in physical therapy. PT filled me with the opposite of dread. It made me elated and hopeful. Sean was exercising two hours each day, and every eyes-wide-shut, grunting, moaning showdown inched him homeward. One time, I watched Sharon, the therapist, knead Sean's scapula for twenty minutes.

"Look at that," she said, her muscular fingers gripping Sean's trapezius. "Feel here." Without question I obeyed her, a Svengali with a short androgynous haircut wearing a tan-colored pullover. Sharon's firm tone and solid presence commanded authority. As instructed, I felt Sean's shoulder muscle. It was hard as a slab of frozen beef. "It's tight," Sharon said, "from trauma, clenching, and underuse. We're working to release the tension."

Sean and I had learned about muscles six years ago. We'd taken a massage course together when I was pregnant with Fiona. Sean liked when I pressed the heel of my palm to the small of his back. When we traded places on the black laminate science lab table, Sean mastered effleurage, light stroking movements used as warm-up. But when we practiced at home, Sean reverted to his usual drive-by back scratching. "I know how to massage my woman!" he'd joked.

Once, a therapist at the nursing home named Tim asked me how to budge Sean, who would stand just a minute or two before saying, "Stop! I have to stop!" I told Tim the kids had been a powerful motivator. "Remind Sean how much he wants to come home to be with Fiona and Finley," I said.

"Yes," Tim replied, "but what about a more immediate reward?"

I paused. "Try chocolate."

At work, I attended events where I pretended I wasn't churning with heartburn and bitterness at everyone else's bizarrely normal lives. People who knew about Sean would ask how he was doing, and I'd provide a polite snapshot. "He's getting better. Slowly." People who didn't know Sean would talk about business. I resented having to parrot the same information over and over again when asked about my ill husband, and I resented small talk when people didn't ask about the specter of sadness that stalked me. They could not see I was shouldering a blackened sky.

Facebook Post: November 10, 2009 at 7:33 p.m.
Dawn Picken: *I put Fiona and Finley on the phone with Sean tonight. Fiona said, " I hope you feel better, Daddy." Finn said, "I want you to feel better and come home." Home is a long way off. Sean said he watched the patient across the hall go into cardiac arrest. He says the staff worked on him in his room before wheeling him away.*

That was our normal. Children desperate for their father. Progress so slow it barely seemed to qualify as progress. Death looming just across the hall.

Frankie visited us at NIACH. When it was time to leave, my van wouldn't start. She trudged across the Walmart parking lot on a bed of new-fallen snow under a frozen sky, pushing a shopping cart with a new battery. The hospital's maintenance man installed the black brick at no extra charge. If only we could have installed a new battery in Sean, revitalized his body, and taken him home.

The cost of my husband's illness had been heavy on all of us — not just me and my kids or his family, but everyone who called Sean a friend.

Still, I had yet to meet a person who knew Sean who wasn't willing to pay it.

The toll was heavy, but Sean was worth it.

Chapter 8

Superman

Our friends from California, Leanne and Mark, sent a three-foot stuffed Superman doll to inspire Sean—and me. We perched him on a rocking chair in Sean's room at the nursing home. Mark had the same doll in his hospital room after his helicopter crash, silently cheering him through the hours of physical therapy he said had made him want to cry. Those red briefs and blue tights symbolized superhuman strength.

I was a huge fan of the Superman of my era, Christopher Reeve. Not only because he was hot and had romanced Lois Lane by taking her on a flight over Metropolis to an orchestrated version of "Can you read my mind?" But also because in 1995, he was thrown from a horse in real life and became paralyzed from the neck down. He died of heart failure in 2004. Superman was a man of steel and nearly indestructible. Mr. Reeve was a man like Sean—breakable and brave.

And Sean was making strides. He was standing and walking. I documented his efforts, though I wasn't nearly as good at photojournalism as he was. You could almost smell the flowers he photographed. My pictures were often dark and blurry, taken between chants of, "You're doing it, honey!" and "Almost there, sweetie, don't give up now!"

Standing for Sean was like pulling a team of two-ton oxen uphill. He closed his eyes in concentration, veins bulging from his temples. Weak muscles screeched in anguish. Weariness manifested as tears. Sean was relearning something he had done all his life, and it hurt like hell.

"Push harder, push harder with your legs," said Sharon, seated on a wheeled stool as she supported Sean between two metal parallel bars. "You're not working hard enough. I want to feel those legs quiver just like your arms."

Sean hunched over. He wore gray-blue hospital scrubs. A PICC line (peripherally inserted central catheter) with three access tubes peeked from beneath the short sleeve of his left arm. This was where staff administered antibiotics and other medicines. Sean's left wrist was wound round and round with white gauze. It looked almost like a sports wristband. He stood for several seconds, leaning heavily on Sharon, quivering and quaking with exertion. He eased himself back into the wheelchair directly behind him.

"Okay, let's go again," Sharon said.

Sean's head was bent toward the floor. I could see the side of his head with its balding patch on top. His eyes were half-closed. "Let me just catch my breath," he said.

Sharon allowed a momentary pause, then said, "Okay, one-two-three. Let's go," as she pulled Sean to a standing position while gripping the too-large pants around his hips. "Nice, quick, walk it out." Sean's forearms strained as he shuffled his hands along the metal rails. His fingers were fused to the beams, never lifting, only scooching forward, inch by inch.

"Good job. Good job. Good steps." The voice in the video was mine.

Sharon and Sean repeated the anguished steps backward. Near

the end of the bars, Sharon instructed Sean to lower himself into the wheelchair. "Stay forward, stay forward," she said.

His breathing intensified. It reminded me of when I was in labor with Finley. I had stayed home, determined not to repeat the experience of the cesarean section I had with Fiona. Despite taking courses in husband-coached labor, I writhed and paced alone all night before waking Sean to drive me to the hospital. While my uterus cramped and felt beaten like a bass drum, some primal instinct had taken over my mind and body — this was my work to breathe through and bear. I was a lone wolf, not in the forest, but on the floor of the TV room, on the same oriental rug where my children would one day wrestle naked.

Sean continued to bow his head as the video ended, as if in prayer. Or extreme pain. He didn't look up. Didn't look at me. But I knew it had been a heroic feat.

Only later did he have the strength and breath to say, "I couldn't have done that yesterday."

November 11, 2009, I posted the video on Facebook. Sean's fans went wild, flooding us with encouraging comments.

Later that week, I strolled the labyrinth at St. John's Cathedral. Entering the sanctuary, I smelled incense and old limestone. The labyrinth itself was a purple maze painted on large canvas, designed as a balm for fast-paced, fast-food lives. It encouraged slowness and meditation. A pamphlet at church said:

A labyrinth is a pattern with a purpose, an ancient tool that speaks to a long-forgotten part of us. Walking a labyrinth is a gift we give ourselves, leading to discovery, insight, peacefulness, happiness, connectedness, and well-being.

I slipped off my shoes and padded the maze wearing thin black socks. At first, I couldn't quiet my monkey mind. How much longer will Sean be in Idaho? How much longer before he's home? I wonder if the kids will go to bed on time tonight? Have new bills arrived?

Finally, the chatter dissipated. I stopped seeking the quickest way out of the puzzle. New thought bubbles surfaced: What if we make it through this? What if I don't have to figure out everything right now? Hang on, what if I don't have to figure out everything RIGHT NOW? I'm not Superman. It wasn't about reaching the end. It was about what happened as I shuffled one foot before the other, turned one tight corner, step, step, stepped through another straight stretch, pivoted on the next corner. The process was progress.

The labyrinth shows us that no time or effort is ever wasted; if we stay the course, every step, however circuitous, takes us closer to our goal.

Shortly after the labyrinth epiphany, a doctor removed Sean's dialysis port. Staff believed Sean's kidneys were recovered enough he could forego dialysis, possibly forever.

Fiona asked if Daddy would be home in time for Christmas. I told her I didn't know (my stock phrase for questions from the kids involving Sean), but we'd bring him Christmas and Thanksgiving wherever he was. Fiona pointed a tiny finger at her chest. "Daddy's always right here in my heart."

Facebook Post: November 12, 2009 at 9:48 p.m.
Dawn Picken: *Maybe two months of illness is our breaking point? Sean told me on the phone he's felt lousy all day; he received two units of blood after getting his dialysis port out yesterday, he missed physical therapy because he was busy getting transfused. He was tearful, very upset. And I found Fiona crying in bed after I tucked her in. She wanted her daddy.*

Sean's mood sank further. Some days, he walked ten more steps than the day before. Other days he couldn't even scooch from bed into his wheelchair. I could tell he felt abandoned when I wasn't there. He told me no one understood what was in his head. It was so hard to be a helpless infant, learning to walk, eat, and resume normal speech patterns at the age of forty-eight, all the while secreted away in some far-off octogenarian corner.

November's chill gripped my disposition too. Darkness descended around four o'clock each afternoon. One day Sean said to me, "I can't take it anymore."

He started refusing PT. He wanted to sleep. To sit in his room and be sad. To barf. Sharon, the physical therapist, came in during one of my visits and asked me to leave the room. Moments later, Sean hoisted himself into a wheelchair and wheeled down the hallway to work. Sharon later told me what she'd said to him:

"I need you to focus. You have twenty-two hours a day to be depressed. You have one hour for occupational therapy and one for physical therapy, and that's it. You're not doing this on my watch. For this hour, I need you to do what I say."

I wanted to kiss her.

Another necrotizing fasciitis survivor, this one from San Francisco, called Sean to offer hope. His attitude improved.

Finley spiked a fever of 102. I took him to urgent care, where he was diagnosed with an ear infection and strep throat. I was terrified Sean would catch Finn's sickness, since the kids had just visited him.

Sean started plodding longer distances using a walker. An entire fifty feet. He unlocked the key to curbing nausea: saltine crackers, the pregnant woman's savior. Sean asked to be weaned off more meds, which also decreased his urge to vomit. We ate dinner together in his room. My husband, in an imitation of his old self, devoured fried shrimp and an ice cream bar. During those rare times when Sean was feeling good and we weren't besieged by nurses, aides, and therapists, we talked about his upbringing, our relationship, and how hard we had worked to be together.

Sean was the oldest of four kids. His siblings had a different father than him, someone Sean grew up with for the first part of his life but was never close to. The disconnect was clearly demonstrated even when Sean was in his forties. The stepfather died, leaving an inheritance to Sean's siblings and nothing to him. After his parents divorced, his mother worked long hours to support the family, leaving Sean to look after his sisters and brother. He laughed about how they used to quickly rake toys from the carpet before his mom got home.

Sean told me he didn't have many rules or structure in his life until around age twenty, when he moved from Seattle to Maryland to live with relatives. Uncle Oley was an airline pilot and Aunt Chickie had been a flight attendant. Sean stayed six years, attending community college on a soccer scholarship and mowing the enormous lawn surrounding their stately brick home. He and his aunt and uncle learned to scuba dive in their pool before a sailing trip to the Caribbean that also included his siblings.

We had only been dating six months when I staged my own cross-country move to be with Sean, even though I had been unwilling to do that for my previous boyfriend of four years. That had always made Sean feel special. He asked me why I had been willing to uproot for him.

"I couldn't bear to live without you," I said. "You're the guy who brought me ice cream and Chinese food when I was too sick to leave my apartment; the one who sent me a plane ticket to visit you in Seattle; the friend who made me spit water while laughing."

Sean smiled, and I reminded him that pre-kids, he couldn't get enough of my time or my body. He rolled his eyes.

I also reminded him how he had wanted to marry me despite fears that my liver disease could part us early. When he proposed he said, "You're the one I want to share my life with, no matter how much time we have together. You're the one I want to have children with. We'll face this together. I'll give you part of my liver. My liver could kick your weak-ass liver with one hand tied behind its back."

I wasn't the sick one now. He was. Cheekbones jutted sharply on his once boyish face, aging Sean twenty years in two and a half months. And I loved him more than in those first wonderful days.

Facebook Post: November 13, 2009 at 3:49 p.m.
Dawn Picken: I could write a book about the past three and a half hours. Sean went from dark depression to feeling as though he'd climbed partway out of hell by the time I left. He thanked me for being his wife, and I thanked him for being my husband. And we both agreed that we made two kids who need both of us.

Another milestone: Sean walked up and down four steps. Sean walked two laps around the gym. All with his walker to support him, but it was tangible progress.

November 20, two staffers from a rehab hospital in Spokane, St. Luke's, evaluated Sean and declared him fit to graduate from the nursing home to their facility. Sean cartwheeled at the news. Not really, but we were elated.

And then we got stung by another medical drama. One of the NIACH doctors wanted the mass on Sean's pancreas removed before he was transferred to the rehab hospital. I called Dr. B, Sean's Spokane surgeon, who said he wouldn't operate on Sean without proof of cancer or a lung infection until Sean had improved more. A continuum of care battle had erupted between the two doctors. But I trusted Dr. B way more than this newcomer I'd never even met.

I called St. Luke's and our insurance provider, pushing for the transfer. And we finally got a date—the day before Thanksgiving. We could celebrate with Sean much closer to home.

Facebook Post: November 25, 2009 at 11:20 a.m.
Dawn Picken: Practically prancing around NIACH. Goodbye, goodbye, goodbye! Sean says he's ready to go to St. Luke's

and ready for some hard therapy. I drove past the St. Luke's sign en route here and smiled. Also wondered how many other people were grateful a spouse was entering rehab. Strange wish.

That day, as if he was performing his victory lap in advance, Sean took several tentative steps without a walker. Afterward, we went back to his room, him proudly exhausted, me so happy he would soon be closer to us. I was in awe of his strength. Maybe he wasn't *the* man of steel, but he was my superman.

Chapter 9

Is Life More Than Struggle?

Salmon swim upstream to spawn future generations. Most are anadromous, a term which comes from the Greek *anadramos*, meaning "running upward." Are we humans also consigned to a vertical run? We bathe in illusions of control and comfort while gobbling calories, earning paychecks, and storing memories in advance of the next struggle. Sean had scaled enough hills. I was willing the rehab gods, or fate, or whoever the fuck is running this shit show — please let him coast. At least let him walk flat ground. Any kind of walking would be fine, preferably at home.

Sean sat in a wheelchair for the ambulance ride to St. Luke's, where three former colleagues from the TV station, Duane, Russ (a.k.a. Moose), and Todd were waiting to greet him. Sean broke into a huge grin when he saw the guys. "This is so cool. Thank you for being here." A staff member eased Sean from the van's wheelchair lift to the grounds of a two-story stone building set on tree-lined grounds on South Cowley Street in Spokane.

I had asked Duane to bring his video camera, thinking he could capture Sean's triumphant arrival at rehab. Staff looked at the large lens and lost their minds, thinking this was a TV news effort. It wasn't. By the time Duane filled out paperwork to film, Sean was in his room. I got my own shot of Sean sitting up in his hospital bed, scrawny right arm raised, hospital band visible. He smiled, giving a thumbs-up while his mates stood behind him, doing the same. Duane shouldered the video camera. Just like Sean used to.

The facility had a different vibe than the advanced care hospital in Idaho. With its hardwood floors, it was stately without being stuffy. Most patients were still older than Sean, but they were here to get well and go home, not to linger and die. Superman came, too — the stuffed doll from Leanne and Mark. I had shoved him into a purple and orange striped beach tote my mom had brought back from the Bahamas. Superman listed to one side, arm hanging from the bag.

Because swine flu precautions were still in effect, Fiona and Finley weren't allowed in Sean's room. But they could meet him in the chapel. The facility's medical director introduced himself, a burly guy who used to play professional football for the Chicago Bears. He arranged for the kids and me to eat Thanksgiving dinner with Sean.

Sean had regained his appetite and his taste buds were reawakening, too. The first night there, he pronounced St. Luke's chicken and noodles "spectacular." The next day he ate a slab of lasagna for lunch.

Facebook Post: November 26, 2009 at 2:35 p.m.
Dawn Picken: Thanksgiving meal at St. Luke's was a bit chaotic with the kids. The room we were initially going to use was locked, so an aide showed us into the library. By the time we got lunch, we had about 15 minutes to eat. Ah, well. Sean got to see the kiddos and eat turkey with them, and that's the important thing.

Sean continued pushing the limits of his exhaustion, walking laps around the rehab's gym and pedaling a stationary bike fifteen minutes. He told me he was working hard to come home. And I knew he was, even though sometimes he only managed twenty minutes of physical therapy — half his allotment — before quitting.

Facebook Post: November 29, 2009 at 9:07 p.m.
Dawn Picken: Sean said a staffer at St. Luke's told him this joke: "What's the difference between a terrorist and a physical therapist? You can negotiate with the terrorist." Actually, Sean said he's told the staff they can push him harder. He said, "I'm pretty motivated to get outta here."

I set up our Christmas tree with help from our neighbors Greg and Jennifer. Another friend, Laura, helped decorate. Even during good years — normal years — I cried unpacking decorations because so many memories were attached to them, like the ornament in the shape of a pregnant brunette I bought at a craft fair when we were expecting Fiona. Another hanging charm featured Finley's baby footprint.

There was an aluminum globe painted with a bride and groom, a gift from my Aunt Janet the Christmas after Sean and I got married. I knew I couldn't manage the tree on my own this year. Laura also covered every available surface — mantel, piano, counters — with Santa figurines, reindeer, sparkly tinsel, and glittery balls.

"No one decorates for Christmas like a Jew," she joked.

Sean's doctors agreed to give him a pass to leave rehab so we could celebrate our tenth wedding anniversary, which was December 3. Friends from church stopped by with a check for $1,000. Sean said, "That's crazy!" I searched for words and stammered, "Thank you!" We felt insanely loved by our community and insanely cursed by fate.

Fiona, during a bath, while I was scrubbing her long dark hair, asked, "Mommy, is it fun being a grown-up?"

I stumbled and stuttered and answered something I don't remember, because the real answer was, "No." At least not much of the time. But telling that to your little girl would be like scalping her doll or confessing Santa Claus isn't real.

I spent more of my scarcest resource — time — on the phone with the health insurance company. I was sorting three dozen statements from a dozen providers spread over two months. How did anyone without degrees in health policy and accountancy solve this riddle?

Sean called me the day before our anniversary. "I have bad news," he said.

Never ever say that to someone stumbling through catastrophic illness. My heart pounded loudly in my ears. *What is it? The mass is cancer? You have a serious lung infection? Pneumonia? Plague?*

"They found a blood clot in my lungs and several in my legs," Sean said. "I have to be on blood thinners and bed rest. I can't leave for our anniversary dinner."

That was all? Blood clots? More meds? No hall pass for the anniversary dinner? Big deal. We'll eat in.

Facebook Post: December 2, 2009 at 7:46 p.m.
Dawn Picken: *It's not the fact that our anniversary night out has been cancelled that upsets me, as much as the fact that we have ONE MORE THING to deal with. One more thing. How many times can a body betray itself in the span of a few months? Wait, I know the answer. The number is infinite.*
JH: *Nah it's not infinite, sis. This is one of those "blind men exploring an elephant" scenarios. This is all one bad thing, but it keeps revealing itself in small, confusing, re-traumatizing bits. Most importantly, each time a bit is revealed, you and Sean kicked its ass. I know you're tired, but you're batting 1,000.*

Anniversary morning, I surprised Sean with a seven o'clock visit. I brought baked oatmeal, which we shared. I also brought our wedding album. I felt a lump in my throat as we turned pages together. So young-looking. Innocent. Naïve. Sean said, "That's when I saw you in your dress the first time. Look how beautiful you are."

My first thought was, *Wow, we look healthy.* On December 3, 1999, we were pink-cheeked and smiling, eyes locked in a lover's gaze. In one photo, Sean's arm held my waist. I was clutching a bouquet of red roses. My hand encircled Sean's neck. I wore a beaded headpiece and back-length veil. Yesterday's Love Princess. Today's Queen of Sorrow.

"Look at my handsome groom," I said.

"Yeah, I had a lot more hair back then," Sean quipped.

Facebook Post: December 3, 2009 at 5:49 p.m.
Dawn Picken: *Staff at St. Luke's have set up a table in Sean's room with a white tablecloth, fake flowers, plus real plates and silverware. It's a much nicer setup than the usual mealtime here, when I hunch over food in my lap. A nurse (who doesn't want recognition for this) is buying our dinner at Anthony's and bringing it to us. We had planned to order lobster. She's buying us lobster.*
PM: *When you and Sean celebrate your 50th (and I really think this is in your future), you will remember this anniversary. You will have many other dinners, fine dining and exquisite serenades, but this is an anniversary you won't forget.*

I had smuggled a small bottle of red wine into Sean's room. We toasted to ten more years and Sean skipped the merlot. He opted for sparkling cider instead. With all the meds he was taking, his body didn't need booze. We dove into an appetizer of beef tenderloin, followed by salad with blue cheese, lobster, shrimp, apple crisp, and crème brûlée.

Our friend Cheryl, a local singer/songwriter, serenaded us during dinner. She sang about love, loss, and taking chances. I videotaped, panning the camera from our plates piled with food to Cheryl, dressed in a lacy black shirt, with light brown and blond-streaked hair styled in a shoulder-length flippy bob. She strummed her guitar, smiling, rocking back and forth.

And I dare you/I double dare you. I dare you to fall in love with me...

I panned the camera again to Sean, who was using a knife and fork to saw something on his plate. The corners of his eyes crinkled as he smiled. He hoisted a forkful of lobster toward me, then inserted it, effortlessly, into his mouth. He chewed and smiled again.

I dare you. Oh, I double dare you. I dare you to fall in love with me...

My eyes watered.

The next day, a church friend, Karen, presented a gourmet picnic lunch of potato and leek soup, salmon, salad, and custard with strawberries. She handed us a tiny silver bell we could ring when we were ready for our next course, to summon her from the hallway.

Dr. B proclaimed Sean well enough to set a surgery date to remove the grapefruit-sized mass on his pancreas: December 17.

I took Fiona to see her first Broadway show, *The Lion King*, in downtown Spokane. She cowered as the performers processed down the aisle next to her wearing face paint, enormous headdresses, and costumes of lions, giraffes, zebras... I cried when they sang "Circle of Life."

Later that week, I hosted a gaggle of girlfriends, sixteen women, to eat and drink with me. The house got so warm from all those bodies and laughter, I opened the sliding glass door for air. The warmth and energy was reassurance from the Universe: *You are not alone. Life is more than struggle. You're allowed moments of peace, away from the smells of hospital laundry, hospital food, and hospital medicine, removed from beeping machines and blaring televisions, apart even from your husband, who's half spouse, half project. Hell, you're not driving. Get drunk if you like.*

Our friend Jean took the kids overnight, allowing me to sleep late, in the manner to which parents of young children have grown unaccustomed.

Facebook Post: December 6, 2009 at 6:49 p.m.
Dawn Picken: *Kiddos and I had dinner at Frankie's with Brad, Lucinda, Jane, and Chi. Yummy chicken soup. Perfect for this bitterly cold weather. Finley broke into Luc's pre-dinner prayer that included a request for Sean's healing by saying, "Daddy's walking without a wheelchair!"*

Fiona and Finley were excited Sean was walking using only a cane. Technically, they still weren't allowed in the rehab, but we could visit together in the common areas. I joked about smuggling them to Sean's room inside a Trojan horse. Or maybe a meal cart.

One day, in the chapel, Sean performed a magic trick by rising unassisted from his wheelchair. He took several steps. Finley kicked his legs in the air. Fiona applauded. Another day, Sean walked 200 feet with a cane and navigated fourteen stairs, the same number connecting the ground floor of our home to the second story.

Friends and neighbors continued holding fundraisers. The latest were a series of chili feeds at a neighborhood restaurant, Chaps. Seeing friends and supporters warmed my heart like chili warmed my stomach.

The bishop of Spokane's Episcopal Diocese visited Sean. My husband, whose catastrophic hospitalization had unleashed from him only trickles of emotion, told me the bishop's prayer made him cry.

Six days before his scheduled surgery, at 9:00 p.m., Sean called me and said, "I'm never gonna get out of here. My legs won't stop bleeding." After many surgeries and skin grafts, it was no wonder

Sean's wound dressings needed to be changed — a lot. His body was a bloody mess, an infinite reservoir of fluids and pain.

I offered to come to the rehab, but he told me to stay home.

Sean and I enjoyed a kind of date at St. Luke's. The facility had an apartment suite where patients practiced living before returning home. I brought a movie ("Last King of Scotland," which we stopped watching before the most brutal scenes). Sean ate five Christmas cookies as I cheered his appetite. We were starting to feel like a real couple again, laughing, eating, watching a movie. I'd even started joking we might someday have sex again. "Take it easy on me," said Sean. "I don't think I'm ready to get jumped just yet."

Between jokes and longing lurked fear. It buzzed at the corner of our senses like a mosquito, invisible but threatening. The surgery was coming up and what if something went wrong? What if it set Sean back again? I wasn't sure he or I could take another setback, another boulder to push up another unrelenting hill. It was hard to relax when struggle was all we'd known for so long. Hard to believe in a life without it.

The next day, Sean got his first hall pass. He'd asked to see the kids walk in the Christmas pageant at church. I drove Fiona and Finley in the morning to St. Luke's, where I blinked in wonder at Sean, who was dressed and waiting in the lobby. *We're taking Sean out into the world! We've sprung him loose from prison! He's ours again!* The kids ran to Sean and gave him gentle hugs, afraid they might break Daddy. "We love you, Daddy," said Fiona. "I'm a donkey!" said Finley, wriggling his blackened nose.

The reaction to Sean walking (with cane) into St. John's was what one might expect if Jesus or Elvis entered the building. Members of our church family stared, wide-eyed with amazement. Some people later told me they cried during the service after Sean wobbled up front to thank everyone for their prayers and support. Sean had never been religious; early Catholic teaching and a church that had seemed to forsake his divorced mom had contributed to him not so much abandoning faith as ignoring it. However, he appreciated the love and strength of community.

I took video of Finley, dressed in a brown burlap donkey suit for the pageant, as he traipsed down the aisle. His blue eyes became saucers when he saw Sean sitting at the end of a pew. He stopped to wave and touch his father, who motioned for Finn to keep going. Between "Away in a Manger" and "O Little Town of Bethlehem," I lay my head on Sean's shoulder and wept. My husband has risen from the dead to hold my hand in church.

Chapter 10

Our Bodies Betray Us

Sean was sent to the hospital for a preoperative consultation with his old surgeon, Dr. B. At first, Sean claimed he had no recollection of the man, his primary caregiver at Sacred Heart. After the meeting though, Sean leaned his head toward me and said in a conspiratorial whisper, "I remember him. He had no mercy. He just ripped out my staples."

> **Facebook Post: December 14, 2009 at 9:41 p.m.**
> **Dawn Picken:** *Sean seemed reassured after a visit with Dr. B who said the pancreatic mass appears cystic. But even masses that are not cancer can become cancer later. It's gotta go. Along with half Sean's pancreas, plus spleen, since blood vessels to the spleen are involved.*

The doctor said he would cut Sean from the bottom of his breastbone to his belly button to get at the large tumor. Then Sean would spend a week post-op at the hospital before returning to the rehab facility. There was even a mention of allowing him to spend

Christmas Eve at home.

Dr. B said he was ecstatic about Sean's progress. He told us the medical community would be talking about Sean for a while, because he had survived necrotizing fasciitis without losing limbs.

Back at rehab, Sean said he was grateful I was sharing his story via Facebook, because he continued receiving visits and phone calls. "Lots of people here don't seem to have anyone. It's like they're forgotten. I'm glad people haven't forgotten me."

Church friends shoveled our driveway. They hadn't forgotten me either.

Sean got more time off for good behavior — a pass for several hours so we could eat dinner together. I was so *over* the single parent thing, all I could think of was taking Sean to a quiet restaurant where we could eat julienned vegetables and seafood in neat vertical stacks, drink overpriced Shiraz, and hold hands across a candlelit table. Instead, Sean insisted on coming home to eat with the kids. "They'll be maniacs," I told him. "You know they're extra crazy at dinner time!"

Sean said, "I know, but I wanna be home. I wanna spend my last night before surgery with you and the kids. I know it's more work for you, but I need to be there."

Facebook Post: December 16, 2009 at 8:33 a.m.
Dawn Picken: *When I told Fiona and Finley that Sean was going to join us at home for dinner, Fiona smiled and said, "I saw a present under the tree." And Finley said, "But we're not gonna open it." Hey, kids, are you paying attention? Daddy gets to come home for a while!*

Facebook Post: December 16, 2009 at 9:08 a.m.
Dawn Picken: *Fiona's holiday program at Mullen Road is this morning. I've seen a preview in rehearsal and can't wait to see the real thing. It'll be kindergarteners wearing reindeer antlers fashioned from their own handprints forgetting the*

words to a half-dozen songs. That's what I call special. I get misty just thinking about it.

I missed the holiday program. I screwed up the time and arrived a half-hour late, catching the last two minutes. Fiona cried, "Mommy, where were you? I didn't see you!" Her teacher graciously asked the kids to re-sing James Taylor's "How Sweet It Is To Be Loved By You," which I'd heard in rehearsal. I wiped away tears watching Fiona's crestfallen pixie face. I apologized, saying I'd make it up to her, stopping short of promising a pony or trip to Disney.

I drove alone to a Starbucks parking lot, put my head on the steering wheel, and sobbed. *I can't do anything right. I can't do this anymore.* I called Sean at St. Luke's. I told him the story between snorty gasps, sucking in air and blowing my nose. He was sympathetic.

"Wow. I bet you didn't cry like that when I came off the ventilator. I think there's something more here than you missing the performance. Fiona will forgive you. You need to forgive yourself. You've been running pretty hard trying to keep up with work, me, the kids, your friends. Give yourself a break."

My husband could still comfort me, even from a bed in rehab.

My friend Beth had videotaped the entire show with Fiona standing right in the front and sent me a copy.

I fetched Sean from St. Luke's and we drove home together. He had shuffled out of the building using a cane, a massive improvement from the walker. I stood behind him as he inched his way into the passenger seat of our minivan. During the ten-minute ride, Sean talked about how he looked forward to coming home, even though he felt very tired. He couldn't wait to see the kids in their natural habitat, to watch them playing, eat dinner as a family, and tuck them into bed. But instead of a joyful reunion, Fiona and Finley barely acknowledged their dad, whining instead about how hungry they were. They started fighting. I bit my lip, staving off tears, then inhaled deeply.

I'd ordered pizza. I nearly tripped over myself after Sean requested a beer. *Beer! Beer! Healthy men have a taste for beer.* This would be Sean's first brew since September. The kids settled after several bites of pizza. *What is this miracle? We're sitting in our own dining room, eating dinner. Just like a normal family.*

All the trappings of middle-class life in suburbia were here: a kitchen with oak cabinets and granite tile countertops, thanks to the work of Sean and our friend Greg, who replaced the old laminate slabs. We had an island with a large pot rack hanging overhead, a double ceramic sink, and separate dining room. It featured a tray ceiling and housed my mother's old cherrywood dining set, custom-upholstered with scenes of 13th-century China.

After the meal, Sean slowly, very carefully, climbed the stairs to our home's second floor. He read the kids a bedtime story called *You Can't Go to School Naked!*

Sean was happy but physically shattered after three hours at home. He asked me to take him back to the rehab. There, I tucked him into his hospital bed with a kiss. I smelled the starch of the sheets, the aroma of cleaning fluids and laundry soap. We didn't talk much. Fears about the surgery had paralyzed our vocal cords. Doctors had tried to reassemble Sean for three months. Now, they were going to take him apart again. To me, that didn't make a lot of sense, but what choice did I have but to trust things would be okay?

Before I crashed into my own bed, I croaked out a weak prayer for strength — not just for Sean and me but for the community that had held us in its embrace.

Facebook Post: December 17, 2009 at 11:43 a.m.
Dawn Picken: *Reverends Bill and Jeff met us at the surgery check-in at Sacred Heart. We had a pre-op huddle; prayers*

sent out for skillful surgeons, strength, and health. Very moving. Made me cry, of course.

We waited an hour and a half in an exam room, a kind of surgery holding pen. The door opened and closed as staff wandered in and out, administering IVs, taking blood pressure, asking the same questions Sean had answered dozens of times during his three-month tour of regional medical centers. "What's your name? How old are you? When did you last eat?"

Shortly after one o'clock, I kissed Sean and handed him to a nurse, who wheeled him away for surgery. Bill and Jeff had left. I didn't want to be alone with my thoughts, so I returned to the main floor waiting room, where I took up the task of personalizing seventy-seven photo Christmas cards. The caption read, "Hoping for a better 2010."

At 2:00, doctors started slicing Sean open. According to the National Institutes of Health website, the death rate from pancreatic surgery had dropped from 25 percent in the late sixties to less than 5 percent now. Morbidity rates (serious complications such as heart problems, pneumonia, infection, and abdominal bleeding) remain high—30 to 60 percent. Sean's surgeon had outlined these risks before the operation.

Father Jeff returned. I asked how he knew what to say to families in crisis. He had been an Air Force chaplain for decades, helping in places like Iraq and the Dover Air Force Base mortuary, where he would shepherd military families through grief. Jeff said, "I believe God gives me the words. But mostly, I listen. Mostly, I'm just present."

I wanted to beg him, "Stay. Keep telling stories." Not only is Jeff a master raconteur, he'd become part of our ad hoc Sean/Dawn team. Our group of friends had survived war, organ transplants, stillborn babies, divorce, infertility, brain tumors, breast cancer. They had learned to spin strands of sorrow into empathy. We were

107

bound to each other in compassion gleaned from struggle.

It took them four hours to remove the grapefruit-sized growth from Sean's pancreas. They also cut out part of the organ itself, an adrenal gland, spleen, and a section of colon.

Several hours after Sean's surgery, I learned he would spend the night on the eighth floor, in an overflow Intensive Care bed. He required four units of blood and his blood pressure was low: 95/65. I was relieved my husband wouldn't return to the second floor ICU. Still, I was frightened he was branded critically ill. He was teetering–lying on that slim, cold rail with life on one side, death on the other.

My friend Kathleen arrived at Sacred Heart around ten thirty that night. She was a veteran of the health care game. Her husband had received a lung transplant and spent months in and out of hospitals and rehabs. She was an all too familiar student of the Ways in Which Our Bodies Betray Us. She didn't dispense clichés like, "One day at a time," and, "God has a plan." She spoke from experience and environment.

We shared a survivor's vocabulary with truisms like, "Sometimes, life is really shitty," and, "People mean well, but they say stupid things."

We met in the eighth floor hallway. Kathleen wore her dark hair wrapped in a headband, mascara'd blue eyes sparking with concern. Kat used to model. Now she painted landscapes and sang with an angel's voice — an angel who sounded as if she lived on the Mississippi Delta and trained in Ella Fitzgerald's gospel choir. Kat, a fifty-six-year-old with high-set cheekbones and porcelain skin, still bore the bloom of someone half her age.

"You okay, honey?" she asked. "Let me give you a hug." She wrapped her arms around me. I smelled perfume, tea, paint. We sat in chairs outside Sean's room, because staff wouldn't let us inside. One RN told me they were having trouble managing Sean's pain. Twenty minutes passed. Finally, a nurse said, "You can see him now."

Kathleen and I padded into Sean's room. He was lying in bed, wires and tubes snaking from beneath the sheet. Thin filaments monitored his heart rate, breathing, and administered fluids.

"Hi, honey," I said. Sean looked tormented. After all, someone had just sliced through his internal organs, then stitched him back together. "We won't stay long. The nurses said you need to rest."

Sean said, "Thanks. I'm having a lot of pain." Shakily, he tried to locate his morphine button. He floundered the first time, succeeded the second. "The meds," Sean said. "They're not really helping a lot, but I keep pressing the button."

I was lost. Powerless. I had no idea how to make it better. I touched Sean's forehead and planted a soft kiss.

"Try to sleep, sweetie. I'll see you tomorrow."

The next day, Sean's doctor said he was looking good and could soon be weaned from blood pressure meds. Pain control proved elusive. Sean was resistant to narcotics after three months of heavy morphine. He was so tired of being in constant pain, and now we'd reset the pain button again. Sometimes, when I looked at my husband and all he'd been through, I imagined he was Job from the Bible, rife with painful boils from the soles of his feet to the top of his head, crying out, "Why me, Lord?"

Except Sean had never asked, "Why me?" Instead, he had said, "It's a good thing it's me in this bed and not one of you guys. You and the kids couldn't handle it."

I pushed aside images of Job and posted videos to Facebook as a distraction: Fiona in gymnastics walking the balance beam, turning cartwheels and somersaults on the mat; singing "How Sweet It Is To Be Loved By You" in the school holiday program I missed.

I shared three videos of Sean at home the night before surgery. In one, he opened and drank his first beer in three months, standing in our kitchen against the marble countertop. Behind him, the refrigerator displayed pictures of Fiona as a baby and Finley and me sitting beneath a cobblestone arch in Italy. *Bella familia. Beautiful family. Bella casa. Beautiful home.*

In the second video, Fiona placed her baby tooth in Daddy's hand.

"Look how tiny it is," Sean said.

"I know," said Fiona.

The final video lasted nineteen seconds. Sean was walking the last of fourteen stairs from the second to the main floor. He clutched a cane in his right hand, the railing in his left. One railing was wrapped in pine garland and tied in a red velvet bow. A five-foot-tall piece of leaded glass hung behind Sean. *My husband made that frame. When he was healthy.*

"You're doing really well, honey. I can't believe you made it up and down our stairs," I said in the video, playing the part of Unseen Narrator. My words have a carefully chosen quality — I knew I'd be posting those episodes online.

"Yep. Ta-da," Sean said breathlessly. "Okay." He huffed down the last step. Then the video ended abruptly, as if Sean had said, "That's enough taping. Please help me, I'm really tired."

The day after his pancreas operation, December 18, Sean told his surgeon the pain was unbearable.

Dr. B said, "We can give you higher doses, but then we'd have to put you back on the ventilator, because we run the risk of relaxing your muscles so much you don't breathe."

I could see it in his eyes—Sean was terrified of returning to a ventilator. If it was hellish pain versus having to start all over again, he'd take the pain.

Facebook Post: December 19, 2009 at 8:00 a.m.
Dawn Picken: *Ran two miles on treadmill, three in spitting rain. It was good. Until phone call from Sean saying the hospital may have been administering continuous Heparin blood thinner by mistake. He could bleed a lot when they remove his epidural. Staff trying to find his surgeon. Anesthesiologist told Sean not to move.*
CM: *Oh, Dawn. I wish for you just one day of no worries. If I could put that in your stocking Christmas Eve, I would.*

Sean called, saying he needed me. I was due at a girls' luncheon in half an hour, which I grudgingly pushed aside. Looking back, it's amazing I tried to do any socializing while Sean was in the hospital, battling pain and fighting for his life. Part of me wants to wag a finger at that woman: *How dare you!* Another part understands how being away from the sights, sounds, and smells of a facility and hobnobbing with normalcy recharged me.

At the hospital, a nurse told me not to worry about the Heparin scare. She said the anesthesiologist was outlining the worst-case scenario, but the Heparin should leave Sean's system in a couple hours.

I was only twenty minutes late for lunch in The Safari Room at Spokane's four-star hotel, the Davenport. I joined a dozen other women in a toast to life and happiness. I told them my hope for the coming year: get Sean home whole and relatively healthy. And to find pants that fit. Mine were sliding from shrinking hips.

Sean called again as the lunch ended. I could nearly hear his teeth gritting. "It's like an elephant is sitting on me," he said.

"On my way," I told him.

Sean seemed better after I'd spent several hours at his bedside. A nurse slipped me a note scribbled on a napkin reading, "This is the calmest he's been all day. Thanks for being here." I felt simultaneously charmed and chastened. *How nice that she noticed. She must not think I'm here enough. I was off eating a swanky lunch while Sean lay in pain.*

I couldn't shake the made-for-TV image of the Devoted Wife who never leaves her husband's hospital room. That wasn't me. I had been ready to surrender after three days. Forget three weeks or three months. I was sick of it. Sick of visiting my husband. Sick of groveling before the Almighty Hospital Machine. Tired of bills and platitudes and constraints of the glass-house fish.

As I thought that, one of Sean's machines starting beeping like a reversing dump truck on crack cocaine. He looked at me, eyes wide in alarm, breathing in rapid huffs, like he couldn't fill his lungs. I jumped up, grabbing his arm, trying to hold him together, as two nurses and a doctor rushed in.

One of the nurses took my arm, guiding me out of the room. Then she went right back.

As I stood out in the hallway, I could hear the team working, trying to keep my husband alive.

And I could hear the sounds of his body betraying him once again.

Chapter 11

Tidings of Pain and Punishment

Sean's right lung had collapsed, and they inserted a chest tube right there in his room. The doctor said it should come out in a few days. I was thankful Sean was alive and didn't have to go back to the ICU. For now.

Sean might not have been asking why this was happening to him, but I sure was. It was all I seemed to ask these days.

When I asked the doctor why Sean's lung had collapsed, he said they didn't know.

Of course, they didn't know. No one knew why any of this was happening, which was the cruelest joke of all. If we'd known why, maybe we could have stopped the train from de-railing time after time. But control was not a thing I'd felt for a very long time.

Facebook Post: December 20, 2009 at 8:09 p.m.
PM: *Well, of course his lung collapsed. It is a test to see how much can go wrong. Next his eyeballs will turn green and mucous will come out of his ears. Toenails will turn upwards for no reason and, I mean, really. If you want to make medical*

PM was one of my favorites. She was a member of our church, a sixty-something sociology professor at a community college. She had survived blood cancer and formed a special connection with a young woman with breast cancer who later died. PM wore flowing rainbow-colored clothing and plastic clogs and was unafraid to swear in church. She was unafraid. Period.

Bad news arrived by mail. Once again, Sean's insurer had billed his pancreas surgery as out-of-network, so it was covered at a lower reimbursement rate. Their records said we had referred ourselves for surgery. PM had connections with our insurer and offered to help.

Sean's chest tube was causing him more pain. So was his incision. He alternated between sleeping and moaning. Watching his agony made me wince. Trying to imagine being zipped inside his blotchy, scarred skin made me want to cry.

Three days before Christmas, I donned a lead shield to help Sean stand for a chest X-ray. I ended up holding two bags—one half-filled with banana-yellow urine, the other with clear reddish fluid draining from his chest tube. "Lean on me," I told my husband.

Doctors removed the chest tube early that evening. "They went light on the pain meds," Sean reported. The full pathology report on the pancreas mass said it was benign. But already, Sean had a quarter-sized infection along his incision, indicating he might have a fistula, or hole, in his intestines.

I escaped to go see Fiona and Finley for the first time in more than twenty hours, and fell asleep after dinner watching *Scooby-Doo* with them on my lap.

This post-surgical moonscape was fraught with one emergency after another. Grooming became a memory. Saving Sean's life took precedence over shaving his face. He looked even more ragged — slightly sinister and homeless — with a five-day growth of beard.

Sean's doctor said his liver biopsy — one of many procedures done in the previous week's medical fishing expedition — was likely the cause of his lung collapse. What happened to *primum non nocere*, or "first, do no harm?" The Hippocratic school of medicine in ancient Greece focused on the patient, not the diagnosis. Care was passive, based on the "healing power of nature." Hippocrates believed the body must be treated as a whole, not a series of parts.

In the hospital, it was easy to visualize Sean's body as a machine on an assembly line, with each organ, system, and procedure assigned a specialist: kidney doctors, cancer docs, surgeons, anesthesiologists, pulmonologists. We routinely fielded questions from staff such as, "Why are you on IV Heparin? Who ordered it?"

DON'T YOU PEOPLE FUCKING TALK TO EACH OTHER? WHAT ARE YOU DOING ON THOSE COMPUTERS? PLAYING POKER?

Sean told me, "I wanna get out of here," but the doctors insisted he couldn't return to St. Luke's Rehab until his pain was controlled and he was eating more.

Meanwhile, friends took the kids for overnights, on play dates, Christmas shopped for me, and brought treats for Sean's nurses. They gave us home-baked goodies and cabbage rolls.

Christmas Eve, Sean found the energy to shave. The kids were allowed in his room despite the eternal Swine Flu ban. Fiona and Finley took turns raising and lowering Sean's bed. Afterward, I took them to the St. John's Christmas Eve service, finding a soupçon of peace in the eighty-four-year-old Gothic cathedral, despite Finn's running up and down the aisle and endless chatter.

Facebook Post: December 24, 2009 at 8:16 p.m.
PM: When I saw Finn at church tonight, he looked like such a cherub! See what a gift he is! When you are thinking about strangling him, you are feeling normal again...really normal. Healthy normal. Strangling the son on Christmas Eve has a sort of metaphoric ring to it.

Facebook Post: December 24, 2009 at 11:40 p.m.
Dawn Picken: Sean called tonight; sounded much more like himself. He was concerned I was stressed when the kids were in his room. Concern's a sign he's getting better.

Fiona awakened me at 7:00 a.m. Christmas morning, saying, "Mommy, let's go downstairs and open presents!" She and Finley shook out their stockings, tore candy canes from the tree, and started ripping wrapping. They each received a bicycle, plus a mountain of presents that screamed, "I have overindulged you because you have a sick father."

We made our Christmas hospital pilgrimage, all six of us: my sister Heather, Mom, and her husband, Dick, had arrived from out of town, plus Fiona, Finley, and me. We shoehorned into Sean's room carrying presents like we were the Three Wise Men (times two). Six loud wise men. I gave Sean a digital photo frame he could take with him as he bounced from room to room, facility to facility (though I was hoping that part was nearly done).

A photo from that day shows Fiona and Finley, pink-cheeked and smiling. Fi is wearing a magenta puffer jacket and Finley wears a blue and gray hoodie. I'm sporting a Santa hat, wan smile, and no eye makeup, adding to my haggard look. Sean sits up in his hospital bed behind us, wearing a gown with pink and burgundy stripes running down either side below his shoulders. His hair is even sparser than in pre-hospital days, his grin narrower, too.

Sean returned to St. Luke's rehab December 30, even though he was still weak and nauseous. It was his fifth relocation in three and a half months. His face was gaunt, eyes sunken with a purplish tint beneath. In one picture, he looked like he was smiling at knife point. Sean's weight had dropped to 149 pounds. Twenty pounds had vanished in two weeks.

Facebook Post: December 30, 2009 at 10:54 p.m.
Dawn Picken: *My friend Heidi said she spent New Year's in Ecuador, where they burn a straw man to represent banishing bad things. Another acquaintance has an annual burning party in spring or summer. I'm all for burning. I already have the what: copies of medical bills, explanations of benefits, extra bandages, medical journal entries on necrotizing fasciitis. Just show me the fire.*

The morning before New Year's Eve, I made pumpkin bread pudding and took the kids downtown for a family-friendly celebration called First Night. We listened to a gospel choir. I sniffed back tears activated, like a traffic light, at the intersection of beauty and sadness.

Sean called me, insisting to be discharged from the rehab that day, partly to save us another four-thousand-dollar deductible that would come with the new year. His case manager and I discussed it and agreed that was a bad idea. Sean required twenty-four-hour care, and our insurance only covered brief daily nursing visits.

There was no way I could manage his high level of care, our kids, my job, and the house. Plus, we had no ground-floor bedroom or shower. We literally had nowhere at home for Sean to sleep or bathe in his current condition. But his request got me thinking about how we would handle it when he finally did come home.

As usual, our community stepped up to the challenge. Someone I didn't even know offered to lend us medical equipment for Sean's ultimate homecoming.

For New Year's Eve, I hosted a dozen neighbors and their kids at our house, while Sean remained imprisoned in the hospital. But I needed the party, the happy, the noise and energy, plus a few stiff drinks. I had to live, even if Sean's living was still so limited.

New Year's Day, despite infection and nausea, Sean took fourteen steps at rehab. I snapped a photo as he maneuvered from his chair to a wheelchair. He wore a grimace atop a white hospital gown with blue trim. His arms, etched with red striations of disease and medications' side effects, looked like matchsticks against the chair armrests. Sean's nostrils flared, eyes squeezed shut, as he bore his yellowish teeth against the pain like a cornered dog.

Back at home, I shot pictures of dancing children — Fiona wearing nothing but white little girl undies with pastel-colored stripes, her finger pointed in the "Stayin' Alive" gesture. Finley stood next to her, wearing his sister's black shimmery tutu, pink long-sleeved shirt, and silver shoes.

The holidays were officially over. We had given the gifts we could, but not received the one we wanted most — Sean, well, whole, and home.

Chapter 12

Don't Tell Me It's Raining

January 4, I got a midnight phone call. Sean was having lots of pain.

"Do you need me to come in?" I asked the nurse.

"Not yet," she said.

At six the next morning, I got another call. Sean had been readmitted to the hospital.

Facebook Post: January 4, 2010 at 8:10 a.m.
Dawn Picken: *Sean woke up last night covered in blood with nurses cutting off his clothing. Apparently, the drain tube from the pancreas surgery had gotten clogged by blood clots and was leaking. They took him by ambulance to SHMC and did a CT scan. He may have another infection. More surgery possible.*

Dr. B later told me that inflammation and bleeding are normal after surgery. He called Sean's bloody nightmare "a minor setback." He then postulated that Sean's pain might be colon-related and laxatives could help. I was so tired of doctors downplaying everything as normal or minor, when it obviously wasn't. Don't tell me it's raining when Godzilla is standing over me, pissing all over my life.

January 5, the doctor removed Sean's wound drain. Sean said he felt better, knowing he wouldn't wake up with the equivalent of a bloody horse head in his bed, like in *The Godfather*.

I had promised myself a night of exile—just one night alone. No kids. No sick husband. No hospital. The check-in clerk at the Davenport asked me if I wanted to upgrade to a suite for an extra fifty dollars. Yes, I did.

I opened the door of my ninth floor parlor suite to reveal a sitting room with sofas upholstered in terracotta-colored silk, a marble wet bar, and a ceramic vase with an oversized arrangement

120

of lilies and gladiolas. I had a marble shower with Frisbee-sized head attachment and a soaking tub. The room smelled clean and floral. It smelled like expensive fabrics. The pièce de résistance was the king-sized bed with Irish linens and a mattress so luxurious, plush, yet firm, I wanted to sleep there forever.

I went to the bar instead. I ordered a wine and sat alone, relishing my solo status. No kids. No sick husband. No hospital.

"Hi there, you look like someone I went to high school with," said a thirty-something man two bar stools away.

Great line.

"You look like an actress," he said. "They shoot movies around here, don't they?"

Instead of blowing him off, I embraced the moment. I talked to a stranger about where I went to high school (Ohio), what I used to do for a living (TV), and what he was doing in Spokane (business trip). We did not discuss sick spouses, surgeries, or setbacks. I let him buy me a mojito. I made no mention of the fact that my husband had been in the hospital, critically ill, for four months. It felt a little like cheating and for just that moment, on that bar stool, in a lounge featuring taxidermized animal heads and faux animal skin fabrics, I was free. I felt young, attractive, and unfettered by sickness. My non-illicit encounter lasted twenty minutes, and it was twenty minutes of bliss.

Refreshed and sheepish about my solo night of luxury and comfort, I returned to Sean the next day. He was curled in a fetal position, despairing of his new feeding tube. He kept saying his stomach was on fire and added, "Everything tastes like rotting flesh." Then he croaked his familiar refrain, "I want to come home."

Hating myself for it, all I could say was, "You need to be able to eat first."

It wasn't an easy request. My husband, who only a month before had eaten five large cookies in one sitting, now had a psychological aversion to food, like an anorexic. Staff estimated

Sean was only receiving 300 calories per day, about one-eighth what an adult male requires, before they inserted another feeding tube.

Despite the eating issues, Sean's social worker said he had gained more independence. He could dress himself and use the toilet alone. She set a tentative discharge date of January 27. Fiona's sixth birthday. I wanted to be excited, but I could barely muster the belief that it would happen.

Facebook Post: January 9, 2010 at 9:28 p.m.
Dawn Picken: Expectation is a bitch. She leads you on, letting you think you're in her league, that you stand a chance. Then, she stops returning your calls. Then, when you confront her, she punches you in the gut and tells you, "Stop dreaming. I'm not yours. Never was."
Kathleen Cavender: Okay...now I need to hold you.
KW: Punch her in the face and look for a new chick! ;)

Sean started taking a steroid to build muscle and increase appetite. He received two units of blood January 14 and reported no difference in energy. The same day, I watched, for the first time, while a nurse changed bandages on Sean's pancreas surgery incision. Two wounds gaped from the canvas of Sean's torso, like coin slots in a Salvador Dali painting. I felt hot while watching the nurse wash out the wounds and reapply gauze. *The trick is to learn without staring, so I don't faint. How will I do this at home, when it's just me and two noisy, needy kids?*

Facebook Post: January 14, 2010 at 9:45 p.m.
Dawn Picken: Today marks four months Sean's been incarcerated, I mean institutionalized, I mean hospitalized. All of the above. I had to step outside today to get some air. Started getting choked up while writing an e-mail. Was thinking how small our world has become. We're like old folks whose biggest event each day is walking to the mailbox.

Friends Mark and Leanne flew in from LA. Mark offered insight about what it's like to be as badly broken as he was after his helicopter crash in 2007. "One of the hardest things for Sean is thinking you can't understand how he's feeling." And I didn't. I tried to imagine having little contact with the outside world, lacking appetite for food, exercise, even for writing. I liked to think we weren't just body — that there was so much more to cling to than our physical existence. But I had to realize that body came first. Stopping the pain was Sean's priority. How could he focus on anything else until that was fixed?

I took the kids to Olympia on January 16, to visit Stephanie over the long Martin Luther King, Jr. holiday. Mark stayed in Spokane most of the weekend to keep Sean company. Driving such a distance, 320 miles, was thrilling. We left behind trees and entered the desert that engulfed the middle of the state. We were miles from any sort of hospital or medical facility. Spending two nights at Steph's house felt visit-Paris good, basking-on-the-beach good, eating-gelato-in-Italy good. Away from hospital sounds, smells, and routines, I was free and comforted.

But not for long.

Facebook Post: January 18, 2010 at 1:56 p.m.
Dawn Picken: Sean is being taken to ER. I'm in Maple Valley, en route to hospital. Lucinda going to ER to be with Sean. I'll need someone at the hospital for kids.
MB: Are kids taken care of? If not, let me know.
Lucinda Kay: I'm just arriving. Pray, don't worry.
AR: What's wrong with Sean? I thought he was better!

AR's question was my forever question and my continual lament. Since the pancreas surgery, Sean had taken one step forward. Then five steps back. And now, we were in the emergency room again, and I wasn't going to let anyone minimize what was happening to us. This sucked. It wasn't rain, it was hurricane after hurricane, tearing down everything we'd ever built, leaving us in a pile of rubble, then blowing the rubble away.

On my cell phone, in the car, a nurse told me that fluid around Sean's lungs needed draining. He was still having wrenching abdominal pain. My friend Lucinda, who had prayed over Sean and teamed up with her husband, Brad, to create our fundraising website, was still recovering from a hysterectomy. Less than two weeks post-surgery, she and Brad rushed to the ER to be there with Sean until I arrived.

> **Facebook Post: January 18, 2010 at 3:22 p.m.**
> **Lucinda Kay:** *Sean's resting, said his ribs hurt and he couldn't breathe, but meds are making him feel better. Hopefully a doc will come talk to us soon.*
> **Stephanie Stanelun Holttum:** *Lucinda, thank you for cancelling your stuff and being there when Dawn was still en route from here. THANK YOU!!!!*

> **Facebook Post: January 18, 2010 at 5:22 p.m.**
> **Lucinda Kay**: *Sean has had a bunch of tests, including a CAT scan with dye. He's pretty miserable, had three doses of powerful meds. I'm holdin' his head and replacing a cool washcloth as needed. But I'm no Dawn. She has someone to pick up kids and she'll be here soon.*

The scan showed pneumonia in both Sean's lungs. He wretched and writhed as I sat in his fifth-floor hospital room. I wanted to run away when my husband heaved, bringing up greenish-black bile. But I had already abandoned Sean by carting his children away for a weekend. The least I could do was sit there and watch him puke. I sat there, doing my duty, thankful that my dad would arrive in two days. I'd asked him, weeks before, to come help me manage Sean's transition from hospital to home.

The next morning, January 19, I missed Sean's surgeon, who did his rounds at seven o'clock while I was home, readying Fiona and Finley for school and myself for another day of strategic travel, navigating snow and ice between home, schools, hospital, work, hospital, home.

I called the surgeon on his cell phone. He told me Sean had pleural effusion, an abnormal amount of fluid around the lungs, which could be caused by pneumonia, abdominal inflammation due to surgery, and poor nutrition. Sean's lungs would have to be suctioned. The doctor confidently told me my husband would heal with antibiotics and time.

He pretended it was just raining.

How long do you trust what others are telling you—the experts—when all the facts and your gut keep telling you something completely different? Everyone, even on Facebook, insisted everything was going to be all right with Sean, and at first, that had been comforting. But now it wasn't. Now I just wanted someone to tell me the truth—that this might never be over. That Sean might never be the same. That he could die.

Chapter 13

Not The End

The next day, I had lunch with Sean. His color and mood had improved. Maybe he felt better after doctors suctioned fluid around his left lung. We watched part of the local news together, and I asked why the female anchor was leaning away from the male anchor.

"Maybe he farted," Sean said.

The doctors had siphoned the equivalent of three-quarters of a large bottle of soda from an area between Sean's left lung and chest. The next day, January 21, he coughed up a beer bottle's worth, and staff suctioned another cup and-a-half.

When I finally cornered the gastrointestinal specialist, Dr. S, he had more bad news. During a scope, he had discovered a fist-sized blood clot in the middle of Sean's stomach, indicating a possible bleeding ulcer. Ever since the surgery more than a month before, Sean had complained about a feeling of having blood in his stomach (he specifically mentioned blood, not fluid, though I wasn't sure how he could tell the difference). He had even asked when it would be suctioned. The doctors and nurses had ignored his claims, saying it wasn't necessary.

And here we were finding out Sean's self-diagnosis had been right all along.

> **Facebook Post: January 21, 2010 at 1:00 p.m.**
> **Dawn Picken:** *Giving up on the idea Sean will ever be well enough to come home. Don't know what that looks like. Have no evidence he's getting better. Just setbacks.*
> **Lucinda Kay:** *Dawn. Stop looking at the evidence. In faith WE walk forward.*
> **AH:** *My friend was in the hospital for nine months. But she did COME HOME. Setback after setback. But she's back with her husband and daughter now. Let me know if you want to talk to her, OR her husband.*

I left the office to interview a woman for an online story about small business owners. She was a beautician and threaded and plucked my brows as a demonstration. I returned to the hospital in time, I believed, to see Sean before his next procedure. I sat in the first-floor surgery waiting room, texting friends, checking Facebook, eating lunch while waiting for the doctor to emerge. After ninety minutes and no doctor, I gave up and returned to work.

> **Facebook Post: January 22, 2010 at 12:56 p.m.**
> **Dawn Picken:** *The receptionist in the surgery waiting room at the hospital looked at me while I was checking in and said, "You again?"*

I didn't see Sean at all that day or in the evening either. I was hungry and wanted to eat dinner with my dad and the kids instead of standing over a tray in Sean's hospital room while he retched and moaned.

Sean called me around seven o'clock that night. He sounded weak and tired. He didn't talk long. "Something else is going on with me. I want you to talk to the doctor."

The new complication, according to Dr. B, was a pseudoaneurysm behind Sean's stomach. Blood was pooling in a pocket leaking from an artery. He didn't think the bleeding was substantial. Still, a radiologist would try to cork the hole tomorrow morning. He would insert a catheter through Sean's femoral artery and snake it into the abdominal cavity in a quasi-cauterization process.

Facebook Post: January 22, 2010 at 9:57 p.m.
Dawn Picken: And all the King's horses and all the King's men couldn't put Humpty Dumpty back together again. Because after the cracks started, they wouldn't stop.

That night, I went for a drink with my friend, Rebekka, who was visiting from out of town. I restrained myself (barely) from ingesting eight ounces of Shiraz in one swallow. I returned home and thanked Dad for watching the kids—for doing laundry, fixing the front door lock, emptying the vacuum canister, diagnosing the refrigerator's problem, and for just being present; for standing in for the most significant male in our lives, while he couldn't.

I trudged to bed at 11:00 p.m., relying on my usual half-Ambien to conk me out before my mind could start spinning. My nighttime medication was an escape hatch, a relatively safe, legal trapdoor in hell's floor. Unconsciousness deferred complications, questions, procedures. They all must wait until morning. Sleep is what Homer, Shakespeare, and Shelley have called the "brother of death."

Just as I was slipping into slumber, my cell phone buzzed from the nightstand. It was a call from Sacred Heart.

Facebook Post: *January 22, 2010 at 11:33 p.m.*
Dawn Picken: The hospital called to say they're considering moving Sean to ICU for the abdominal bleed. Wanted to know

if I would be coming to the hospital. But I'm zonked on Ambien and so tired I can't think. I started crying into the phone. Waiting for the next call saying Sean's in ICU.

KW: *Dawn, I am so sorry. Sean has had enough and so have you. You have had more than you should have and it's time for you to have a break. Our dear Lord needs to start handing you good news and heal Sean so he can get healthy and come home.*

MO: *Praying for your strength, Dawn. I'm so glad your father is there. Wish I could take the stress and sadness away, friend.*

Lucinda Kay: *I wish I weren't in Seattle. But I'm keeping my phone by the bed if you need to talk.*

Unable to get back to sleep, I walked downstairs and flopped onto the living room couch. My dad came in as I tucked my knees into my chest and tried to "just breathe." In. Out. In. Out.

"I don't know what to do," I said, my throat tight with sorrow. "I'm scared, but I don't want to go back to the hospital. I can't drive—I just took a sleeping pill. I want to sleep. I'm so, so tired. If I can get some sleep, I can handle the next crisis in the morning."

"Go to bed," Dad said. "You've been dealing with this for months. You need to sleep."

So I pushed aside my inner raven, harbinger of doom, and crawled back into bed.

Still, I couldn't sleep, so I called Kathleen to tell her about Sean and staff asking if I was coming to the hospital. My mind was fuzzy, but that question seemed more significant than it ever had before.

Kathleen offered to meet me there, and I managed to explain that I'd taken a sleeping pill and needed just a few hours of sleep.

"Call when you need me," she said. "Anytime."

I must have finally fallen asleep, because my phone woke me up at 1:55 a.m., its large red eye with white orb beaming at me from the blackness. The screen read, "Sacred Heart ICU." I slid my thumb over the screen to accept the call. "Hello?"

Even Ambien couldn't stop the thump-thump-thumping of my racing heart.

"Hi, this is Doug, the hospital chaplain. I need you to come here. Sean is in the ICU, and his team is performing CPR. Have someone drive you. Do you understand? I don't want you driving yourself."

I acknowledged his request, then started to ask, "Is he—?" I stopped. In all the time Sean had been in the hospital, I had never been called by a chaplain. That was when I knew something was wrong—horribly wrong. My hands shook with hasty purpose; I couldn't move quickly enough. My throat felt dry. I wanted to cry, but there was no time.

I found Kathleen's name on my phone and pressed send. Kat answered within three rings.

"What do you need, hon?" she asked.

"Kathleen, the hospital just called. The chaplain. He said—" I felt something catch like fish hooks in my throat. "He told me not to drive. Can you come?"

"I'll be there as soon as I can," she said. "It might take a while because I need to shovel the car out of the snow, and it's old and slow to start. Don't go anywhere, I'll be there. I love you."

"I love you too, Kat." Those words flowed from me with ease. Despite everything, there was love in my life, possibly more than there had ever been before. Sean's illness had bound me more tightly to family and friends, caused me to let down all my defenses because there was no energy to maintain them. I was like a sponge, absorbing support and love and light—because it had literally been keeping me alive. I had never felt love so deeply, side-by-side with the inky terror of loss and darkness.

I flung off my pajamas and dressed in jeans and a sweater. I brushed the metallic aftertaste of Ambien and wine from my teeth and splashed my face with water. In the mirror, I could see the pale etching of the number eleven between my eyes — worry lines. I resisted the desperate urge to leap into the minivan and drive to the hospital myself. There was nothing to do but wait for Kathleen. That's what I thought. I had forgotten Heidi and Kyle across the street, or Yvonne and Jeff, or Jennifer and Greg, Lisa and Mike, Debra and Vince. There was a plethora of helpers living less than half a mile in all directions who would have driven me to the hospital at a moment's notice. And I was waiting for Kathleen to arrive from seven miles away.

But it wasn't just that I'd forgotten about those people. I knew what was coming — the moaning and wailing, the flesh and blood and pain. Like a woman preparing for childbirth, I had to ask myself who I would need in that room. Who was brave enough, kind enough, strong enough? Who had the stomach to withstand it? Kat's presence did more than shore me up. It comforted me. So, I waited for her, just as I had for Finley's doula, who lived a half-hour from the hospital. The doula had arrived just in time to hold my legs as I pushed my boy from womb to doctor, to Sean's waiting arms. Now Kat would be my doula for something else just as profound.

And perhaps, deep down, I didn't want to be at the hospital in these darkest moments — especially not in the ICU. Was that denial? It seemed impossible, after all those months, the ups and downs, tests, repeat trips from near-death and back, that Sean would die. Did I imagine I had more time? (I *always* thought I'd have more time for one more phone call, one more e-mail, one more house chore. I am Marge in *The Simpsons Movie,* who scrubs one last dish as her house burns.)

Yes, I could have been at the hospital in fifteen minutes instead of thirty. I could have asked my dad to drive and had a neighbor stay with the kids. Now, I see that, and I'm not sure I would have changed a thing.

Instead, I updated Facebook and waited for Kat.

I made another phone call, this time to my priest, Bill. He lived a block away from the hospital. He picked up on the first ring.

"I'll go the hospital right now. I'll meet you there," he said.

I paced the kitchen, checking my phone, opening the refrigerator, closing it, drinking a glass of water, pacing. I let the rest of the house sleep: Dad, Fiona, Finley. I had been summoned. No one else. I alone would represent the family inside the abyss of the ICU.

After an eternity — ten minutes, fifteen, nearly twenty — Kathleen arrived. I pulled on my Ugg boots to wade through six inches of new snow, carefully closed and locked the large red front door, and stepped into twenty-five-degree air. As I exhaled, I could see my breath.

I slid into the passenger seat of Kathleen's husband's 1970s Buick.

Kathleen hugged me and said, "Sorry it took me so long. I had a hard time starting the car, and then I had to shovel out the tires because it's been sitting for a while. You okay?"

I nodded and said, "Yeah. No. Scared. Let's go."

We crept along Highway 195 heading north. The roads were buried beneath a thick crust of ice and snow. Windshield wipers dispersed tiny flakes dotting the glass. I alternated between wanting to tell Kathleen to hurry and biting my lip, knowing that hurrying, especially on these snowy roads, wouldn't get us to Sean any faster. I told Kathleen I'd already phoned my priest, Bill.

"Kathleen, I think it's too late. I'm too late. I should have gone when they called earlier, around eleven, but I told them I needed sleep. This time a chaplain called. It wasn't the nurse, it was the chaplain," I said, rubbing my hands together for warmth. "What if I'm too late?"

Kat placed her right hand on mine, where it stayed for most of the trip. "You'll be okay. Bill will already be there. Sean's not alone. Whatever we find when we get to the hospital, we'll handle it."

What kind of wife doesn't make it to her husband's deathbed? I pictured Sean wearing a thin white hospital gown with blue squares. I could see his aspen branch arms and scarred matchstick legs. I wondered if he had the wide-eyed look, the one I'd seen when he was rendered half-unconscious by drugs and exhaustion. Were those blue eyes I loved so much searching the room for me one last time, not finding me there?

Fifteen minutes of grinding at thirty miles per hour got us to Sacred Heart Medical Center. It was our hospital. I'd had Fiona via caesarean section on the ninth floor. I had practically lived there with Sean for months.

The hospital chaplain met us at the elevator doors outside the parking garage. He introduced himself as Doug. He was tall, with sandy brown hair and a thirty-something face.

What happened next was like water swirling in a bog—murky, moving, alternately revealing and concealing what lay beneath. I imagined one scenario where I didn't leave the elevator. The doors opened, Kathleen and Doug exited, but I remained. I pressed the button to shoot back to the bottom level of the parking garage. I pressed another button, gliding to the ninth floor. Maybe I'd peek at babies.

Anywhere but the ICU. Instinct screamed at me to run and never look back. If I didn't go forward—if I didn't find out, if I didn't witness it—maybe my heart wouldn't break.

I ignored that voice and followed Doug and Kathleen onto the main floor, plodding the maze—left, right, left. I'd walked this path hundreds of times already, past the photos of the Sisters.

We entered the main set of elevators that would take us to the

ICU. I grasped Kathleen's hand as we walked the polished tile corridor toward a destination I never wanted to arrive at.

The chaplain opened the door to Sean's room. I knew immediately. Without words, I knew. I looked first at the face of my priest, pale and pained. Then, to the doctor, who cast his eyes down briefly, mouth set in a straight line.

Finally, I looked at Sean. My husband. He lay beneath a white sheet that no longer rose and fell with his breath. His eyes were closed. I wondered who closed them. His face was whiter, even, than I was used to seeing. His surroundings and his body were blood-free, which surprised me. I was used to his blood flowing everywhere, leaking out of him like he was a sieve.

I stood for just a moment — in that moment — then gasped and started sobbing.

I knew but did not want to know. I felt stricken and scared to touch Sean, because he wasn't there anymore. I forced myself to kiss his room-temperature forehead. It was some kind of sacred act. This is the pact we sign when we love — to touch and smell, to hug and caress a corpse. It is an act of love and courage. I didn't linger over his body, sitting down at his bedside, instead, wordless. The vortex of his suffering had left me laconic. Mute. Kat later told me I sat staring at Sean for forty-five minutes as she stood silently behind me, hands on my shoulders.

"He's not here anymore," I said, cracking the quiet as if breaking an egg over a bowl.

"No, he's not," said Bill. "When I got here, they were performing CPR. They tried for half an hour. It was already too late."

The doctor, one who had overseen Sean's care while in the ICU, explained that Sean had a ruptured pseudoaneurysm, which is a pocket of blood that forms as a result of a hole in an artery. It was most likely caused by enzymes leaking from the pancreas, which damaged blood vessels. Iatrogenic trauma — a complication of surgery to remove the benign tumor on his pancreas a month earlier. Sean's surgeon, Dr. B, had called last night to tell me about the pseudoaneurysm, saying Sean was scheduled for a procedure to try to stem the bleeding the next day. Today.

A day too late.

The ICU doctor, Dr. H, said the pocket of blood had burst, causing massive internal bleeding. "After the rupture, there was nothing we could do. We performed CPR for so long because he was young, and we wanted to know we'd done everything we could."

This young doc, the one who'd worked so hard in the middle of the night to save Sean, was pacing, frantic, crying. She kept repeating, "We did everything we could do. I don't know what else we could've done."

Kathleen turned to embrace the doc, comforting her as she has comforted me.

Dr. H offered to write a letter outlining what had happened, which I accepted with some vague idea I might need it in the future. I imagined myself saying, "My husband died. I have this paper to prove it." Maybe I would need the doctor's note to prove it to myself.

The doctor left and it was just me, Kathleen, and Bill. Kathleen pulled me close, saying, "I'm so sorry, baby. So sorry. But you're gonna be okay."

Bill said, "He'd lost so much blood; it happened fast. I am sorry."

I later learned that blood gushed from Sean's mouth and nose as hospital staff pressed on his chest. Dr. H said, "It was a bloody mess. It was a blessing you weren't there."

I saw empathy on Bill's face and in his posture as he worked to console me: the sad eyes and bent back. He was not just doing his job as a priest. He was there to stand with me as a fellow human, one who's known love and loss and questioned why. "Would it be okay if we prayed?" asked Bill.

Of course.

He read "Litany at the Time of Death" from the Episcopal Book of Common Prayer:

"…That it may please you to grant *him* a place of refreshment and everlasting blessedness, *We beseech you to hear us, good Lord.*"

I started noticing more and more how hot the room was. Uncomfortably hot. Just then, Bill teetered forward, his head slumped on Sean's chest. Had he fainted? What had just happened?

Kathleen gripped Bill's shoulder and pulled him upright. He paused, then continued, "That it may please you to give *him* joy and gladness in your kingdom, with your saints in light."

Facebook Post: January 23, 2010 at 10:20 a.m.
Kathleen Cavender: *This is Kathleen. I picked up Dawn at 2 a.m. to take her to the hospital. Upon arrival, we were told that Sean had passed away just a moment before. I am here with her. We are asking that everyone protect Dawn's space in this difficult time. You can call my cell to arrange meals, if you like. She feels your love and prayers. Thank you so much. Love, Kathleen & Cheryl-Anne*

Chapter 14

Aftermath

Kathleen and I stayed with Father Bill in the waiting room after we left Sean's body. I had sat there so often keeping vigil, but now it was done. There would be no attempts at mechanical resurrection; no more surgeries to remove diseased flesh and restore missing skin; no more CT scans, blood tests, dialysis, or rectal tubes to drain my husband's shit into a bag. Physical therapy was done, occupational therapy too. Operation after operation after operation, ultimately leading to the one that would eventually kill Sean and make me a widow — over and done with. No more results to hang hopes on, only to have them strangled. No more suffering and pain for Sean.

And yet, I still felt that something more must be required of me at the hospital. Surely someone needed a form signed on Sean's behalf; surely I must wait with him in radiology or accompany him to a procedure. There was still hospital food to cajole Sean to eat. My wifely duties couldn't be done.

A hospital staffer appeared with a clipboard. "Mrs. Picken, we need to know what you'd like done with your husband's body. Are you having him buried or cremated?"

I'd known the answer for years, because Sean and I had had the conversation one day en route to a feature story about a father and daughter who'd built a casket from a kit. What would we want for ourselves? We'd agreed on cremation. We believed our bodies would be shells after we died; why spend thousands of dollars embalming them and choosing a gleaming stainless steel casket with innerspring mattress and adjustable headrest, then lower it into a grave?

I signed the form authorizing cremation.

Father Bill, Kathleen, and I sat, immobilized, talking for another forty-five minutes.

Bill asked how Kathleen and I knew each other.

"We met at a writer's group," I said. "It was about nine months ago."

Kat and I had bonded over medical hardships: she had guided her husband through a lung transplant; I'd prepped for a liver transplant I hadn't needed. We swapped stories like war vets over lunch at Madeleine's or drinks at Churchill's.

"Kathleen's been here for me in profound ways. But I don't think I'll ever forgive myself for not being here with Sean when he died."

Bill, who could appear shy and even socially awkward, looked me in the eyes and said, "If you need to carry that guilt, go ahead. I would never hold you to it, and I know Sean wouldn't either. If it gives you something to hang on to, I understand."

We talked about the way Sean died — I had only a vague idea before now what it meant to bleed out, but I was sure Sean wouldn't have wanted me to see him that way. The medical term for bleeding out is exsanguination, from the Latin *exsanguinatus*, meaning "drained of blood." Catastrophic internal hemorrhages like Sean's ruptured pseudoaneurysm can cause fatal blood loss within minutes, which sets off a vicious cycle of hypothermia,

138

increased blood acid, abnormal heartbeat, and impaired clotting function. The comprehensive medical phrase for this is fucking implosion.

And CPR? On TV, 70 percent of attempts succeed quickly, but in real life only 37 percent of patients receiving in-hospital CPR survive immediately. Just 13 percent make it long-term, according to researchers at the University of Southern California.

I knew Bill was right. I couldn't free guilt from its metal cage, yet I was spent, like the last time I crossed the finish line at a marathon. Maybe I could've run even farther than 26.2 miles in Portland, but my legs screamed, "NO!" Muscles winced with each step. I was bone-weary. Wasted.

I let Kathleen take me home. We didn't return to Sean's hospital room. My lips and hands understood, with that final kiss of pallid flesh, that who he was—essence, soul, sense of humor, mannerisms, and speech patterns—had disappeared when Sean breathed his last. I'd read about widows who spent hours sitting with their beloved's body. I would later watch a documentary called *Losing Layla*, where an Australian mother whose baby died hours after birth stayed in the hospital to hold and snuggle her child's cold-preserved cadaver for four days.

Yet I was leaving the hospital as if checking out of my parlor suite at the Davenport hotel. No corpse-cradling, no hand-holding. My physical relationship with Sean—the man I had kissed deeply and made love to, that corporeal co-mingling—was over. Joyce Carol Oates wrote, "In love there are two things—bodies and words." I was left with words: Sean's letters, his voice on video, his voice in my head.

Kathleen and I returned home at 5:00 a.m. I had to decide how to tell Fiona and Finley. I wouldn't wake my children to tell them Daddy had died. I wouldn't wake my dad to burden him with bad news. I'd sleep for a couple hours, then face those tasks after sunrise. I peeked at the kids, curled together like teaspoons in

Fiona's bed, breathing in tandem. I kissed each one, feeling life and warmth inside their forty-pound bodies, realizing I would be the person who, with a single phrase, would bisect their lives into "before" and "after." But not now. Not until I'd slept.

I crawled under my covers fully clad (save for shoes), laid my head on my pillow, and fell unconscious. Two hours later, I woke from a dreamless sleep, almost surprised to be alive while Sean's body lay in the hospital morgue. I padded downstairs to make breakfast.

Dad entered the kitchen, standing at the counter. I turned to face him as I poured water into the automatic drip coffee maker. Could he read my face?

I stopped pouring. "Dad, Sean didn't make it. He died this morning."

I didn't cry. I was still processing, slowly, soberly, purposefully. Still reconstructing the timeline of Sean's illness, surgery, complications, death. Still figuring out how I would tell the kids. I clutched my reporter's shield, though I wouldn't update Facebook that day. I didn't need to. Friends had already disseminated news of Sean's death. Nearly 200 messages of condolences flooded my page overnight, a torrent of love and regret.

Facebook Post January 23, 2010 at 10:34 a.m.
SB: *God has a special place in heaven for the people who have brought so much joy, love, and happiness to those around them. Feeling so blessed to have known Sean, if even for a short time, and so very sad for his young family. Much love and hugs to Dawn and kiddos.*
JW: *Prayers are coming in for Dawn from every direction. Dawn, there is no easy way to tell the children, but God will give you the words to say, I just know it. I am truly thankful you have these awesome friends who will walk you through the next days, months, and years ahead. (((HUGS)))*

RH: My heart grieves with you, Dawn. I can't express my feelings in words. You are loved. God has not abandoned you. You and Sean fought a very good fight.

BW: Oh my God. I don't know what to say. Dawn, if you see this, I am SO sorry. Sean's a great guy and I am SO sorry. If you need anything, please let me know.

TG: Dawn, we are so very sorry. Sean and you and your kids have been through so much. We were so hopeful that you all had made it through the biggest difficulties. May Sean rest in peace, and may you find peace wherever you can in this most trying time.

DP: UPDATE ON FOOD ASSISTANCE: This is Debra and I just spoke to Kathleen about coordinating food. St. John's friends will assist for the near term. Call me or Kathleen if you wish to help please. I'm also checking on the website, which some of you have used in the past. Sleep is what Dawn needs most at this moment.

MD: Our hearts are full for you, Fiona, and Finley. Your devotion and love were immeasurable. Mark and I are so deeply sorry.

CR: For Sean: Unto the ends of the universe and time eternal do I send this prayer, dear Sean, cast into the waves of stars and space and by our hands let go; and we do now open our aching souls and commend your spirit and personhood to the keeping of God as you walk into that beautiful door to know and be known in the ways that remain still a mystery to us here. Goodbye dear person and hello dear spirit of you. We give thanks for you and hold your family for you as you watch over them and bless their way ahead.

I was wrapped in a fog of numbness and indecision over choices big and small: Was I supposed to set out food? How would I break the news to Fiona and Finley? The homecoming we had planned would never happen. *Mommy was wrong. The doctors were wrong. It's all wrong.* I'd lost my husband to sickness, surgery, to fate's fatal slip, when the Universe set Sean's foot on the edge of a crumbling cliff. And that made me a widow. Was I really not married anymore?

I gazed at the one-carat diamond, flanked by baguettes, on my left-hand ring finger. Sean and I had found it together at a Seattle pawnshop. He gave it to me when he proposed on Valentine's Day, 1999, at Paradise trail on Mt. Rainier. How could ten years of marriage be undone in a moment? Death had caught our family. But we weren't ready. It shouldn't have been Sean. With my weak-ass liver, I had always thought I would die before he did.

Dad hugged me and said, "I'm so sorry. He had such a hard time and was in so much pain. I'm sorry, hon. I hate seeing you so sad."

I began to cry, finally, the kind of tears I could only cry in my father's arms. Tears of a broken-hearted child.

Kathleen had napped on our family room sofa and rose to marshal the team. Within minutes, our mutual friend Cheryl-Anne stood at my kitchen counter, answering the phone, making lists of people to call and people to thank.

"What am I supposed to do?" I asked. I'd never dealt with the death of someone close to me, let alone my husband. Late husband. Who was he to me now?

Cheryl-Anne, a writer and mother of four mostly grown children, knew about these things. "People want to see and hold and comfort you. We could host an open house. Don't worry about food. Your friends will bring things."

She gave me a list of tasks, because it was better to do something. My first call was to Sean's sister Steph. She didn't answer her cell phone. I called her husband, John. I asked where they were. It was 8:30 in the morning. John said, "We're on our way to Steph's race." I had forgotten Steph was running her first ten-kilometer race. I wanted to hang up, but it was too late.

"John, are you driving? I need to tell you something." John pulled over to the road's shoulder. "Sean died this morning around 2:30. A ruptured pseudoaneurysm. They said it was a complication of surgery."

John said, "I'm so sorry. I knew when I saw you were calling at this time of the morning it must be bad news. I'll give you to Steph."

Steph sobbed as John passed her the phone. "I can't believe it," she said. "He fought so hard. I'm sorry. For you and for me."

I delivered the news with guilt and regret, as if I had somehow played a role in Sean's death, though I wasn't sure how. What if I had insisted his surgeon operate last night? If I had visited him earlier that day, maybe they would have rushed him to intensive care sooner. There were a thousand scenarios in my head where Sean didn't die. Where he wasn't dead.

Over that first day, my Facebook wall became a tribute to Sean. Some messages came from former coworkers and news colleagues, like Wendy and Devon in Spokane and Jim in Illinois.

> **Facebook Post: January 23, 2010 at 11:05 a.m.**
> **WS:** Dawn, I am just back to internet connection and am shocked and saddened to hear about Sean. I know you two are soul mates. I am so sorry. Stay strong for your beautiful children.
> **DH:** Dawn, Cara and I are truly sorry for your loss. Sean was such an amazing person and we'll never forget the time, effort, and care that he put into shooting and editing our wedding day! We have something to remember who Sean is and what his passion was forever. We love you, Dawn!!
> **JL:** Dawn, I was heartbroken to hear the news. It all seems so unfair after the battle you and Sean waged. I want you to know what an inspiration you've been to all of us who watched your fight from afar. Your determination and selflessness on his behalf has been remarkable to behold. The loss won't go away, but the pain will diminish in time.

It was comforting to know others wept with us. Yet I thought of the people in our inner and outer circles dipping their toes in grief's pool while I remained submerged in the waters of bereavement. Our friends could flee the pool. The kids and I could sink or swim, but we couldn't leave. And Finley would pee in the water.

An acquaintance whose wife died of cancer offered advice about how to help Fiona and Finley cope with Sean's death.

Facebook Post: January 23, 2010 at 3:30 p.m.
MP: *Give the kids several months and then have them work with the wonderful children's counselor at Hospice of Spokane. They do art projects, tree plantings, and have other outlets for their feelings and grief. They will deal with it differently than adults do. They can't put their feelings into words right now. But you will see it in actions. I would avoid driving anywhere near a hospital for a while. They know more than we realize.*

My church family was ever-present, in person and online. Stalwarts like Kay, Polly, and Skip provided proof of what people might consider the Holy Spirit, or at least Community Spirit, in words, meals, and help with chores around the house.

I continued my death duty marathon, which had started at the hospital and seemed to stretch far into the future. I made several more calls that morning — to my mom, my Aunt Leslie, my friend Shelly. By far, the toughest call I made was to Sean's mom. I was about to tell her her eldest son had died. Our relationship had grown especially frosty after Sean got sick. She visited several times while Sean was in the hospital, and he would report afterward being stressed each time. "She hovers," he said. "And asks lots of questions. It doesn't help." Whenever she visited, an uncomfortable tension hung in the air, and Sean was already miserable.

My heart started thumping as I dialed her number.

"Helen, it's Dawn. I'm so sorry to tell you this, but Sean died this morning." I told her how he died, how the doctors and nurses had worked to save him. There was a pause. I closed my eyes and waited — it was coming.

"Well, I'm sorry, too," she said. "I wish I could've seen him more."

I didn't refute her. From my perspective, she could have visited Sean at any time — I had not held him under armed guard at the hospital. Sean always had a phone at his bedside (whether he felt well enough to use it was another matter).

She asked when the service would occur. I told her I didn't know, I hadn't gotten that far.

I hung up, thinking once more that Sean's death was my fault. Wouldn't everyone blame the widow?

I researched my most important duty: telling Fiona and Finley. It was 10 a.m. and they were watching cartoons on TV, ignoring the hubbub around them. I bought myself time by asking our neighbor, Yvonne, if the kids could play at her house. "Of course," she said. "Send them over."

I called my brother-in-law back. (Was he still mine to call brother, now that Sean was gone?) John was a child psychiatrist. He told me Steph had run the 10K in Sean's honor.

"How should I tell the kids? I don't want to traumatize them more than they already will be, and I also want them to understand Sean's not coming back."

John said, "The most important thing is keep it simple: 'The doctors tried to make Daddy better, but they couldn't. He died.' The kids won't understand details."

I called Paul the priest for advice. He said, "Don't tell them God made this happen. And keep it simple."

It was 11:30 a.m. when I asked Yvonne to send the kids back over. It had been nine hours since their father had died. I sat Fiona and Finley on the brown leather couch in the family room, the one connected to the kitchen where my dad, friends Frankie and Cheryl-Anne stood, sipping from large mugs, talking quietly. The room smelled of fresh-brewed coffee and toast.

I looked at Finley, wearing the green shirt emblazoned with a truck he got for his fourth birthday. A sweep of long, dark lashes guarded his blue-gray eyes. Fiona wore a pink shirt (her favorite color) and stretchy black leggings. I focused on the constellation of light brown freckles sprinkled across her button nose.

I said, "You know how we thought Daddy would get better and come home? Well, last night, he got worse and the doctors and nurses couldn't save him. They tried as hard as they could, but Daddy died." I examined their faces, Finley's large eyes more saucer-like than ever. Fiona blinked. Neither burst into tears. Not at that moment.

> **Facebook Post: January 23, 2010 at 1:39 p.m.**
> **Dawn Picken:** *This is Cheryl-Anne posting an update from Dawn. She wants to thank everyone for the prayers and kind words. She's told the children and they took the news as only children can. Finley asked for a cupcake and Fiona asked if Daddy was in heaven and then wanted to look at photo albums. Looking at photos of Sean at Fairmont Hot Springs, Finley asked, "Is that heaven?" Dawn replied that yes, it was. The children are now with neighbors, being cared for and loved. Frankie and I are here with Dawn, as is her father.*

I wondered if the kids understood what I'd just told them. They weren't sobbing. Not laying on the floor, beating hands and fists. Not clutching Sean's picture, crying, "NO, DADDY, NO!" Instead, Finley asked, "Can we go back to Ryan's and play?"

"Yes, go play."

Visitors ebbed and flowed all day, bringing flowers, food, cards, hugs, and stories. Our living room looked like we had raided the exquisite floral beds at Spokane's Duncan Garden in Manito Park. Our space was festooned with flowers, including lilies, orchids, roses, carnations, and sunflowers, smaller versions of the ones Sean planted in our garden. The top of the baby grand piano was an Impressionist still life of pinks, yellows, greens, and purples.

For nearly an hour, I escaped to the neighbor's, too. Like the kids, I wanted a playdate — somewhere condolences, bouquets of sadness, and consolatory baked goods couldn't find me.

Chapter 15

The Comfort of Widows

Sean's sister Steph arrived the next day with her five-year-old son, Sam. She was aloe vera for my wounded brain, soothing and cooling. We held each other and cried for who and what we'd lost: a brother, husband, a future of joint family holidays, of childhood stories, sibling teasing, and solidarity.

I set the date for Sean's memorial after visiting the funeral home with Kathleen and Bill, but it wouldn't be for three weeks. I wasn't ready to host a funeral yet. Besides, Father Bill was headed to Minnesota and Kat was leaving for Arizona, and I needed him to officiate and her to sing. So we would have it on February 14 — Valentine's Day — after they both got back. It also happened to be the day Sean had proposed marriage, a date I had been dreading. Why shouldn't everyone else have a shitty Valentine's Day?

Two days after Sean's death, I awoke to blackness outside and tiptoed downstairs to sit at the glass-topped kitchen table that faces photographs of fruit, vegetables, crabs, and flowers Sean and I had taken at Seattle's Pike Place Market. This was where, a month before, Sean had sat marveling over Fiona's lost tooth. I called

Joanne, a friend of my friend Paul. He and Joanne had attended college together. Her husband had died eight years earlier, leaving her to raise four children. It was 5:00 a.m. Pacific Time when I called, 8:00 a.m. on the East Coast, where Joanne lived. We talked nearly an hour during that first conversation. I took notes. We started by commiserating over awkward things people said to console a widow.

Joanne said, "'He's in a better place' is such a problematic statement. But in the horror of the situation, I saw God through the support of others. Those who turned out to be the most helpful were not necessarily closest to me before my husband died." She encouraged me not to look too far ahead. "Just put one foot in front of the other."

Yet we did talk of futures, of how her life had turned out and how mine might. She told me of a friend whose father had died when the friend was a child. The mother quickly remarried a man for security, not love. "Don't try to replace Sean," she said. I agreed that would be impossible, and besides, my children would never have another father. Joanne suggested getting the kids into sports and scouts, where they could have male mentors. She provided tips about the money side of widowhood only another widow could offer, like letting people know about Sean's benefit fund. "There is a short shelf life for generosity at times like this. People move on with their own lives." She recommended getting a cheap box at the funeral home for Sean's ashes, since I could later choose my own urn. And the funeral I dreaded? "It's more for the community; it's almost a show," she warned me. "I hated being the subject of all that pity."

But there would be an afterward—beyond the service, the thank-you notes, the giving and receiving of condolences. Only after the hurricane blows in can rebuilding start. Joanne said, "I've come to a place where it's part of my life, but I'm mindful it's not a defining thing in my life."

149

This smacked of truth for me. Who wanted to be defined by death? *She's the one who lost her husband.* Then what?

Joanne's children had grown into smart, tenacious adults. Her son wrote a college essay about his father's talents and their lasting connection. "They're strong and resilient. It's gratifying to see them grow and see what you loved in your husband coming out in them. It's bittersweet."

She continued, "We honor him by living the best and most vital lives we can. Whatever you have to do to get through this time, do it. Everything in your life has prepared you for this in some way."

Joanne and her kids had created a small altar in their home after her husband died. It included his picture and candles. She recommended two books: *Getting to the Other Side of Grief* and *One Year Off*. The latter is about a family who left San Francisco to travel the world for a year. I could scarcely believe someone would encourage my passion for travel so soon after Sean's death. But Joanne was a fellow widow, and we shared a similar world view.

She continued, "I've tried desperately to embrace all life has to offer. There is another side of the valley. When I was in Berkeley, two or three weeks after Richard died, I saw a big truck barreling down a hill and, for a moment, I thought of jumping in front of it. But I saw that in some ways, that was the easy way. There's really a beautiful light on the other side. But those kinds of thoughts are normal during grief."

I exhaled. Finally, someone understood what this was like, being left alone to raise your kids. Joanne had internalized the message of *One Year Off* and took a year to redefine herself and her family. She found a good financial planner who helped her chart a course that allowed her to live abroad, to walk an exciting path that honored her husband's presence. She researched where she might go: an English-speaking country with a good climate and year-round schooling. She chose New Zealand. "It was liberating to be able to walk the aisles of the grocery store and not bump into people who'd say, 'I'm so sorry for your loss.'"

It was too soon to buy plane tickets, but it wasn't too soon to dream. While I planned Sean's memorial, I also plotted my escape.

My best friend from high school, Shelly, arrived three days before the service. In our teens and early twenties, we talked nearly every day. The past fifteen years, we talked maybe once a year, so this was a rare chance to reconnect. We had once swilled pitchers of Michelob Light at a pub; now we sipped lattes at a café.

"I'm thinking of taking the kids and leaving the country for a year," I told her. "I want to go somewhere new, maybe France and Italy, stay where the kids and I stayed with Sean. I need to go —" I started crying, because I had just admitted one of my deepest desires. It was mandate masquerading as wish. I felt I might die if I didn't leave. My runner's instinct made my legs twitch and my heart race. Running away felt normal, even necessary.

Instead of saying it was too soon or cautioning me against making big changes, Shelly said, "We get emotional about things that mean the most to us. You have to do what feeds your soul. Travel is part of who you are. And it's not too soon to plant the seed."

But first, I had to endure the memorial. Friends and family traveled from Western Washington and the Midwest, packing St. John's Cathedral. Sean's brother, Steve, whom we rarely heard from, had even flown in from Australia. Leanne and Mark traveled from Los Angeles.

At the time, I knew so little about death rituals, about what I could do that might offer a sliver of peace in this moment, and in years to come. My Irish ancestors would have held a wake, the most ancient of death customs. Women used to wash the body, dress it in its finest clothing, and place it on a table in the main room of the house with candles around it. The wake would last a few days and the body would never be left alone. Everyone was encouraged to touch it. The Irish wake was not a solemn occasion. Maybe it's an outgrowth of the Irish love of partying, but a funeral was cause to celebrate life rather than lament death.

The old custom of living with a loved one's body in your home, a more dignified version of *Weekend at Bernie's,* stands in stark contrast to Western funerals, where mourners stoically occupy pews in a church or seats at a funeral home for an hour-long service. They might catch a glimpse of the dead person for a few seconds as he/she lays inside a gleaming casket. Crying happens quietly, like sadness is a shameful secret.

We estimated the crowd for Sean's service at more than 500. I wrote and delivered a tribute to Sean, describing his sense of humor, love for family, and love of flannel shirts. I'd bought a new pair of black patent leather Nine West shoes with four-inch heels and a zipper up the back seam. I wore the same black dress I had worn for Fiona's baptism six years before. Something old, something new — like our wedding. I did not allow myself to cry. Not during that most public display of mourning where I felt on display like a zoo monkey. Instead, I sat in the front of the church holding Kathleen's hand, giggling about nothing.

It would not be the only funeral I had laughed through. Years later, when my mom's mother, Florence died, I attended the service with Mom and her sister, Cheryl. Grandma Flo was an eccentric who lived the last years of her life in a hoarder's paradise– a double-wide trailer stacked with magazines and other detritus of impulse and indecision. She was also a respected organist and pianist in her church community. After she died, her church friends paid tribute to her in song. At the service inside a tiny sanctuary in Elyria, Ohio, a large woman in a bouffant blonde wig punched a button on a boom box, grabbed a microphone, and belted Christian karaoke. I can't remember her song, but I do recall she was off-key and croaky. Cheryl and I sat, hunched over, shoulders convulsing with laughter. People probably thought we were sobbing.

Crying is supposed to be okay, but how many people can sit

with you while you wail and not offer platitudes or suggestions? I may have been better off had I bawled at Sean's service, since psychology tells us tears are good for mental health and well-being. But I was too focused on my tasks: speaking, corralling kids to sing, thinking about the reception afterward.

At least one of Sean's relatives — let's call them Pat — kept their distance during the memorial. They were livid I hadn't invited them to see Sean's body before he was cremated. Pat called one week after he died, saying they might have wanted to bring their children to the funeral home to watch the cremation. "It would be a learning experience for them and provide closure," they said. I hadn't thought to ask the funeral director when Sean's body would be burned. It wasn't something I wanted to see.

Pat wanted to speak at Sean's service. I told them it would be a formal Episcopal affair with communion, lasting at least an hour. Anyone who wanted to pay tribute could do so after the service during a church reception. I later learned that Pat also called Father Bill; the associate priest, Margaret; and the bishop to complain about the way I had planned Sean's memorial. I told Margaret I was sorry for Pat's behavior. She said, "We never apologize for family, because everyone's got one."

Widows are often a lightning rod for other people's grief. We need someone or something to blame for death, especially the death of someone as young as Sean. I was Sean's auxiliary, his keeper and caretaker. Whatever happened to him would be my responsibility. And my fault. It wasn't enough to have my heart caught in my throat, to realize Sean's arms would never hold me again, to know he would not see his children grow. As the widow, I must also take other people's emotional temperatures and discern how to help them hurt less.

We held an after-party for Sean at the Irish pub, O'Doherty's. Sean would've loved seeing his friends and family drinking Guinness, eating shepherd's pie, laughing, and sharing stories.

Steph wrote Sean's name on a dollar bill and stuck it to the wall above a booth. Fiona and Finley raced through the pub, eating fries and begging for quarters for video games. They'd been looking forward to "Daddy's party" for weeks.

After the hubbub of the memorial, receptions, dinners out, and brunches with out-of-town guests, I welcomed the return to something resembling normalcy: at the Chamber, I had a desk, a computer, a cubicle. It seemed sane, safe, and ordinary. I worked twenty hours a week, just enough to distract from "what next?"

I was about to leave work one day, when I received a call from a Spokane police sergeant, who'd been contacted by someone in Sean's circle (whose name I'm not disclosing for obvious reasons, like that the incident makes them look like a shitty person).

He introduced himself, then said, "We received a complaint from Z. Smith that you didn't allow your husband to use the phone while he was in the hospital, and that you'd neglected him when he was sick at home. I know this sounds silly, and I'm sorry for your loss, but we're required to look into these things."

My hands shook as I started writing notes on a yellow legal pad. How could they? Wasn't it enough that I'd lost Sean? Now the cops were investigating too? I had started to sputter and cry as I told the officer, "My husband died after four and a half months in the hospital. It's true that I left him alone for one night at home when we both thought he had the flu. But he died of surgical complications after spending more than four months in the hospital and rehab facilities. And he always had a phone by his bed, though he was often too weak or drugged to use it."

The officer's low, soft tone of voice showed he believed me. "I'm really sorry, ma'am," he said. "You understand, though, we have to follow through when we get a complaint like this, even though, obviously, this one has no merit. I'm not going to do anything else with the matter. I'll tell the caller we won't investigate."

Two nights later, I was putting the kids to bed upstairs when the phone rang. It was almost 10:00 p.m. My first thought was, *Someone is calling to report Sean's condition to me*, but no, no one would call to do that ever again. It was late and the kids were safe at home, so I let the call go to voicemail.

I listened to it later and it was Z.

Um, I just wanted to say we did not call the police. They called us. And uh, that was an interesting conversation to have with them, actually. I was just curious as to what happened before he went into the hospital, if he was actually left alone, because we heard that he was, and we really want to know what happened. So I'd, uh, appreciate if you could give me a call. I know you're at home, I know this is not a comfortable conversation for you to have, but it's important for me to be able to discuss this with you. I'm not gonna bite you, I would just like to clear some of this stuff up. So, um, please give me a call. I know that I'm not your favorite person, um, and you know, you're not my favorite person. But I hope you will have the courage to call me back. Thank you very much. Bye.

I listened to the message twice. And saved it. Z lived far away, but their actions spooked me. Calling the police to harass a widow was evil. What if they sent someone to the kids' school? Fiona and Finley were my "hearts walking around outside my body," as Elizabeth Stone wrote. I was shaky but had enough wits about me to marshal help.

I called a lawyer friend, Mike, the next day and told him about calls from the police and Z. He offered, pro bono, to send a letter ordering them not to contact me by phone, letter, or e-mail. They were also not to come to the house or the kids' school.

Mike said, "There's often a manic phase these people go

155

through. They'll be even more upset when they get this letter, but eventually they'll figure out there's nothing more to do. At least you'll have a record you've told them not to contact you."

I pulled my friends and family closer, like a fleece blanket you snug against your body on a cold night. Kathleen said, "You have so many people who want in to your life. You're a local celebrity. Everyone wants a piece of you, to be part of your story. Be very careful to protect your safe inner circle."

Four days after Sean's death, Fiona turned six-years-old. I held her birthday party at the house, as planned. I basked in the warmth and joy a dozen little kids brought to our home as they wolfed chocolate cake coated in white icing and pink sprinkles with Hannah Montana's (Miley Cyrus) picture. Fiona let Finley help her blow out the candles.

But later, grief's roller coaster sent me careening earthward, as it so often does, at night.

Facebook Post: January 28, 2010 at 10:30 p.m.
Dawn Picken: *Fiona was crying as I put her to bed tonight. She said, "I wanted Daddy to come down from heaven for my birthday present." I told her he's in her heart.*
MM: *Even though we are miles apart and were friends for a short time, I find myself thinking about you often throughout my days. What a struggle you've had and how well you've dealt with it. Make sure you don't stay too strong. Grieve yourself and make sure you cry plenty. As time goes on, you will heal, but you'll never forget Sean and the time you had, and those two wonderful children will always remind you of what a great husband and dad Sean was. Have people send their memories of Sean so the kids can read them someday.*

Tara, who had lost her daughter's father, often checked in on Facebook.

A friend from my exchange student days made me smile with the following:

I defaulted to Supermom mode, believing for a brief time I could work, take care of the kids and my home, and maintain a sliver of social life. Until I got tired and cried myself to sleep, missing Sean. Missing his comforting presence, his words of encouragement, his warm body next to mine in bed. Sometimes I forgot my support systems were as close as the phone or computer. I talked to Steph and she encouraged me to take time off for myself, to remember to enjoy those just-for-me moments when I ran, wrote, and read. And to cry whenever, wherever. I had assumed the loneliness and drudgery of single parenthood would be temporary when Sean got sick in September. Only now, the gig was permanent.

At home in Spokane, 2008

Sean with Fiona in Lisbon, 2004. Our children were early travelers.

Sean with Finley on Quadra Island, British Columbia, Canada, 2006.

Sean at Heriot Bay, Quadra Island, 2006.

Lastra a Signa, Italy, 2008.

Italy, 2008

Pisa, Italy, 2008.

Florence, Italy, 2008.

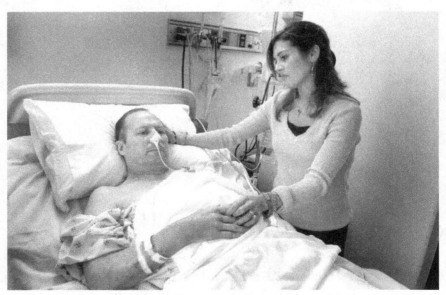

With Sean in hospital, September, 2009.

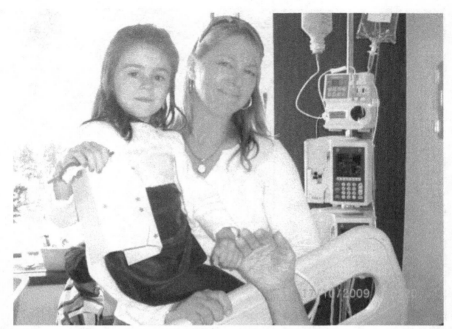

Stephanie Holttum (Sean's sister) and Fiona in Sean's hospital room.

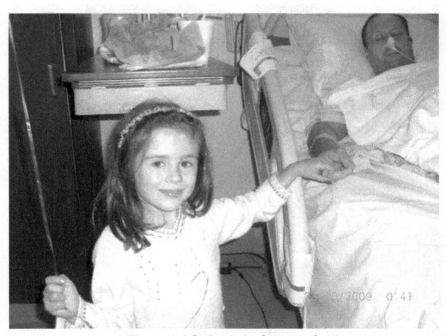

Fiona with Sean in hospital.

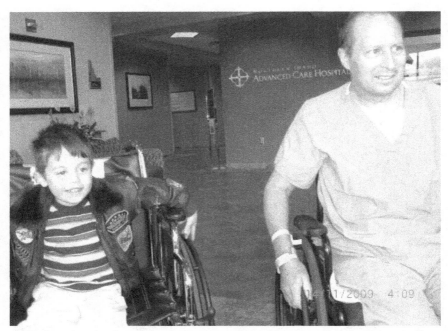

Finley is ready to race Sean at the advanced care hospital.

Former TV colleagues Duane, Russ and Todd surprised Sean at the rehabilitation hospital in Spokane.

Sean, Fiona and Finley reading at home, December, 2009.

Sean got a pass from the rehab center to come home for dinner.

Christmas pageant, St. John's Cathedral.

Grand Canyon, August, 2010.

Emulating The Thinker at the Rodin Museum.

Paris, September, 2010.

Allen (and Picken) family reunion, Portrush, Northern Ireland, September, 2010.

Giant's Causeway, Northern Ireland.

Knysna Elephant Park, South Africa, December, 2010.

Tip of South Africa

We met a Koala named Sean near Sydney, Australia

Kids were enthralled by a man playing a didgeridoo in Sydney.

Scattering Sean's ashes at Mount Maunganui, New Zealand, 2011
(Photo: Bridget Nickel Photography).

Near our new home in New Zealand, 2011
(Photo: Bridget Nickel Photography).

Part 2

After

"It is not more surprising to be born twice than once;
everything in nature is resurrection."

— Voltaire

Chapter 16

Making My Escape

September, 2010

Seven months after Sean died, I rented out our house for a year. I stored my Honda, sold Sean's Volkswagen, and donated, sold, or jettisoned three vanloads and two pickup truck loads of junk. I was ready for escape, to put distance between myself and the places where Sean had suffered and died. The summer of 2010, the kids and I explored parts of the US we'd never seen, like the Grand Canyon, before hopscotching the country, touring friends' and families' guest rooms. Our American adventure ended in Florida, where we wandered Walt Disney World and Epcot Center and spent a week with my friend Nyla and her family. I slept on an air mattress in a dining area converted to guest quarters via a curtain pulled across the room.

The hospital bills might continue dribbling in, but we had met our $7,500 deductible for 2009, meaning our insurance covered 100 percent of the bills beyond that. We paid the deductible plus 2010 bills with funds from Sean's benefit and other donations that had rolled in via the HelpSeanRecover.com website. Thanks to our community's generosity, I wasn't burdened by medical debt, the leading cause of bankruptcy in the US.

In the book *One Year Off,* which had inspired my travels and guided my planning, the author had written beneath the title page, "June 15, 1996 to July 7, 1997." During six days of bliss on St. Croix with friends Chris and Jason, I reclined in a hammock on Carambola Beach, carefully penning my own dates in the book: "June 1, 2011 to July 7, 2012."

I'd mapped out our year: two months in Europe, one month in South Africa, three weeks in Australia, and six months in New Zealand. I had been inspired by my conversation with fellow widow Joanne to choose New Zealand as the place to enroll the kids in school. Under the Southern hemisphere sun, we'd plant new roots and see what happened.

Friends and family supported my mission, though not unreservedly. My mom worried, especially about the Africa part of the trip, asking, "Isn't it dangerous there?" but eventually conceded I was a wanderer who loved to travel. Plus, I'd be staying with a friend in South Africa. "I'll miss you and the kids, but I understand," she said.

Dad, too, at first questioned my urge to travel so soon but finally said, "You've always had a bit of gypsy in you. Your plan sounds unconventional, but then again, so are you." Aunt Leslie asked whether it might be better to wait a few years after Sean's death to travel so things could settle in. At the end our conversation she said, "You know, if you wait a few years, you'll reach a new normal and then you might feel it's irresponsible to take Fiona and Finley out of their home in Spokane. Maybe now's the time." Dad offered to meet us wherever our first port of call might be.

I talked to my financial advisor, John, pre-trip, explaining I'd use a portion of Sean's life insurance payout to fund our travels.

The money wasn't enough to retire on, but it would sustain the kids and I for a year of globe-hopping, provided I stuck to a budget. We'd stay mostly with family and friends, minimize eating out, and use public transit where available (the last part of that plan would only happen in Paris and London).

"A spending plan isn't set in stone," said John. "But it gives you something to deviate from. Just know you can't visit every attraction, or you'll be cutting hair on the beach six months into your trip." I pictured tourists with bowl cuts and Fiona holding a sign saying, "Haircuts: $10—I'm hungry!"

The world tour idea felt more like prospect than promise. I was still grieving Sean and licking my wounds. But Sean and I had planned two holidays together that we never took because of his illness and death. And if I couldn't have him back, at least I could still travel. Planning the trip had already given me something indispensable: hope. I clung to the words of a friend of a friend who'd embarked on a world journey with her husband after unsuccessful attempts to get pregnant. She said, "We divide our life into two segments: before the world tour, and after." My life was already split by Sean's death. I wanted a new line of demarcation.

Joanne described her metaphor for life after her late husband's death. She said, "It's like a cut redwood. The tree is raw and fresh when it has just fallen, and eight years later, you may see a hole, but it's softened, and flowers are growing inside." I needed to learn what would grow from extended travel rather than focus on what grew from misfortune.

Facebook Post:
Dawn Picken: *After three weeks on the road in the US, we're due to head out early this evening for Paris. I ran six miles this morning in the Florida heat and humidity and thought about the fact that it would be my last run in the States for a while. I don't know how long it'll be till we're back. Could be a month. Could be the full year.*

The first flight of our world tour left me worried and weary. I tried to knock the kids out with melatonin, which other traveling parents had recommended. Fiona slept nearly the whole flight, but Finley awoke after forty minutes, crying and screaming, "I'm cold! I'm cold!" The double-decker Boeing 747 was chilled for champagne, not children. Miami's haze and heat had impaired my preparedness. I'd forgotten jackets on board, leaving me just two thin airline blankets with which to drape Freezing Finley. My four-year-old burrito-wrapped himself, leaving his feet exposed and dangling to kick the seat in front of him. Then he started crying like a banshee.

Somewhere over the Atlantic, I meditated on how best not to beat my child.

I cradled Finley like a football and dashed to the lavatory, where I flung myself on the tyrant's mercy: "Finley, you have to help Mommy. You have to stop crying. There's only me. You have to help."

"You hate me. You don't like me," he cried.

I told him, "No, Finn. I don't hate you. I just don't like the way you're acting. You need to calm down." I squeezed back tears and Finley clamped his own waterworks. We returned to our seats, where I asked a flight attendant for *lait chaud* (warm milk, and even though Air France employees spoke English, I figured I might as well start practicing my exchange-student French). "*Avec du chocolat?*" (With chocolate?) "*Oui,*" I told her. Yes.

Facebook Post:

We spotted my dad at baggage claim in the Charles de Gaulle airport. Our flights had landed simultaneously. I waved as he and his wife, Kathé, trudged forward with enough luggage to last from Paris to Peking. *And they're only spending four weeks in Paris!* A taxi driver with a fifteen-seater van whisked us away, forty minutes to the city center, charging about $130 for the journey. *Bienvenue à Paris, tout le monde!* (Welcome to Paris, everyone!) *C'est très, très cher.* (It's very, very expensive.)

Even after a night locked in a metal tube with Finley The Merciless, I was delighted to inhabit the City of Light.

"Are we going to la Tour Eiffel?" asked Fiona.

"Yes," I answered.

We drove past centuries-old Art Nouveau apartments wrought with iron balconies and scrolling masonry designs. There were umbrella-laden sidewalk cafes where chicly-attired patrons and equally crisp servers interacted as though in a Balzac play. At last, above densely stacked buildings, I glimpsed the lattice spire of the Eiffel Tower. "Look, kids, that's it!" I said. Fiona asked for the fifty-sixth time if we were going there.

The apartment my dad had rented for us sat in the très elegant sixth *arrondissement* (district) in a neighborhood called Saint-Germain-des-Prés. *The Unofficial Guide to Paris* described it as "Chic shopping meets the best of Parisian literary and artistic elements with scores of excellent and charming hotels and restaurants. But be prepared to pay for quality and style."

For three weeks, we would reside on the left bank of the Seine River, near a sixth-century Abbey, the Académie Française, and the Jardins du Luxembourg. I imagined strolling along the river in wildly fashionable clothing out-of-character for an American mother of two demitasse-sized, feral kids. In the daydream, I found a quiet cafe where I ordered a glass of Bordeaux from a handsome, smiling waiter. (This was, after all, a daydream. I'm not sure French servers smile).

Back in the land of reality, we entered a security code next to a ten-foot-tall door with black ironwork at the apartment on rue Jacob. Once inside, we tilted our heads to gape at the spiral stairs with green carpet runner and polished wood banister, and heaved bags up four flights of stairs.

The kids raced through the renovated seventeenth century flat named *Isadora* before returning to the hallway to drop their shoes from the fourth-floor balcony to the checkerboard tiled lobby. They opened cupboards and doors and slid across hardwood floors while inspecting our three bedrooms and two bathrooms. I tucked fragile knick-knacks into corners of high shelves. Finley asked me to open an ancient, creaky window overlooking a courtyard at the center of the apartments.

"Hey you guysssss!" he screamed.

"Finn," I snapped. "Stop it! Other people live in this building, too."

The kids soon passed out on the couch, the soles of their bare black feet touching white leather. Minutes later, our friend Chelsea rang the doorbell. Chelsea was twenty-two years old, a recent university graduate and friend of a friend in Spokane who had agreed to nanny in return for room, board, and travel costs. She stood about five feet three with short reddish hair, laughed loudly and easily, loved Disney movies, and adored shopping. Chelsea and Dad were part of my paragliding-as-world-travel metaphor: I could launch from this cliff more securely with an instructor and a second chute.

Sean and I had taken the kids to meet Dad and Kathé for family vacations since Finley was a baby. We stayed at the Oregon Coast, Vancouver, B.C., Lopez Island (near Seattle), plus Mexico and Italy. These trips bridged three generations and 1,800 miles separating Spokane, Washington from Ashtabula, Ohio. Sean and I had been grateful not only for free accommodation and extra help with the kids, but also for travel memories we'd never forget. We had laughed about how chasing Toddler Fiona and feeding Baby Finley would be character-building for the grandparents.

When Dad sold his business in 2008, we had all celebrated with a stay in a Tuscan Villa near Florence.

But my dad, Tom, came to traveling much later in life. He had founded his fiberglass company at age twenty-three. During most of my childhood, he had worked long hours, often returning home at ten o'clock at night. I can still remember the smells of plated dinners my mom had left warm in the oven — steak and asparagus, meatloaf and mashed potatoes.

Dad's clothing had been covered in scratchy fiberglass filaments and smelled of resin and polyurethane. He had been quick to yell at us for infractions such as leaving lights on (kids) or spending too much (Mom). He drank Cabernet Sauvignon and Chardonnay the way an athlete might top up with water to avoid dehydration. Dad blamed his Irish heritage for his temper and intemperance. Sometimes, when I heard my parents fighting at night, I crawled beneath the covers and cried. Then they would make up, take us on a trip, and things would get better. For a while. I had a front-row seat at the implosion of a marriage. I was terrified my folks would divorce and terrified they wouldn't.

For years, my mom kept the books for my dad's business, cooked like Julia Child, decorated like Dorothy Draper (and apparently spent nearly as much, according to my father), kept house, and shuttled my sister and I between six or eight activities. My mother's talent for beauty extended to designer shoes and clothing (Stuart Weitzman, Donna Karan, Escada, and St. John were some of her favorites) and full makeup, no matter if she were schlepping me to play practice or attending the symphony. I often recognized my mom's laugh before I could distinguish her voice in a crowded room. Her kindness attracted a coterie of friends. She and Dad stayed together until Heather and I graduated college. They divorced when I was twenty-six.

The marital meltdown and grandkids mellowed Dad. He got more chill with each gray hair. By the time Fiona emerged, he'd aged like a seasoned wok, or a pair of formerly stiff hiking boots. Twenty months later, around the time Finley was born, Dad kicked the smoking addiction he'd carried like a camel on his back since age twelve. He said, "I want to be here for my grandchildren."

Neither he nor Kathé had ever changed a diaper prior to becoming grandparents, though they once tried to put one on Fiona — inside out. They were reliable for short stretches of time as infant sitters, but by the time the kids were four and five, the grandparents were introducing them to Wii video games, teaching them to drive a golf cart, and watching cartoons on TV with them. Dad would tell me afterward, "We had a great time with the kids. I really enjoyed keeping them up till ten o'clock at night watching *Phineas and Ferb*. We'd love to have them stay a couple weeks when they're older."

And now, we have three weeks together. In Paris. *Quel rêve.* (What a dream.)

When the kids emerged from their jetlagged coma, Fiona twirled from the bedroom wearing her ballet costume, bodice covered in pink sequins. The skirt had two layers of black tulle hemmed with silky pink ribbon. The ensemble was capped off with a black-sequin and pink-feather fascinator. She had anticipated an immediate ascent at la Tour Eiffel and wanted to dress accordingly.

She was disappointed to learn we would lunch in the neighborhood instead.

Dad was not pleased with Fi's froufrou tutu. "Fiona, that looks weird," he said. "Can you put on normal clothes, please?"

"No," said Fiona. "I want to wear this." I told her it was fine. Six-year-olds have few fashion dont's.

En route to lunch, Fiona received smiles and more than a few comments like, *"Belle, si belle."* ("Beautiful, so beautiful.") Just a block from Isadora, we chose a touristy sidewalk café with a translated English menu. Finley took several bites of chicken nuggets and fries before falling asleep in his chair. He slumped onto the table like a lily wilting in the sun. Lunch was pleasant and quiet with Comatose Kid. *"Il a trop fait la fête hier soir?"* asked the server. ("He partied too much last night?")

Chelsea won my heart when, after lunch and a long nap, she suggested feeding the kids at the apartment while Dad, Kathé, and I enjoyed a grown-up dinner for my birthday. We walked five minutes to *Le Comptoir* (The Counter). Even on a Sunday night, a line stretched out the door. The maître d' was searching for a party of three in a queue of couples: *"Deux, deux, non... Il y a trois?"* ("Two, two, no... Are there three?") *"Oui, on est trois,"* I said. ("Yes, we're three.")

The madame led us past the line, directly to a table inside the tiny restaurant. Birthday luck. Sated by salmon, champagne, and a pyramid of perfect pink raspberries, I looked to the side, imagining Sean sitting there with me. He had been fond of saying, "Just wait till you get to be my age!" And I'd respond, "But you'll *always* be nine years older than me!"

Now, that was no longer true. If I lived eight more years, I was going to catch up with him. And then, if I was lucky (and unlucky), I would grow old without him. But I wasn't alone. Even in Paris, I could connect with friends, family, and acquaintances on Facebook. **One special comment that day, tucked among dozens of birthday** well-wishes, came from a twenty-something woman from our home church, St. John's. She had a young daughter who had been left fatherless when her dad (T's boyfriend) died.

Facebook Post:
TS: *My daughter and I went to church today, and she asked where Finn and Fiona were. I told her they were in Paris with their mommy, and then she said, "Oh good, they can meet their daddy there!" No joke. So, it got me wondering. Do you REALLY think that Sean would leave you by yourself on your birthday?*

That night, on my fortieth birthday, I fell asleep alone. But I didn't cry.

Chapter 17

Losing It in the City of Light

At the Rodin museum, Fiona and Finley (as most children must) imitated The Thinker's pose. They sat, elbows on thighs, chins resting on the backs of their hands. The museum brochure said, "The concentration and the tension of this thinker, rendered universal in its nudity, constitutes a compelling symbol of hope and of faith in mankind."

My faith in kid-kind was shaken when Finley threw a tantrum. Chelsea scooped him up and brought him outside as if he were a flaming skillet.

The brochure continued, "Sometimes a bit morose in his daily life, Rodin nonetheless continued his search for the truth of the bodies of his models."

The veracity of our anatomy disappoints. Sean's body had revealed truths about bacteria, infection, betrayal, reconstruction, renewal, risk, and ultimately, failure. His blotchy, bloated skin was reality's road map. I tried to imagine Sean climbing four flights of stairs in the Parisian apartment. *Pas de chance.* No luck. The truth of his body was that even if he had survived surgery, he may not have been able to climb those stairs.

Though I'd been to Paris several times, this was the first time with children. Their routine involved waking around eight o'clock, eating Cheerios or chocolate cereal, and watching *des dessins animés* (cartoons). With Chelsea, Dad, and Kathé at the apartment, I was free to run every morning. The first day, I ran two miles to the Eiffel Tower. The first glimpse caused me to draw a sharp breath. The symbol of all things French stood like a 900-foot-tall iron dream.

Our family visit to the tower ended (as so many outings with small kids do) more like a nightmare. We decided to descend the 300-plus stairs instead of taking the elevator from the first level to the ground. This broke Fiona, who shed fat tears, saying, "It's too far! I don't wanna walk down anymore!" When I bribed the kids with ice cream, Finley scampered off with his cone, dropping the whole thing—an offering to the Parisian pigeons.

Most days during our Paris September were pleasant and sunny, and sometimes I ran along the River Seine to Notre Dame. The easiest place to run was Luxembourg Gardens. Within its sixty acres, I could pound a gravel trail between beds of marigolds and pansies without stopping at traffic lights and cheating death by crossing traffic-choked Parisian streets. I saw something different each time. One morning, students in a gym class lunged in unison in the grass. The next day, men in tight shorts and t-shirts with the words, "*Sapeurs pompiers,*" (firefighters) ran ahead of me, and I considered lighting a fire to meet those fit young Frenchmen.

For our daily family adventures, we usually left around noon to see a "boring" museum like the Impressionist d'Orsay, followed by a playground (the Tuileries near the Louvre and giant playground at the Luxembourg Gardens were the kids' favorites).

Sandwiched between running and sightseeing (and more important in Paris) was eating.

The Unofficial Guide to Paris said Parisians spent more money per capita on food away from home than residents of most other

European cities. Dining out is an *experience gastronomique*, an education in French culture I wanted my kids to appreciate.

Sometimes, I designated Fiona our taste tester. Like one Saturday morning, when we took the Metro to the end of the line to Porte de Clignancourt to visit the **Marché** aux Puces at St. Ouen, just north of the city limits. It was a flea market with trendy clothing—military jackets, leggings, and cut-out shirts. Trash overflowed the bins, and music blared in market stalls—gangsta rap with references to felines and doin' it. I hustled the kids from one stall quickly to avoid explaining "doggy style." I bought a magenta and blue sundress for ten dollars and a pair of leggings whose garbage bag-style material reminded me of something Stiffler's mom in the *American Pie* movies would wear.

We refueled after shopping. We left Chelsea to explore on her own and Dad, Kathé, the kids, and I ate at Café Le Voltaire. The reader board announced a prix fixe special with *oeuf dur avec mayonnaise* (hard-boiled egg with mayonnaise), *tomate crevettes* (shrimp and tomato), and something called *salade de gésiers*. "What is that?" I asked our server in French. "*L'estomac des oiseaux*," she replied. (Bird stomach.) "Interesting," I told her, dismissing the idea of sinking bird guts into my own gullet.

After our server left, I rethought the *gésiers*. Maybe it was time to stretch my taste buds beyond baguettes, Salade Niçoise, and salmon. I ordered the gizzards. When they appeared in front of me, they were warm, red, and smooth, sitting on a bed of lettuce, surrounded by tomato wedges. It didn't matter that these were probably chicken gizzards—I pictured Paris's ubiquitous plump pigeons aligned beneath mini-guillotines.

"Go ahead, Fiona. Try this. You'll love it," I said. Let the six-year-old be the guinea pigeon, er pig.

Fiona asked, "What is it?"

"It's meat." I speared a quarter-sized gizzard and gave it to Fi. She bit into it without hesitation, chewed, then swallowed.

"You like it?" I asked.

"Yeah, it's good. Can I have another?" She ate four of the muscular pouches. I munched the rest. They tasted like you'd expect an internal organ to taste. Smooth, rich, and a *petit peu* weird. Salt and salad sauce disguises nearly anything—except maybe cow tongue. I tried it once in Luxembourg but couldn't stomach having another animal's taste buds on mine. I gave it to the dog.

> **Facebook Post: September 21, 2010 at 10:08 a.m.**
> **Dawn Picken:** *Had a wonderful day with the Foucher family, who live near Paris in Rubelles. They fed us déjeuner (it was much too nice to call "lunch") and took us to a chateau five minutes from their home: Vaux-le-Vicomte.*

Two of our most enjoyable meals in France happened thanks to a man I met through work. Hervé Foucher was a computer software engineer in his mid-thirties whose company had considered relocating him and his family to Spokane. I showed his wife, Fabienne, around town when I worked at the Chamber of Commerce and saved Hervé's e-mail address.

Several days after treating us to lunch at an excellent non-touristy restaurant called Le Caramelle, Hervé invited the six of us to eat at his home in the Paris suburb of Rubelles, about an hour's commute from Paris.

The Fouchers had two children: eleven-year-old Antoine and eight-year-old Jeanne. The kids were happy to show Fiona and Finley their rooms and their guinea pigs, named after Bond Girls: Octopussy and…(wait for it)…Fiona.

Lunch began with champagne, followed by Basque chicken (a roasted bird whose meat falls from the bone) with vegetables, rice, and homemade bread. Dessert was Cherry Clafoutis, which consists of fresh sweet cherries suspended in a pancake-like batter, and Charlotte, cake with pears and caramel, plus cream. Fabienne was a preschool teacher, who, despite creating beautiful calorific meals, remained slim in that casual Gallic way. I never imagined French women running ten kilometers each morning. Instead, I pictured them nibbling cheese, sipping wine, chewing bread and a few tranches of meat before walking to their next appointment in four-inch heels.

Hervé and Fabienne had been so smitten with Spokane when they visited in 2008 that even now, Hervé's computer screen displayed pictures of the Davenport Hotel, Riverfront Park, and other Lilac City landmarks. He said he bought little American flags to give friends for a moving-to-the-States party, but the assignment never happened.

We spent all afternoon with the Fouchers. They unfolded a large map of the United States and outlined their dream trip through the West, featuring Route 66, part of which I had traveled with the kids and Shelby a month ago.

Vaux-le-Vicomte was just five minutes' drive away. The seventeenth century château is a masterpiece of French Baroque architecture. It was also the venue for the wedding reception of actress Eva Longoria and NBA star Tony Parker in 2007.

Never mind the slate dome, pitched roofs, or stone façade gracing the château's exterior, the kids saw the Versailles-style gardens as another wide-open space to zoom around. I snapped a photo of Fiona atop Hervé's shoulders, smiling. The kids clambered up stone pillars and leaped onto the grass, over and over.

Hervé drove us to the train station after our château visit. Spending time with his family had left me with a sense of connection and a moment of melancholy, wondering whether I would ever see them again.

Facebook Post: September 21, 2010 at 10:19 a.m.
Dawn Picken: We were sad yesterday to say goodbye to our

French friends after spending the day with them. While it's interesting to visit monuments and museums, what I most want from this trip is to connect with other people and my kids. The Mona Lisa won't invite me to her house, and the Eiffel Tower doesn't care about my day.

TS: *What? The Eiffel Tower totally cares about your day. That's why she's so nosy. I mean really, you can see her ALL over Paris!!*

Dawn Picken: *I can almost feel her arms of steel. :)*

Alternate mornings, I treated both kids to breakfast in the neighborhood. Fiona's mother-daughter *petit déjeuner* happened on our block at Ladurée, a famous tea and pastry shop on Rue Bonaparte whose gold-rimmed china, botanical prints, and velvet side chairs whispered luxury. Fiona ordered hot chocolate served in a heavy silver pot. The drink's rich, velvety consistency was pure melted chocolate and cream. Fi's first taste left a thick mustache above her upper lip. After the second taste she said, "It's too chocolatey." I felt duty-bound to taste the silky cocoa to determine if the drink was, in fact, "too chocolatey." A second sip inspired me to swirl the concoction into my café au lait.

I asked Fiona how she felt about leaving Grandpa and Grandma Kathé in a few days. "Sad," said Fiona. "I'm going to miss them."

Finley and I shared a mother-son breakfast the next day at PAUL café. Our server gave Finley a brown piece of paper to draw on while we waited under an olive-green tray ceiling, watching pastry chefs and bakers in the kitchen turning out specialties like crusty bread loaves, tarts, pies, and mille-feuille. I inhaled a petit pain au chocolat with black coffee while Finley drank hot chocolate and munched a football-length chocolate éclair stuffed with rich chocolate pastry cream.

Finn scribbled a large stick figure with long hair and arms protruding from its head. "That's you, Mommy," he said. "And that's me." A much smaller stick figure with short hair stood beside the Mommy stick.

"I really like your drawing," I said, as Finley raised his arm in a victory salute. Finley pointed to his half-eaten chocolate football. "Can I take the rest to Fiona?"

That September would've been Fiona's first year of full-time school in the States. Finley would have attended three half-days of preschool. While other kids their age were reading and writing, my kids were learning how to insert tickets into the Metro machine, how to tell when the next train was due, and how to find a spot to park their *petits derrières* when the metro cars were packed. They also visited the Mona Lisa and occupied three hours inside the Louvre watching Scooby Doo on my iPod. I taught my tiny tourists not to accept trinkets from vendors at the Sacré Coeur or Eiffel Tower. I warned them the woman who "found" a gold ring on the Pont Neuf was trying to con tourists.

Finley learned to lock himself inside the public toilets but didn't always remember how to get out; he made a game of unhooking elastic cordons at museum queues, swiveling high-powered hand dryers to blow back the skin on his face; and he surveyed the "big Band-Aid" vending machines in the ladies' room. (Ha! Maxi-pads.) He relieved himself on a tree at the Tuileries Gardens while yelling, "I'm watering the plants."

"...The American in Paris is the best American..." –F. Scott Fitzgerald

Unless that American is Finley.

Finley did his best to act his worst. Just as I was trying to demonstrate I could handle a year of (mostly) solo travel with kids, Finn unhinged me. He fought so fiercely with Fiona about a scrap of paper at the American Cathedral that I asked Chelsea to remove both kids from the church service. One day, Finley pressed a button at the Louvre Metro stop, which sounded an alarm.

The underground provided performance space for Finley's

disappearing act. He'd exit the entrance door and purposely stand apart from us. One day, as we swayed to a string quartet at the Franklin D. Roosevelt Metro station, I lost sight of Finley for an interminable five seconds. Somewhere, among businessmen in suits, backpackers, women in saris, and the universe of beggars, hoodlums, and chic French *mesdames,* wandered Finley. My heart thump-thump-THUMPED as I searched for him. Suddenly, Chelsea yelled, "There he is!" Finley had moved closer to the quartet for a better view. I hugged Finley before telling him off: "Finn! You *have* to stay with us!" Just then, a man wearing a suit sidled up to me and asked Finley's age. He said in a clipped Indian accent, "You must be very, very careful. They steal children in the Metros."

Above ground on the Champs Élysées, Finley darted to and fro, directly in Fiona's path and anyone else's unlucky enough to risk getting tripped. My snarly mom warning to cut it out sent Finn into a full-on, everything-but-fists-on-floor tantrum for the twelfth time that day. "You're tired, Finley. It's time for a rest." I asked Chelsea to return with Finley to the apartment, where he cried for an hour while Fiona and I detoured to walk around the Eiffel Tower. How much do we love Chelsea? A lot.

Facebook Post: September 21, 2010 at 10:10 a.m.
Dawn Picken: *Fiona and I scattered a tiny bit of Sean's ashes near the base of the Eiffel Tower today. Sean visited Paris with a work colleague in the '90s and the colleague told me Sean knew he was "really in Paris" when he saw La Tour Eiffel. Fi's idea was to put some ashes in the middle of a three-trunked tree. Later, she said, "Maybe we can grow lots of new daddies."*

That night, we watched 20,000 lights twinkle on the Tower. Sean would have loved it. I pictured his star in the vast sky.

I lived in constant fear of that truth. Just before we had left Spokane, Finley ran into the street in front of our house, just as a car was rounding the corner. The car slowed and Finley stopped, but that didn't prevent me from screaming as if my son had been hit. A nurse at church later told me that exaggerated response — fear of losing another family member — was common. I was a normal crazy person.

One afternoon, Chelsea and I split up so she could buy bacon at the store, and I could fetch fresh bread at the bakery. Fiona said she would stick with me. Finley went with Chelsea. I walked with Fiona (wearing her ballet tutu) to check out the line at PAUL. I peeked inside for, oh, three seconds...turned around, and Fiona was gone. GONE. GONE.

That was when my "exaggerated loss response" kicked in. I panicked. Heart-pounding-in-throat panic. At the crossroads of Rue de Buci and Rue de Seine, I could inspect four streets. I started screaming, loudly: "Fee-OH-nah... Fee-OHHHH-nah!"

"Have you seen a little girl wearing a ballet dress?" I queried patrons at a corner café in French, and two men on the street.

What if Fiona had followed Chelsea and Finley into the store when I wasn't watching? I raced into the Carrefour market, yelling as I approached the meat section: "Fee-OH-nah! Fee-OHHHH-nah!" The din of the store, crowded with after-work shoppers on a Friday night, diminished, and Parisians stared at the strange, screaming American. Finally, in the meat aisle, I spied them: Chelsea, Finley and...Fiona. I seized her and started to sob. "Never leave me. Don't ever leave me. How could you just leave me?" Fiona blinked, wide-eyed. I grabbed both kids by the hand and led them from the store. An employee said, "*Ça va, madame. Ça va.*" ("It's okay, ma'am, it's okay.")

Dear Sean,
We miss you terribly.
I wish you were here with me.
Love forever,
Your wife, Dawn

I sat in a pew to stare at the cathedral's enormous rose stained-glass window, which reminded me of the windows at St. John's Cathedral in Spokane. I cradled my head in my hands and wept.

Outside, at Notre Dame's left portal, St. Denis held his head in his hands, too.

Chelsea and I, plus kids, would leave Dad and Kathé in two days to fly to Belfast, where we'd visit distant relatives and tour both halves of Ireland. But two days after I booked the flight, French unions announced one of their infamous and frequent grèves: a general strike that would halt most public transportation. They were protesting President Nicolas Sarkozy's "austerity" measures, which would raise the retirement age from sixty to sixty-two.

I was angry the demonstration could interrupt our travel plans but torn about leaving Paris. I was enjoying our "bubble" — the gorgeous Left Bank apartment where music and laughter bubbled up from the sidewalks below and mice skittered behind our accommodation's walls.

For a final outing, we visited Monet's garden with its sunflowers and hollyhocks in Giverny; the place where Joan of Arc was burned at the stake in Rouen; the Rodin Museum; a flea market; the cheese, meat and flower stands of rue Cler; the Louvre and the Eiffel Tower. We ate lunch together. In an imitation of my exchange student days, when I'd led my parents around Paris following my year in Luxembourg, I read menus, asked questions, and ordered meals. Dad paid, another souvenir from my student days.

After years of being so utterly responsible — as the main breadwinner, juggling kids, volunteer work, social activities and money — it was comforting to slide back into funky, shiny daughter shoes (El Cheapo freeloader style).

Facebook Post: September 22, 2010 at 8:02 a.m.
Dawn Picken: *My dad asked me, the first day in Paris, if I thought I could manage a year of traveling the world with the kids. I told him no, I can't think about a whole year. I can, however, think about this day, even this week. It's not all fun and sunshine (remember, there's always weather and Finley, both of which are beyond my control). Still, I'm grateful for this opportunity to spread our wings.*

Our last night in Paris, Dad, Kathé, and I toasted with champagne at Paris' most famous literary café, Café de Flore (Sartre, Simone de Beauvoir, and Hemingway were patrons) before dinner at another literary legend across the street, Les Deux Magots. Between bites of six enormous prawns, I answered Dad's questions. He asked, "What are you going to do for schooling for the kids? They need stability." I assured him I'd already enrolled them in school in New Zealand. "What if you meet someone? What if you never come back? Please, don't take my grandchildren away." His voice caught and I could almost see angst-and-champagne-induced tears. My best answer was I wouldn't hook up with some foreigner and leave the US for good. This was a one-year escape.

"I'll come back next July," I promised. "And then I'll decide what to do and where to live. Maybe we'll even be closer to you."

Facebook Post: September 23, 2010 at 5:39 a.m.
Dawn Picken *Our flight to Belfast tomorrow is one of the few that still hasn't been cancelled. That could change at any minute, of course. As we were talking about leaving, Finley said, "I don't wanna leave." I thought he would say he didn't want to leave Grandpa and Grandma. Maybe, but the concern he voiced was, "They don't have cereal in Ireland!"*
Stephanie Stanelun Holttum: *Gotta love a kid who knows what's important, knows what he wants! Sean loved his cereal too. Miss you all!*

We fêted our last day in Paris with a long lunch around the corner at café La Charette, a tiny neighborhood bistro with a long wooden bar. I stifled the lump in my throat enough to wolf half the bread basket and finish the kids' fries. I was nervous our flight to Belfast would be cancelled. And I was nervous it wouldn't be.

We arrived at the airport three hours early. I asked the ticket agent, "We're going to Belfast. It's not cancelled?"

"No, madam, it's going."

We were going. Taking with us the city Hemingway had called a "moveable feast."

Au revoir, Paris. Au revoir, mon *père*.

Chapter 18

Finding Family in Ireland

Traveling on easyJet from Paris to Belfast is like exchanging your crusty French baguette with smoked salmon and brie for two slices of Wonder Bread with Spam. A brief survey of fellow passengers revealed pasty-faced paunchy chaps and lasses in gray Disneyland t-shirts, faded '80s jeans, and chunky cardigans designed to ward off the isle's clammy chill and the opposite sex. I strained to read expressions: were Irish people unhappy, cheerful, depressed? Even the flight attendants looked dour and frumpy in white shirts and orange scarves, unlike their counterparts on Air France, sleek in navy skirts and nipped-in jackets defining slim Gallic waists.

My paternal grandfather was born in Ballymena, Northern Ireland. My paternal grandmother's mother came from Hungary. Ancestors on my mom's side emigrated from England and Germany. *Je ne sais quois* fails to flower on my family tree. We're a gypsy, meat-potato-and-sauerkraut ball-eating bunch. We resemble people on this plane—at least, in winter time, when we cocoon into our palest, pudgiest selves.

One Irishwoman, a passenger in her twenties or early thirties with dark hair pulled into a bun, marched her kids to the toilet and commanded, "Ey sade get en thar afore yee wet yer pants!" The same woman later jumped up and down playfully on the Jetway with her children as we waited to exit the aircraft — two sides of one Irish coin.

The captain suddenly garbled over the loudspeaker in barely intelligible, clipped British English, "We'll have [shh-garble-garble] Belfast [shh-garble-garble] schedule."

I hoped he was saying we'd land on time in Belfast, even though I was still mooning over Paris. Locals cheered as the pilot guided the plane onto the asphalt: "Woo-hoo!" I glanced at Chelsea. She shot me a grin of bemusement and relief.

Finley provided color commentary: "We're landing. I see a runway. They speak Eng-uh-lish. I'm squeezing down my pee-pee."

I lacked the sense of my Irish compatriot to force my children into the loo during the two-hour flight.

Chelsea and I guided the kids down the Jetway, into the short immigration queue. I was still fumbling for passports as we presented ourselves to a middle-aged woman wearing a stiff navy uniform and a frown.

"Who da we have HAY-uhr?" she asked. "These are yar children?" She inspected Fiona and Finley (who was still tapping out the bladder-bust shuffle). I told her they were my kids as my heart thumped a quick-time mambo.

Immigration Lady set her crosshairs on Chelsea. "And who are yee in relation to they-um?"

Chelsea said, "I'm a friend. I'm helping with the kids."

"Do yee have a wurk PAHR-mit?" Immigration Lady asked.

"Uh, no," Chelsea stammered. "I'm not getting paid. I'm volunteering."

"Yee can't volunteer without a PARH-mit. It's Ell-EE-gal. I could NOT let yee in."

Heart mambo: *left foot forward, right rock back, step back close, pause*. After fretting over the transport strike in France, wondering whether we'd have to paddle to Ulster like its earliest inhabitants 9,000 years ago, was our undoing going to be the fact that I had a helper?

Chelsea and I had arrived in Paris separately, so we hadn't faced this issue. Were we really going to be held up at the border, prevented from entering a country where 27 percent of young people were neither employed nor seeking work? A place that received one-tenth the tourists of the Republic of Ireland?

Immigration Lady grimly stamped our passports and sent us away with a warning. I told Chelsea, "Remember, if the kids run in front of a bus, don't chase them. You're not allowed."

We collected our bags and found William Wallace waiting for us near the airport's exit. I recognized my distant relative because I'd met him in Switzerland in 2004. He stood about six feet tall, with a bald, shiny head. William had a joking manner and accent I strained, at first, to understand.

When I recounted one of Finley's naughty episodes that night, William said, "We'll jist half to SHIT [shoot]him." Total joke, which was funnier with the Ulster accent.

Our William Wallace was not the Scottish warrior of Braveheart fame, but instead, a Northern Irish deep-sea oil worker. Rather than raid or rebel against American forces, he had invited us into his home.

Our invading army had landed well: William's house in the seaside town of Portrush, eighty-four kilometers (fifty-two miles) from Belfast, stood two stories high, with a white cement facade contrasting the red brick driveway. He told us he'd remodeled the home while retaining its original character. Even though floors and walls were refinished, replaced, or otherwise renewed, the home had an old-fashioned feel, with its narrow hallway separating living room from study. The kitchen floor was tiled in muted shades of terracotta, while cupboards were enrobed in light-colored wood. An old-fashioned stove belonging to the original kitchen sat at one end of the long room, across from a blond wood table that could seat twelve people. Polished gray and brown granite countertops gleamed beneath a backsplash of cream-colored tile.

I slept on a double bed with a light-blue fluffy down duvet. Chelsea and the kids slept in the other room, whose orange wallpaper appeared sponge-painted. My favorite room in the house was the large bathroom, with wide-planked wood floors, corner soaking tub, and white sink basin hovering over a cement slab. I rarely used a bathtub, but enjoyed the fantasy of long, child-free, carefree immersions. The shower was complete with full glass door. In Paris, the half-door fixed above the claw foot tub failed to prevent streams of water from splooshing onto the floor.

Facebook Post: September 25, 2010 at 2:57 a.m.
Dawn Picken: We're staying with my distant relative, William, (I think we share a great-grandmother) on a road called Ballywillin. I kid you not: it runs perpendicular to Crocknamack Road.
Mike Wilder: I think there's a street gang named Crocknamack here in Chicago.

No evidence of street gangs where we were, though I did snap a picture of the side of a forsaken house, where someone had spray-painted "Fuck The Weed." School students walked along this road of row houses neatly painted in alternating shades of white, cream, and orange. Many kids wore navy blue uniforms with pleated trousers and stiff white shirts. Some smoked cigarettes.

The kids and I, plus Chelsea, explored Portrush on foot. We walked downtown from William's house in ten minutes. The town took its name from the Irish *Port Rois*, meaning "promontory port." The main part of the old city is built on a mile-long peninsula called

Ramore Head. Tourism officials call the town of about 7,000 "Northern Ireland's favourite holiday destination."

Hordes of holiday-makers had dispersed; school was in session and autumn was in the air. We walked the old stone sidewalks, pausing to admire the 1843 stone church of Holy Trinity, and browsed menus at restaurants along the way like the Harbour Inn, and Coast. I snapped a photo of Finley standing on charcoal slabs of footpath, dressed in gray sweatpants and blue sweatshirt with hood atop his head. He was a *Star Wars* Ewok, white drawstrings dangling from his waist. He flashed a tiny-toothed grin. You could count those Tic-Tacs from ten paces, so straight and white inside their temporary home. Finley's smile stretched his mini-marshmallow nose to the point of flaring. He had tucked his hands behind his back in treasure-concealing stance; you never knew what he had scavenged — stones, wrappers, metal bits and bobs...thankfully, no shriveled condoms — yet.

Late September behaved like Finley, alternating between sunny and bright, petulant and breezy. Coastal causeway winds whipped our hair, slapped our ears, while beams of sun darted and retreated from above the clouds. We ducked into a brightly lit café where CNN blared from a TV mounted below the ceiling. Fiona and Finley slurped mugs of hot cocoa while Chelsea and I sipped cappuccinos.

Chelsea was aide-de-camp, trusted advisor, co-quaffer of coffee and wine. During dozens of hours, over hundreds of kilometers, we shared not just where we were going or where we'd been, but also stories of families, jobs, loves, health, and future hopes. Chelsea didn't have a boyfriend, had struggled with depression, yet mostly maintained a cheery disposition. I met her through my friend Lucinda, another member of the Optimist Tribe. Chelsea had interned at Lucinda's communications business called *Let It Shine* in Spokane. My helper was a young-woman-finding-herself tucked into a cheerleader's shell. "I'm sad I never knew

Sean," she told me. "It sounds like you guys had a really good marriage. That's the kind of relationship I want."

"We did have a solid partnership. No marriage is perfect. Sean wasn't perfect. But we worked well together. We respected each other and joked that even if sometimes we didn't like each other, we were in the marriage for good. Or at least until the kids were grown. But neither of us ever wanted to quit. He was my best friend. And I never wanted to be without him."

I pinched my hand to stem tears.

What I didn't mention were details of that imperfection — the way marriage had allowed Sean to settle into our home, becoming more insular, less social than the man I met more than a decade ago. There were classic issues of aging: hair loss, weight gain, loss of sexual desire. Sometimes I felt I was the anachronism, like I belonged to a place that existed ten years ago. I had my hair, my weight had changed little, I still wanted sex…

Granted, Sean could have compiled a list of my own shortcomings. I was impatient. I kept too busy. I had too many interests and too many friends and never enough time for either. I spread myself in a stretchy layer across an oversized agenda, like pizza dough that meets the edges of a pan only if you pull it enough to create holes in the middle. I write to bottle time because my memory is a sieve, yet I have reserved a couple steel brain boxes where I house my deepest resentments against select individuals. Anne Lamott calls these traits — neuroses, sense of entitlement, narcissism, and envy — the "uncooked egg-parts" that come with being human.

What would I have changed about my marriage? More time together as a couple doing things I admired in my friends' worlds: hiking, cycling, talking about books, volunteering…all those pursuits the cool kids make time for. And sex more than once a month — (and that only happened if the month contained the letter 'e').

I would've spent more time with Fiona and Finley during their babyhoods, not rushing back to work when they were three and four months old. Would I have wanted someone else to shoulder the financial burden instead of carrying most of the load myself? Only in hindsight.

But no one knows how adopting a new name — Mom — will change goals and desires. No one can tell you how you'll feel about not being the center of your own universe, how motherhood means servitude and sacrifice but also great joy and love. I plotted my life's course as an adolescent before I could read motherhood's map. I drew a line from school to university to career. Husband and children lay somewhere on the edge of my chart, over distant borders I couldn't yet see. I was blind to long, winding detours that would whisk me from the twin cities of Ambition and Accomplishment to the four corners of Sickness, Surprise, Humility, and Heartbreak.

I chose a patient partner, one who could change a diaper, push a stroller, and settle two tykes for a nap before retreating to the basement to edit video. Our marriage had worked because neither of us took the other for granted. And we had always joked we were too beat to cheat.

"You'll find him, Chelsea. You're cute, funny, smart. And young. He's probably not the guy you met on the sidewalk in Paris, but he's out there somewhere."

Just as maybe someone was still out there for me, too.

Facebook Post: September 25, 2010
Dawn Picken: I ran this morning in Portrush along the Atlantic Ocean. I came upon 3 Americans in a park; I knew from hearing a few words they were from the States. They'd just been to the Dingle Peninsula (where we plan to go) and recommended we eat at a place called Baker's. Also had my first left-hand-side driving lesson. Sat on the right, shifted gears with my left hand. Egads! My plan is to drive about 20

mph, max.

My Facebook posts in Ireland were often responded to with care and eloquence by Reverend Jeff, who had sat beside me and told stories while Sean was in the hospital. Jeff, with his Air Force background and global life, offered much more than "attagirl" and "LOL."

> **Jeffrey Neuberger:** *We loved the Dingle Peninsula. Take a long walk on the beach. It goes on forever with views on all sides. For old movie buffs, the horse racing scene from "The Quiet Man" with John Wayne and Maureen O'Hara was filmed on that beach. Enjoy some soda bread and a Guinness for me. Killarney was great—some good restaurants. We also went horseback riding (draught horses) there. Left-hand driving is fun, isn't it! And be mindful of the berms on the sides of those Irish roads. Don't let them bamboozle you. Just focus and stay in the land, especially when meeting large buses. Oh, envy!*

Oh, driving! I started by overcompensating, steering too far left, nearly clipping the hedgerows of whitethorn and elder. Chelsea, head glued to the passenger seat headrest (belying any attempt to telegraph, "I'm not worried we'll crash. Not at all.") would squeak, "Little too close over here!"

William had provided my first left-side driving lessons. "Stee CLOH-sahr ta the CEN-tahr line," he'd say. I tried to remain calm but couldn't help thinking skinny thoughts when trucks passed on the other side.

William organized a family reunion for sixty people. His sister, Lily, was flying from Canada. His fiancée, Marion, had arrived from Switzerland. William had proposed marriage to her the day he fetched us from the airport; he'd bought an engagement ring in Dubai on a return trip from his work on an oil rig. They'd had a long-distance relationship for years, shuttling between Switzerland and the UK.

Marion wore short blonde hair and a mountaintop tan. Her German accent was softened at the edges by the French she spoke each day in her village to three teenage daughters and patrons of the hot pools where she worked in nearby Saillon. Later, we would travel to her town nestled in the Alps and soak in the pools, in the shadow of white and purple craggy giants towering as high as fifteen thousand feet.

One night after dinner, Marion helped Finley turn bananas frying in butter in a large saucepan on the stove. He stood on a chair and smiled as he maneuvered the square wooden spoon around the pan.

Facebook Post: September 25, 2010
Dawn Picken: Re: family reunion in Northern Ireland tomorrow: William wants us to make speeches about how we're related. Uh, that's a tough one: we share the same great-grandmother (or great-great). All that matters to my kids is whether other kids will attend (yes!). And I think I'll just stick with a simple American toast. Anyone have one I could borrow?
LR: Yeah. "Who the hell are you guys? CHEERS!"
MB: Here's to those who wish us well. All the rest can go to...
Chelsea Dannen: My toast: I am a random American nanny attending your family reunion. I was raised by wolves and love red wine.

The reunion was at the Royal Court Hotel in Portrush on Balleybogey Road, overlooking the North Atlantic. Its website said the hotel has "panoramic views of County Donegal and the Scottish Isles," which we strained to glimpse under gray skies.

The ladies of our tribe had scrubbed up for the occasion: Fiona wore her pink sequined ballet leotard with black tutu and pink satin ribbon trim. Chelsea had woven small braids at either side of Fi's head, tucking them into a ponytail adorned with black and silver ribbons. Chelsea wore a black and pink floral print tunic with plum scarf, black leggings, and boots. I wore my Parisian black lacy tiered skirt with black long-sleeved top and olive green lacey-edged scarf. Despite whipping Causeway winds, my hair remained camera-ready, stable in its hair-sprayed straightness, long, with side-swept bangs and slightly back-bombed crown. Finley was our slapdash sidekick in his light-blue long-sleeved shirt with hot air balloon appliqué and gray sweatpants.

We stepped into a sea of Irish folk, most of whom I'd never seen before. As the first to arrive, we watched families stream into the room: couples in their thirties and forties with small children, pairs in their fifties and sixties. Another group included Chris, a sturdy young man with curly blond hair who attended university in Belfast. His sister, Sarah, sported a clutch of auburn curls and laughed easily. Teenagers walked amid their elders, looking bored yet trendy.

"Aunties" Margaret and Anna, in their eighties, were there too, but Betty, the other aunty Sean and I had met during our 2001 Ireland trip, had died. I remembered Betty diagramming the family tree, telling stories in her brogue. She described the house my grandfather had lived in until he was about seven years old as a "Tuh UP, tuh DINE" (two up, two down), because the narrow stone house contained two rooms upstairs and two rooms downstairs. Sean and I had visited the place to see remnants of its crumbling façade. We ran from a goat tied up in the front yard.

William's party had a great spread. We filled our plates with salads, potatoes, and slices of ham and beef before sitting at the head table facing Irish kin. As guests of honor, we were the only ones not asked to pay.

William's sister, Lily, had thick silver hair, pale skin, and blue eyes that reminded me of my grandfather's. She took the microphone to explain how the Picken and Allen families were related. "Margaret Picken married Robert Allen and that's the Allen family. That's where we're all connected here. Some of the

Picken boys went to America, to Ohio, including Bob Picken, who had a son named John, who's the grandfather of Dawn Picken, who's here with us today."

When it was my turn to speak, I stood, smoothed my skirt, and said, "I asked my grandfather, before my first trip to Ireland nine years ago, whether we had living relatives over here. He told me, in his usual blunt manner, 'Ah, nah, they're all dead.' Clearly, you're not."

The Irish folk laughed. Thank God they laughed.

My grandfather's contemporaries begat children who had children of their own: one kid sported a foam-muscled Batman costume, another a pink and blue dress with pink boots. A B-52-style bouffant hairdo sat atop a teenager's head, purple flowers behind one ear. A bald grandfather fashioned pins from fishing lures. It was a parallel dynasty on a different continent, a snapshot of what life could have been for my family if my grandfather had remained in Ballymena. Who would I have been? Would I have rubbed elbows with Liam Neeson whilst shoe shopping in town? He was one of Northern Ireland's most celebrated native sons.

Sean and I had visited Ireland shortly before the terrorist attacks of 9/11. We were checking out of our hotel in Dublin when we saw news reports of the first Twin Tower, smoking but still standing. We listened to Irish radio while driving to Castle Leslie in Monaghan to hear the horror unfolding. I was vacationing from my job as news reporter, absent from my country during the worst terrorist attack the US had ever seen. As we bounced along windy Irish roads, I sat in the back seat, wondering when we'd be able to return home. Wondering how we could holiday when thousands of people had died in flames and smoke, beneath falling towers and inside pirated planes. How could we smile for the camera when so many people were weeping around the world?

But we didn't have much choice. It would be at least a week before commercial airlines would fly back to the States. Sean and I decided not to watch TV coverage of the attacks. I felt unhinged and helpless so far from home. There was nothing we could do. We eased back into travel, telling each other to make the most of our three-week belated honeymoon. Wherever we went in Ireland, people would hear our American accents and say, "I'm so sorry for what happened to your country," with genuine compassion. Sometimes they'd touch our shoulders or grasp our hands.

We visited not only distant relatives during that 2001 visit to Northern Ireland, but tourist sites, too. We walked some of the 40,000 interlocking basalt columns along Giant's Causeway, where legend says giant Finn McCool built a bridge linking Ireland to Scotland (the rocks are actually the result of volcanic eruption sixty million years ago). A photo of Sean standing on one of the hexagonal rocks showed him smiling, wearing jeans and a bright blue windbreaker. He looked relaxed. Happy.

Now, eight months after Sean's death, I returned to Giant's Causeway. I inched William's Honda along the access road, waiting for double-decker tour buses to round the bend. I didn't remember this many people being there nine years ago. I only had eyes for Sean, not tourist masses with their macro lenses and teams of children.

As the kids and I walked the half-kilometer to stepping stones that led from the cliffs before disappearing under the sea, I told Fiona and Finley, "Your daddy and I came here a long time ago, before you were born."

Finley asked, "Are we going to see Daddy here?"

Maybe I was trying to bring back Sean by retracing our steps. Part of him *was* there, not just fragments of my memories, but long-ago scrapings from his shoes, the carbon dioxide he exhaled, DNA smudged on rocks and railings. His smallest particles were still there, neutrinos comingled with footprints of those who had trod before and awaited those who would come after. Picturing atoms, envisioning gases is one way to mentally transform what Gail

Caldwell referred to as "life's irrefutable forward motion, a one-way arrow pointed past the dead."

Reality interrupted reverie, as if someone had suddenly blasted Def Leppard inside a monastery.

Four-year-old Finley was scuttling onto rocks, hopping farther away, closer to the frigid Atlantic. Panic curdled in my throat as I screeched, "FIN-LEY! GET BACK HERE! YOU'RE TOO FAR!" The closer I scramble-hopped to Finn, the more he eluded my grasp. I changed course, advancing slowly toward him. He didn't have many more rocks to go before he'd tumble into the water.

He slowed, too, then said, "Hey, Mom, look! I can jump!"

And he did, sending my heart lurching along with my feet.

He landed atop the same column he'd been perched on, oblivious to my wild mother-heart's syncopated rhythms. He was exploring, living with the exuberance of youth.

"FINLEY!" I yelped, relieved. "Stay with me!" I grasped his stubby-fingered hand.

I knew it was an overreaction, but I was still recovering from the ultra-marathon of Sean's illness and death. I couldn't run another sorrowful race. And I needed my boy's comedy to help me heal.

We returned to William's for our last night in his home. Although I missed the food, the language, the noise, and glamour of Paris, we had found family in Ireland, and I really needed that. I had lost one family—the one that included Sean—and found another 4,300 miles from Spokane.

Chapter 19

More Troubles in Ireland

Late September, 2010

Sean and I had visited not only distant relatives during our 2001 visit to Northern Ireland, but tourist sites too. He had knocked back his free sample and mine at Bushmills distillery, where a tour guide told us the whiskey was "triple distilled" to be extra smooth. It still tasted like something I could use to strip layers of paint from the built-in china cabinet at our bungalow in Spokane. We walked sixteenth and seventeenth century ruins of Dunluce Castle, on the edge of a basalt outcropping high above the sea. Wind battered our ears, etching a red tattoo that remained for half an hour.

> **Facebook Post:**
> **Dawn Picken:** *I should be sleeping, but I'm still negotiating roundabouts in my head. Today, I did two things I swore I wouldn't do in Ireland: 1) drive in the city; 2) drive at night. We made it to Belfast during the day, and from Ballymena to Portrush at night. Intact. Chelsea's a great co-pilot. You need a co-pilot for such things.*

Our tour of Belfast transfered me from the driver's seat to the back bench of an enormous black London-style taxi. William's sister, Lily, joined us for the hour-and-a-half trip led by a Catholic cabby named Tommy Hannah. For forty-three British pounds (around seventy US dollars), we'd travel through former paramilitary neighborhoods. We'd drive the same streets where buses, homes, and pubs were petrol-bombed during the Troubles.

Tommy delivered his rendition of the conflict between Catholics and Protestants in Northern Ireland. He said 3,800 people died in bombings, shootings, knifings, and hijackings perpetrated by groups like the Ulster Volunteer Force (Protestant) and the Irish Republic Army (Catholic).

I took notes. I wanted to understand the history of my grandfather's homeland. But after reading books and googling and querying locals (many of whom aren't too keen to talk about the Troubles), I admitted to a scant understanding of Northern Ireland. It was like I'd dragged my fingernail across a ten-pound turkey carcass, when I needed an electric knife.

Despite the 1998 Good Friday Agreement, Tommy said most of Northern Ireland was still segregated, and violence still erupted. The Irish spoke of Protestants and Catholics the way Americans refer to people of different races. Tommy's son attended an "integrated" school. A guide at the Anglican church in Downpatrick in 2001 referred to a union between a Protestant and a Catholic as a "mixed marriage." Sean and I laughed when we realized our Anglo-Saxon Christian union would've been classed a mixed marriage in Northern Ireland.

Our taxi traveled first along Shankill Road in West Belfast. It was a working-class Protestant area of dingy cement row houses. Most of its residents remained loyal to the British Crown. Next, we drove the Catholic area in and around Falls Road. Neighbors there sought an end to British rule and wanted a politically united Ireland. The houses looked equally depressing. Stones had replaced grass in many yards.

A twenty-five-foot-tall corrugated metal wall separating Catholics and Protestants was part of a series of barriers called peace walls. Tommy told us more than forty of these barriers snaked through Belfast. He stopped his taxi to allow us to do what former President Bill Clinton, the Dalai Lama, and rock star Bono had done—sign our names.

Despite the peace deal, people in Belfast were still terrorized by rocks and petrol bombs. Surveys of neighbors showed the vast majority want the walls to stay, even as a movement was underway to begin removing them.

Facebook post:
Dawn Picken: *I wrote Sean's name on the peace wall in Belfast. Our taxi driver/tour guide asked about it, and I told him my husband had died. "Really?" he said, "Ye seem young to've lost a husband." If I were Northern Irish, I would've replied, "Aye. 'Tis a shee-yum [shame], it is. Now, let's go have a wee pint."*

We didn't stop for a pint, driving instead past dozens of buildings with giant painted murals. Just looking at them made me sad and a little scared. Small children—kids the same age as my two—walked past these tributes to violence each day. These children knew who was orange and who was green as soon as they started learning colors. The Protestant/Catholic distinction was not a religious division, but rather a cultural one. Loyalists and Republicans weren't debating the authority of the Pope or the importance of Mother Mary; they were fighting for power and control, clashing over the politics of their land.

One haunting depiction of thuggery showed a man in black balaclava and camouflage jacket pointing a gun. No matter which direction you walked from this "U.F.F Member" his gun barrel was set on you.

Finley said, "Look! The man in the picture has a gun!" He then spotted something shiny on the pavement and scrambled to scavenge the treasure.

"Hey, honey, how about if you catch up to your brother?" I told Fiona, trying to divert the attention of my tenderhearted girl.

That night, I asked my relative, William, about his experiences during the Troubles. William said when he was eighteen, he went home with a girl who later told him she was worried for his safety.

He said, "…because it was in a Catholic area, and with a name like William Wallace, I'm obviously Protestant."

"How do you tell the difference between Catholic names and Protestant names?" I asked.

William said, "Picken is Protestant; it's a Scottish name. But you're an American. They're not going to hurt tourists."

William escaped the Troubles by traveling for work. "We have peace after thirty years of fighting. Obviously, there are always a few nutters running around, because you can't just deprogram after thirty years. And it makes me laugh to see they're making money out of showing tourists the murals on Shankill Road. Whatever. That's good."

People who lived in West Belfast used to have grills in front of their windows and a fire extinguisher in each room to guard against petrol bombs, said William. "My family had a central location in Ballymena, and when July came around for the Orangemen marches, my granny would come to the house to watch. She said, 'You don't much like the marches, do you?' I said, 'No, I don't.' It was like victors tormenting the conquered. My family were all these proud Orangemen."

Finley sat beside me, wearing a green IRELAND soccer jersey. We didn't know this as a Catholic color (not before this trip). I used to imagine the Emerald Isle as a joyful green-hilled island, a singular mosaic of Guinness, sheep, and leprechauns. When I was growing up, I hardly knew anything about the Troubles.

Tomorrow, we'd venture into the more familiar Ireland, one of shamrocks and shillelaghs, driving South to coastal towns to visit castles, cliffs, monuments, and pubs.

We motored from Portrush to Enniskillen in three and a half hours. Locals told us it was a two-hour drive. Every journey takes longer on windy Irish roads laden with tractors sandwiched between hedgerows and a thin stripe of center-line paint. I once drove twenty kilometers behind a tractor, because I couldn't see if anything was approaching from the other side.

Facebook post:
Dawn Picken: I actually enjoyed the drive from Enniskillen, Northern Ireland to Westport, Ireland today. Getting used to the left-hand side. It's like life: I didn't plan to drive on the left-hand side/stay on the left bank of Paris/get left behind as a wife. Yet here I am. On the left-hand side.
Lucinda Kay: It's especially fruitful when you can be ambidextrous.

That night following our day trip to the Marble Arch Caves, the kids crashed around nine. Chelsea and I enjoyed a respite, drinking glasses of red wine from a two-liter cardboard box. Finley had been especially willful. It was his way of saying, "Enough of the grown-up stuff. I'm tired of being a powerless kid. I'll show you how much I can whine/swing my arms/blow raspberries/be contrarian."

We spent the next night in Galway, a major center for traditional Irish music and language on the West Coast.

Facebook post:
Dawn Picken: Ate dinner at a pub called Finnigan's in Galway. Sat next to a young local couple and asked them about lodging options. They pointed us to College Road, which is chock-full of B&Bs. Finally, we're staying in what I imagined: a B&B run by an older couple with two Westie dogs, Victorian furnishings, and a breakfast room just waiting for

hungry tourists.

RB: *I think that is where we stayed...love Ireland! When you go to the Aran Islands and plan to rent a bike, go past the rentals on the pier and up to the shops. Same price but the bikes are brand new. Also, if you go to the ancient fortress, Dun Aengus, hold onto Finn for dear life. There aren't any guard rails at the edge of the cliff!*

We left the B&B to catch a ferry to the Aran Island of Inishmore, where a tour bus bounced us on paved roads over windswept, rocky terrain. Eight hundred people lived there.

Our driver said, "We all know each other, and that's not always a good thing." There were two primary schools and one secondary school. You couldn't buy a home on the island unless you'd lived there seven years and spoke fluent Gaelic. Inishmore had three Catholic churches and one priest. Six inches of soil sat atop the rocks, which was why farmers had created 3,000 kilometers of zig-zagging stone fence — they needed to use the rock.

The ancient fort of Dun Aengus didn't disappoint with its 300-foot-tall limestone cliffs (as Rebecca suggested on Facebook, I didn't let Finley get too close). The prehistoric site overlooking the Atlantic Ocean is the largest of its kind on the islands. Three massive stone walls encased the semicircular fortress; tall rocks set vertically into the ground were designed to deter attackers. Fiona and Finley were mostly interested in a tiny stone house built for leprechauns.

A carriage driver named Tony gave us a free lift and let the kids take the reins. He was enthused about America, saying, "Clinton is brilliant. Lovely man. There would be no peace in the North if it weren't for him."

He told us the current president, George Bush "...turned the whole world upside down."

I tried to push ten euros into Tony's palm at the end of our fifteen-minute ride, but he refused. A half hour later, we spotted him on a barstool in the port of Kilronan at The American Bar. I gave the bartender money for Tony's sandwich and drink. Meanwhile, in a back room, the kids flicked balls across the pool table.

Sean would've loved these places. We'd only visited Dublin and the North together, missing the charm of Southern coastal towns. I pictured Sean pulling up a barstool, taking long swigs of Guinness, and listening to some old Irish salt spin tales. I closed my eyes and tried to feel Sean sitting next to me.

The following day, fog obscured our view from the Cliffs of Moher, which tower above the rugged west County Clare coast. Unlike at Dun Aengus, guard rails keep people from the edge of the precipice, due to previous suicides. On this blustery, gray day, Finley threw a tantrum. He wanted to run close to the edge instead of sticking with us. I set his munchkin nose against O'Brien's stone tower for a time-out.

My patience was threadbare above these 700-foot-tall cliffs, yet I had no urge as others had to fling myself from the rocks in this moment. Even though Sean's death left a chasm, a vacancy, my children stepped in to fill the void. I cherished my life to safeguard theirs. And something in this thin space—the inner voice I alternately imagined as Sean or God—whispered that things would work out.

No one is sure where the phrase "thin space" originated, but it may as well have been in Ireland. A thin space is where heaven and earth nearly collide. Eric Weiner in 2012 wrote, "The ancient pagan Celts, and later, Christians, used the term to describe mesmerizing places like the wind-swept isle of Iona (now part of Scotland) or the rocky peaks of Croagh Patrick. Heaven and earth, the Celtic saying goes, are only three feet apart, but in thin places that distance is even shorter."

Thin places aren't only in sanctuaries (though walking the labyrinth at St. John's felt like a brush with the infinite and unknowable). For me, a serendipitous meeting with a stranger can feel thin, as can the moments when I look into my children's eyes and see their father's soul reflected back. At the Cliffs, I felt connection with the ocean and the air that had held the dreams and molecules of millions of travelers.

Travel itself provides consolation, offering a mantel of newness, like sniffing fresh lilac or falling in love. Travel helped me birth joy inside the deepest void of Sean's death.

We headed south, driving 140 miles from the Cliffs to the fishing and tourist village of Dingle.

Facebook post:
Dawn Picken: *We're still alive and well and now in Dingle, Ireland. Stayed inside much of today due to rain and driving wind. There's a good little aquarium next to where we're staying, so the kids and I gawked at sharks. Spent more than two hours last night at a pub with kiddos, listening to Irish music. Made me teary, because it's exactly what Sean would've loved. Rain has stopped—time to get back outside and explore.*
HK: *Thinking of you. Your wonderful front trees are changing color and losing leaves. I remember Sean spending forever raking them... Miss you.*

One night in Dingle, I took myself out for a drink at Dick Mack's, mostly because I liked the name. It's a former shoeshine shop and haberdashery. There, I filled my metaphorical adult conversation cup and a literal cider cup with one too many pints after the bartender accidentally poured an extra drink, which he gave me for free. I exchanged craic (banter) with a couple Irishmen, including Pat, who motioned toward a young German student with sideswept blond locks, saying, "Yee have the most parfect fockin' hair, like Luke fockin' Skywalker." A few too many drams made Pat philosophical and forward. He said, "I admire what yee're doin'…and yee're fockin' gorgeous. If yee lived in Ireland, I'd get down on my knee now and ask yee to marry me."

Laurie from Maryland told me she, too, had been widowed young. Her husband died of cancer when she was twenty-eight. She was left with three children, ages two, three, and six. This made me cry. I can talk about Sean's death matter-of-factly with strangers, almost as though I'm reporting it for the news. But meeting a fellow widow opened my soul and my tear ducts. "I've had tremendous support from my church family and my father," she said. Just like me. What were the chances the two of us would meet at a pub in Dingle? Laurie's mother had died six months before her husband. Today, fifteen years after losing her mom and being widowed, Laurie has remarried and works as a neonatal intensive care nurse in Washington, D.C. She was living, cider-swilling proof that second lives existed after someone you built your life with had died.

Chelsea, the kids and I returned from Dingle to Portrush, driving nine hours on bendy, hairpin-turn, tractor-crammed roads until the blessed motorway — the M1 — from Dublin to Belfast. We'd have a day to recover before our next adventure. My relative Lily delivered us to the airport.

Belfast International, like other airports before and yet to come, is a table of contents for our traveling souls, the place our brave hearts close one chapter before turning the next page.

Chapter 20

Transitions and Townships

November 11, 2010, the kids and I flew from Frankfurt, Germany to Capetown, South Africa. Chelsea had returned to the States after the four of us spent a week together in Mallorca, Spain. We formed a sorrowful tribe as we said our goodbyes.

We had hopscotched Europe, visiting London, where I rented an overpriced basement apartment in the central city and sobbed while watching the musical *Billy Elliot* in the West End Theatre district. The story centers on a motherless British boy who starts taking ballet lessons. I had forgotten about the letter from Billy's dead mum and her other visitations when I bought my theater ticket. We visited friends in Switzerland and Luxembourg, where I had been an exchange student. It rained almost the whole time we were there, just as I'd remembered it in high school.

We stayed with my friend Jean-Marie whom I had met as a seventeen-year-old at the *Lycée Classique* in Diekirch. Jemmy, as he's known, lived with his wife, Idalina, and two children. Their house adjoined his mother's home. Our first night staying in the downstairs guest suite with tidy furniture and polished concrete floors was marked by a series of sheet changes after Finley threw up—twice. He blamed it on the potatoes we had eaten that day at lunch.

Jean-Marie towered over six feet and, with his dark hair and beard, looked like a Luxembourgish version of Paul Bunyan. All that was missing was an axe, though as a forest ranger, he would have occasion to swing lots of sharp objects. He and I would talk in the living room, often over a glass of fragrant Bordeaux after I put the kids to bed. Finley would inevitably rise, time and again, and I would march him back to the room.

"You must be the good cop and the bad cop," said Jean-Marie, "because it's just you." I told him I knew that, but I was tired of being any kind of enforcer. Jemmy and his family spoiled us during our ten-day stint with large midday meals, Tattinger champagne for Sunday lunch, babysitting, and the use of his car to visit the public pool in Mersch. That was where I tried to shed my Yankee inhibitions during a women's-only buck-naked day. I zipped from sauna to jacuzzi to steam room with a towel draped over my shoulders, half trying not to check out all the other nude bodies to see how my fat rolls, or lack thereof, stacked up with theirs.

In Switzerland, we stayed with two dear friends: Anne had been our angel in Spokane when she au paired for us six months. She brought us to her parents' home in Mex, a town of about 140 souls high in the Alps. Sean and I had traveled there in 2005, when Fiona was a toddler and Finley was in utero. Then, as now, we ate raclette and fondue, savoring the rich sharpness of gruyere mixed with white wine and the smell of comfort.

Our other hosts lived near Zurich, where we bunked with the sister of our former exchange student, Angi. Petra and her husband, Reto, had three children, ages three, seven, and ten. Petra invited me to her neighborhood group, where I feasted on lasagna and swapped stories with other with other mums. One of them told me her neighbor had recently lost his young wife to cancer. "The sadness wasn't just his," she said. "We shared it, too."

Finley celebrated his fifth birthday three times in Switzerland, as Anne, her mother, Colette, and Petra had all made him a cake. I can still picture his squirrel cheeks as he blew out candles on Mickey Mouse.

The kids were surprisingly great during the twelve-hour flight from Europe to South Africa. It helped that the leg from Frankfurt started at midnight. They were out by 1:00 am and slept until nearly 8:00.

Fiona was almost seven: a classic older child, she was mostly obedient, kind, and smart. Observant, too. As we snaked through the Immigration line at Cape Town's International Airport, she asked, "Mommy, why are there so many brown people here?"

"Because they live here," I replied. Fiona had been born and raised in Spokane, Washington, whose population was nearly ninety percent white and two percent black.

Facebook Post:
Dawn Picken: I'm realizing how segregated my kids have been as they make comments like, "The brown man tried to touch my hand." You'd think they'd never seen a person of color before. I told Fiona, "Barack Obama is black." She said, "No, he's not." Maybe she's used to him being president, and that's all she needs to know. Obama's big in South Africa: you see his face on pillows and t-shirts.

The black population of South Africa stood at ninety percent, with whites making up nine percent. No wonder my kids were culture-shocked: they were experiencing an inverse ratio of the demographics they were used to. And I was thankful for it. What else would they experience in South Africa that would change their world view?

Once we were out of customs, we found my friend Heather waiting for us as we exited baggage claim. Heather and I had been best friends during our exchange year in Luxembourg. We attended and ditched classes together, swam together, and drank too much of the local Riesling together.

She may have regretted replying to my e-mail asking if the kids and I could stay with her for a month. On May 27, 2010, Heather wrote:

It really is so good to connect with you again after all these years… I know that our friendship is one that can pick up where we left off, and I hope we can still find some naughty-silly-funny things to do together 20+ years on!

Staying with Heather afforded great freedom and crushing loneliness. Aside from a couple weekends with her and her blended family of fiancé and two boys, the kids and I were on our own. Heather worked full-time in finance, traveled, attended meetings, cycled up to 100 kilometers during a weekend and was busy, busy, busy. She reminded me of me before Sean got sick (minus the long bike rides).

The weather was warm and sunny when we arrived in Cape Town, so we hit the beach.

Finley took one look at the ocean and said, "Am I dreaming?"

Facebook Post:
Dawn Picken: *I'm enjoying the South African version of Fiona and Finley. For the sixth night in a row, they've gone to bed and gone to sleep without getting up or calling for me. And they've been relatively well-behaved. Maybe it's the change of seasons: they get plenty of exercise and hardly watch TV.*

Facebook Post:
Dawn Picken: *Kids and I passed the township of Khayelitsha today en route to Stellenbosch (wine region). More than*

400,000 people, nearly all black, live there in tin shacks. Kids asked why. I tried to explain (a little) about segregation. Fiona said, "I'm glad I'm not brown." NOT the lesson I was trying to teach. I reminded her Barack Obama's brown, president, and rich. Finley said, "So if we need money, we can ask Rock Obama."

Until 1994, when apartheid ended, non-whites were forced to live in townships. Our twenty-four-year-old mixed-race tour guide on Robben Island (where former South African President Nelson Mandela was imprisoned) described apartheid as "mental divide and conquer." Now it's economics, not government, that dictate where tan, brown, and ebony-skinned people live. Flat-roofed tin dwellings sprawl for miles in the dirt.

Facebook Post:
Dawn Picken: *Booked a township tour tomorrow with the kids. It'll be the sanitized version of life in tin shacks. We'll go with a local to see a preschool and have lunch. This is what you do when you travel with small children: partake of the safe, sanitized version of lodging, touring. No more sleeping on trains and wandering the streets at night. I did that stuff in college. Maybe I'll do it again if I'm lucky enough to grow old.*

At the beginning of the tour, we were serenaded by Ella and Sandy, two Xhosa women (to say "Xhosa," try clicking your tongue while pronouncing "cl"). They sang with such joy and vigor, Ella in a traffic cone-orange suit while Sandy sported a Kelly-green shirt and black trousers. Ella's ebony cheekbones were dotted with white paint. She looked regal.

The song's refrain sounded something like, "*Ee-oh, Ee-oh lay-tay lah.*" Sandy fluttered her hands in the air like two graceful black birds. She clapped while Ella pounded a three-foot-long hourglass-shaped drum. "*Ee-oh, Ee-oh lay-tay lah.*"

I hid behind my sunglasses and wondered if tears swam counterclockwise below the equator. Even though I didn't often cry over Sean's death, the exhilaration of beauty my late husband would never see blinded me with tears.

A dozen children stood to the side, singing. They appeared three to six years old, an equal mix of girls and boys. Mahogany skin glowed with sweat and pride. They wore a gumball machine's mix of hues: pink, red, blue, yellow, green, black.

I focused on a little girl, Anna, who was around three. Her thick black hair stood high and proud, waving to the African sky. She wore a yellow soccer jersey with a deep-green vee. With chubby cheeks, almond-shaped eyes, and full lips, she was a miniature Xhosa queen.

While we watched the concert, a skinny yellow dog climbed inside its nearby wooden house, and Finley tried to follow. "Finn!" I croaked a ragged half whisper: "Get out of there!" I yanked him to the front of the group to pound a small drum while I beat the big one. Fiona, in a moment of shyness, abandoned her drumming career.

Still recording video at the Knysna Township tour, I panned the camera back to Finley. He sported a hooded gray long-sleeved shirt with blue felt guitar that said "Rocker Nation." Finn's favorite shirt was too warm for eighty degrees Fahrenheit. At least he was smiling, apple cheeks pinker than usual in this heat.

After the song, Ella told us how grateful she felt to live in this township of 16,000 people, lined with cardboard and cement homes, ringed by dirt, roaming dogs, clucking chickens, and the odd pig. Ella said it was a world away from her childhood farm, where she lived after her alcoholic parents divorced. Even though it was unusual for girls in her village to attend school, she had wanted to learn English and she had practiced on visitors such as Christian missionaries.

Ella returned to school in her early twenties. "No one knew I was twenty-four," she said. "I didn't care. I had to finish school." She found work as a dishwasher in Knysna, earning the equivalent of fifty US cents per hour. "When I became a waiter, I started to realize I had potential," she told us. Ella met Penny at a Baptist church. "She was my first white friend," said Ella. The duo started Emzini Tours ("emzini" means "at home" in Xhosa), which buses tourists to Knysna Township for a three-hour $50 daylight tour in one of South Africa's smaller, safer ghettos.

Earlier, on the way to the tour in the shuttle van with two other tourists, our guide, Penny, had turned to the kids and asked, "What did you do with Daddy today? Leave him in the closet?" I looked down at my left hand, where I still wore my wedding ring. I couldn't bear to leave it in the States and I still felt married. Sean died, but the love never did.

The kids didn't know how to respond to this stranger's query, and I paused before answering, "My husband died in January. The kids and I are on a world tour because I needed to see something new." Nine months after Sean's death, the fact that my husband had died and my children had lost their father was starting to settle into my bones. Our eleventh wedding anniversary would've been tomorrow, December 3.

Penny's face fell. I'd seen that expression before, the "oh-my-God-I-had-no-idea-I'm-mortified" look. "I'm sorry," she said. "I think you're doing the right thing by traveling. It'll be a good experience for you and the kids."

The township tour did provide a new perspective on living in community. After the singing, Ella entered her cinder block home and re-emerged with a plate of fried dough balls. They smelled like American donuts. Our hosts poured tall drinks of red fruit punch. Finley grabbed two fried balls and a punch. He sat beside Lamla, Ella's fourteen-year-old daughter. Lamla barely spoke English, but she was friendly and approachable and appeared taken by my son's impishness. She was coltishly thin, with reddish-brown Don

King hair. I gave her the equivalent of ten US dollars, which she presented to her grandmother, who was sitting on a brown leather-look couch in the living room.

I asked if it was okay to look around Ella's small home. The kitchen, which was small and tidy, adjoined the living room. A blue-painted bathroom contained a sink, toilet, shower, and tub. Lamla's room featured a red-striped bedspread, yellow and orange throw pillows, a small dresser loaded with books, boxes, lotions, and a crucifix. Black drapes were tied back, revealing sheer curtains with a black lace flower pattern. Another bedroom had a black and white leaf print comforter on a double bed, decorative pillows, and black and white print curtains. Ella said their Habitat for Humanity home had cost 25,000 Rand (about $3,500 US) to build. Her share of the cost was 8,000 Rand ($1,100 US). Ella said she was lucky, because many of her neighbors lived for years in wooden shacks with cardboard walls.

After we'd finished the fried dough and punch, we walked to one of those cardboard homes. I snapped a picture of wood beams supporting the ceiling. Cardboard was stuffed in between the beams. Wires snaked up walls and zigzagged above our heads. An electrical box was attached to the wall sprouting three plugs. The place looked like a fire-trap. We were told a shack like that cost about $600 US. Despite its condition, someone had decorated, using a blue circular patterned cover for the sofa and a skein of white flouncy fabric on a wall.

We walked a dirt road toward the preschool. Finley and his new friend, Lamla, were smiling and talking. The tourist pack, plus a dozen little kids, squeezed into a preschool. It was a low, wooden brown building with a wood and cardboard roof and a single room. Drawings of people, animals, and houses decorated walls, matted on gray and pink paper. Inside, mugginess filled my throat like a wad of wet towel. In the opposite corner sat a baby's crib. I wondered how any learning, sleeping, or living happened here. I

229

couldn't wait to escape. Finley's face was shiny from sweat as he picked up a green Lego block and played alongside the township kids.

Back outside, Fiona and Finley scrambled up a dirt pile. Finley borrowed one of the kids' toys, a wheel attached to a wire. This was the greatest thing he had ever seen. "Can we take it back to Spokane?" he asked. I told him no, it was too big and these kids needed their toy.

"You have plenty of toys back home, Finn." I was embarrassed to think about my children driving around the $500 toy Jeep my dad had given them for Christmas. I wished Fiona and Finley were older, so they could understand how good they had it. I promised myself I would thrust poverty in their faces—take them to volunteer in shelters—as they grew up.

Because even as an adult, I could be oblivious. When I had first arrived in Cape Town, before I bought a SIM card for my phone, I asked my friend's char (cleaning woman) to borrow her phone to make a quick local call.

The woman sheepishly said, "I don't have any money on the phone. I can only receive calls."

Duh. Of course she didn't have a loaded cell phone. She lived in a township, didn't own a car, and barely scraped by. And I had asked to use her cell phone.

On the township tour, we walked to a small cinder block building set up as a supermarket. Crates of cabbage, onions, and potatoes sat, mid-store, surrounded by shelves stacked with neat rows of staples: sugar, ultra-pasteurized milk, biscuits, and tinned meats. We were told much of the food was past its prime, and selection was scant. We walked to a metal shipping container that housed a soup kitchen.

One of our group members had brought a box of food to help stock the kitchen's pantry. I scolded myself. Why hadn't I thought of that?

Next time I would bring food.

Because apparently, I had already decided we would return to South Africa.

American poverty differs from third-world poverty. It's Walmart versus a store offering two kinds of stale bread, or the supermarket-that-accepts-food-stamps versus grinding corn for your own tortillas. In the States, you can collect a welfare check and still have satellite TV, a cell phone, and fake nails. You might also have heat, lights, and food. Plywood shacks exist in pockets of Appalachia, Florida, and the Mountain West, but in the US you must seek them out. In South Africa, shacks are everywhere, reminders of the serendipity of our first-world birthplaces. But for the grace of God, we too could've been born in Khayelitsha, the slums of Kolkata or the Hutong villages of Beijing. As wealthy westerners, we can visit poverty, pat its head, throw it a few coins, then return home and whine about the high cost of high-speed internet or the price of college.

MK: Please write it down so you can tell them that story in about 18 years. It is so funny to watch their expressions when you tell them stories like this when they are in their twenties.
Cheryl Branz: *Just the laugh I needed right this minute!*

Our tribe would need laughs and luck to survive the rest of our African adventure.

Chapter 21

South Africa's Wild Life

December, 2010

It wasn't just the experience at the township that endeared me to South Africa. And it wasn't just me. I met many other tourists, mostly Europeans, who returned to South Africa time and again. They, too, have been captivated by the landscape — glistening blue waters around Cape Town, craggy mountains, and salt-white beaches — and intrigued by its people. The cost of lodging, food, and attractions is far cheaper than in most of Europe, and it's kid-friendly. Even the wineries have attractions for children.

At Spier wine estate in Stellenbosch, Fiona and Finley petted a cheetah. I sent them into the cage with a trainer — without me — deciding it wasn't worth $20 for me to pat the cat. The kids emerged unscathed, and the three of us visited the birds of prey encounter, where we donned leather gloves so an owl could perch on our arms.

We fortified ourselves with bacon and eggs one morning before setting off to ride wrinkly gray elephants at Knysna Elephant Park.

Rather, Fiona and Finley rode the beasts. When you leave home, quit your job, and surrender your income, you do not fling money at each tourist trap. One of my best pieces of travel advice came from a friend of a friend who spent a year globe-trotting. Sharon said, "Make a budget. You can't leap at every skydiving tour you find."

The elephant ride, at $50 per child and $100 per adult, was something I could skip.

There were, however, four key facts I failed to investigate before tightening my belt and rejecting the ride: 1) the walk took about forty-five minutes; 2) I would not be allowed to take pictures during the excursion (an employee explained the company had faced complaints after an animal rights group posted pictures online, something that, had I investigated, would probably have led me to skip the elephant ride); 3) I would have to walk behind the elephants; 4) elephants pee and poop a lot while they're walking.

I should've spent the $100.

I tried not to inhale while trampling and tripping over holes hidden by grass in the Knysna Elephant Park. The guide, Matt, asked, "Why are you not riding, too?" I explained I wanted to photograph the kids. "You are not allowed to take pictures." When Matt wasn't looking, I tried a quick snap.

Ha, take that! Photo Enforcer's head snapped 'round. "Hey, you can't take any pictures during the ride." They wanted to sell us photos and a DVD for $30. Shit. The elephant dropped another load.

This is a story I will resurrect when the kids are older. *I walked behind piles of elephant dung and puddles of urine for you when you were young. Be thankful.*

Facebook post:
Dawn Picken: *Took the kids on safari today. Okay, that*

sounds a lot bolder than it really is: we're at a game reserve with a fence to keep animals in and people out (like poachers). You're guaranteed to see the "Big Five." It's still cool that they're indigenous to this area. Saw zebras, wildebeest, kudu, lions, rhino, giraffe, buffalo, cheetah. Rhino sprayed the dirt road while walking. "Look, Mom, he's peeing!" said Finley.
GM: *Well, I felt rather adventurous at the San Diego Wild Animal Park, so I'm VERY impressed! Pictures?*

We took two game drives at the Garden Route Game Lodge, a family-friendly park. The youngest member aboard our open-topped Land Rover was two. Our ranger, Jason, explained that lions at the park were rescued from canned hunts, where tourists paid to shoot the animals on a ranch.

Facebook post:
Dawn Picken: *We fed an elephant tonight after the game drive. The big guy sounded like a vacuum sucking up all the pellets. Dinner at the lodge was a buffet featuring steak (beef) and venison skewers: kudu, wildebeest, and eland (a kind of antelope), or was it springbok? I had springbok carpaccio on salad for lunch. Not bad. Fiona ate two good old-fashioned steaks, plus a mussel, broccoli, and a brownie.*
CW: *Good for Fiona. I don't think I would eat a mussel.*

The most exciting part of the game drive for Fiona and Finley happened at the business end of a rhinoceros: "Look, Mom, the rhino has a giant penis!" That observation was followed by a fire hose of urine. A sharp scent of ammonia stung my nostrils. Why was I always on the receiving end of bodily functions? Because life smells. At least it's not the hospital.

Facebook post:
Dawn Picken: *Drove from the Cape Peninsula today to Hermanus, the self-proclaimed "whale-watching capital of the world." The marketing works, because I was keen to drive out*

of our way to see whales. Took a two-hour boat trip and was richly rewarded: Southern Right Whales, mamas and their calves were breeching, tail smacking, showing off for us. Fiona and Finley kept saying, "Whoa!" Happy, happy...

We caught the ocean safari during one of the last days of whale-watching season. Unlike the game reserve, where animals are fenced, whales are free to roam. It was fewer than thirty minutes before our skipper spots the first whale. "Thar she blows!" he says. Really, just like a scene from *Moby Dick*. A geyser of clear blue spray shot from the whale's "water spout," as the kids called it. I took real and mental pictures of the moment. *This* moment. Blue water beneath us, green slab of mountains before us, and endless surfacing of Southern Right Whales.

"Look over there!" I told Fiona and Finley.

"I can't see it!" said Finley. "Point my head." I cupped his noggin between my hands and angled it straight ahead of him, where a large whale breached and dove, breached and dove.

"There," I said. "Do you see it?"

Finley said, "I see! I see! Fiona, there's a whee-awl!"

After the whale adventure, we drove on fumes to the tip of Africa, Cape Agulhas. Why hadn't I refueled in Hermanus? I was at the end of the world with two kids, running out of gas. I asked Sean for help: "Honey, I know it was stupid not to fill up, but could you get us to the next town?"

We made it to a Mobil station in Bredasdorp, where the black attendant (gas stations in South Africa are full-service) repeats the price twice (about 600 Rand, or $80 US), as if to let me know he's not ripping me off. "I know," I say. "I was running on empty."

The owner of the guest house I called earlier that day to book a reservation invited us to inspect our room and stash our bags. I queried our host, Philip, whether the local beach was safe. You must ask these questions in South Africa: an average of fifty people a day are murdered there, but 80 percent of those murders happen between people who know each other.

Carjacking remains a problem. I drove with locked doors and ignored hawkers selling newspapers at intersections.

A young woman on honeymoon from the UK was found murdered the week we arrived in Cape Town. She and New Hubby were visiting a township at night. The case was everywhere in the news. Tourism officials wrung their hands. Her husband was later found guilty of her murder.

Philip told us the beach in Cape Agulhas is okay, but said, "Be careful. I don't want to sound racist, but there are lots of coloreds, and they play rough." Huh? Only brown-skinned children are rough?

Later, after the kids were asleep, I snuck my starved-for-adult-conversation self to the lounge. Philip poured me a glass of red wine, himself a Scotch, and started talking politics.

"South Africa is going to the dogs. In five years, it'll be nothing. The blacks take over municipalities and employ too many people. It's nepotism, and nothing gets done. There's no water storage facility for our town and roads don't get fixed. I pay taxes into a rate payers' association, a trust, and we hire a reputable company, not a black empowerment company… Jacob Zuma, our president, has three wives and says, 'I took a shower, so I don't have HIV.' It's ridiculous."

Philip is an Afrikaaner, part of an Afrikaans-speaking ethnic group descended from Dutch, German, and French settlers. For decades, he's taken groups on four-wheel drive safaris in Namibia and Botswana. He told me about the Belgian guy who thought lions were scratching his tent. He was hearing squirrels. A group of World War II veterans insisted on sleeping like Philip beneath the stars on a cot beside a river teeming with crocodiles. "They won't climb out to get you," Philip said.

I told him I was taking Fiona and Finley around the world. "I think you won't regret it," he said. "They've been exposed to so many different cultures, and it probably is good to get away from American culture for a while."

We watched animals rest. Does that count? Africa was the place to punch our animal-watching cards, with a visit to Monkeyland near Knysna, where primates pounced from trees, landing at our feet. "Mommy, the monkeys aren't going to get us, are they?" Fiona quivers. I assure her they won't, then wonder myself. We spot seals in Hout Bay and baboons on a hillside in the Western Cape.

The kids chase geckos on top of Table Mountain following a cable car ride 3,500 feet (1,085 meters) to the top.

I'm just as interested in showing the kids injustices humans have perpetrated on our own species as showing them animals at wildlife parks.

I read to the kids how brown-skinned people were stuffed into boats against their will to sail to a new country where they'd work for no pay. I tell them their own country, America, had used slaves.

After I explain circumcision, Finley says, "You mean they cut off his pee-pee?"

I squirm at the image and tell him, "No, just the tip. But it sounds awful."

My friend, Heather, who hosted us at her homes in Cape Town and Kommetjie for a month, met Nelson Mandela once, during a student rally. She's a South African of British descent who had protested apartheid. Even though the whites I met during our trip criticized the class system, they still enjoyed a privileged lifestyle thanks to the brown majority who watched their children, scrubbed their toilets, and swept their floors for far less than the price a white person would charge. With unemployment at around 50 percent in many townships, any job was better than no job.

Whites pay for cheap labor in other ways: installing eight-foot-high spiky security fences, cameras, and alarm systems. They sequester themselves inside posh prisons. Everyone's been burgled, or even knows someone who was murdered. I locked myself outside Heather's house once and set off her alarm system twice.

While I could escape the life Sean and I shared in Spokane, I couldn't outrun loneliness. It waited for me as a lion crouches for prey, and found me in South Africa. Everywhere I turned, I saw families consisting of what looked like Mom and Dad plus two kids. The romance of the landscape was captivating—and sorrowful: the sparkling azure waters of Hout Bay; the rugged rock hills of the Western Cape; the crashing, smashing waters at Knysna Heads. Don't get me started on wine country, which reminded me of when Sean and I toured Napa Valley.

I envied the closeness Fiona and Finley shared. They would play in their own little world, making up stories and confiding in one another. It was sweet and maddening at the same time. I didn't have a peer or companion like they did. Sure, I was their mom, but that also separated me as a solo entity.

I remembered the many letters Sean wrote me before I moved to Seattle to be with him. We lived apart fifteen months, during which time our romance started to bud.

June 1, 1998

…you have been on my mind night and day since your decision to move here. I couldn't be more happy. The longing for you is overwhelming at times…I have always known this, but as of late it has been so strong. That being how much I love you. I find myself imagining scenarios where we are together; each time I get a sense of strength. There is no question that you are "the one."…I know that I am ready. I am ready to share my life with you.

Facebook post:
Dawn Picken: *Today would've been my 11th wedding anniversary. Talked via Skype to Leanne and Mark tonight, who have always remembered our date. Hate to wish away time, but I'm glad the day is just about done. Last year, I had a husband, lobster, singer friend Cheryl…within the walls of St. Luke's Rehab. One of the nurses bought our dinner.*

I spent that anniversary at a guest house in Knysna, eating grocery store salad and bread, drinking five dollar (always good, even at that price) South African wine, and trying to get Fiona and Finley to sleep by eight o'clock so I could wallow in peace.

We married on a rainy Friday, December 3, 1999 in front of 150 friends and family at St. Paul's Episcopal Cathedral in Cleveland Heights, Ohio. There, I read my own love letter.

...You are my rock, my anchor – you ground me...
Sean, I can't promise you wealth, success or perfect health,
But what I can offer you and will give you is all of me.

I posted pictures and video to Facebook of the kids and I at an outdoor summer concert at Kirstenbosch Botanical Gardens. Fiona sat on my shoulders while I danced. Finley slept, wrapped burrito-style in a blanket on the grass. Fiona and I swayed sloppily, happily, on the eastern slopes of Table Mountain between protea flowers and fynbos ferns while listening to a Quaito group (similar to R&B) called TKZee. I bought their CD, listening to it over and over on our South African trip. The kids and I sang the refrain to one song, whose lyrics say there's someone "out there."

Out where? Was that why I was on this journey? Not just to heal from losing Sean but to find someone new? It hadn't been my intent when I'd set out, but the person to whom I had given my all was gone. I still had a lot to give.

Chapter 22

Half a Heart in Australia

December, 2010

Thanks, Sponge Bob Square Pants, for globetrotting with us from South Africa to Australia, a twenty-three-hour-long ordeal in a flying cylinder. The Qatar Airways kids' pack included a mini toothbrush, paste, crayons, and coloring pages inside a fuzzy Sponge Bob bag. Fiona and Finley inspected Bob's booty before plugging in to a Ben Ten cartoon and playing video games.

After three months of traveling, we were old pros free of barfing spells and ear infections, about to land in the Sunburned Country, whose kangaroos, koalas, and golden coasts I'd only dreamed of. The fact that I was getting better at traveling alone with the kids pleased me and made me miss Sean more. I did not want to get used to life without him. We would have our first Christmas minus Sean in Australia. Provided we cleared customs.

I'd heard stories, sober warnings from other passengers about the risk of being caught with contraband at an Australian airport. No fruit, meat, marijuana, cannabis, heroin, cocaine, or amphetamines. And definitely no honey. One woman told me she'd forgotten about a tiny unopened pot of honey in her carry-on bag. That one-ounce jar cost her four hundred dollars.

It was nearly midnight in Oz, and I had no snacks for the kids. Or me. I offered to jettison my South African Rooibos tea, but the customs agent said it was unnecessary. No one asked if I had food and I didn't see anyone inspect our luggage. I could have packed cookies. Even honey-flavored granola bars.

Rain pelted the sidewalks and roads as we exited the terminal. We caught a shuttle bus to the Best Western, where I grabbed three apples from reception, which would serve as breakfast the next day. We fell unconscious around one in the morning.

Eight hours later, I crawled from bed and we caught the van to the airport to retrieve our rental car, which I'd reserved for ten o'clock to capture most of a day in Melbourne. I had vastly underestimated my fatigue, sacrificing rest and renewal for sightseeing and presumably productive travel (whatever the hell that is with a jet-lagged mom and two tired kids). We would spend three weeks in Australia, surely I could have scheduled a couple days of nothing. But no. Doing nothing led to extreme feelings of loneliness. It was better to always be doing something.

I drove into downtown Melbourne like a bumbling hamster, or half-blind Mister Magoo, unsure where I was going. We had half a day before we were due to arrive at our travel hosts' home an hour east of the city. I wanted to explore, but where to park? I sat in traffic on Flinders Street fifteen minutes before pulling into a parking garage charging sixteen dollars per hour. I could park all day in Spokane for that. I was tired of the relentless travel and traffic.

We popped into St. Paul's Cathedral, a block from the parking garage. Its website said it was built in the neo-Gothic transitional style, which means it's only partly decorated. Thick pillars guarded the sanctuary. These soldiers, wearing bands of black and tan, stretched to yoke-pointed arches. The cathedral's processional doors depicted the story of St. Paul the moment he was blinded by light on the road to Damascus.

Fiona and Finley asked if they could light a candle for Daddy. I wondered if playing with fire was part of what drove the kids to repeat the ritual. "Mommy, can we sit near the front? I want to see stuff and pray for Daddy," said Fiona.

We perched on a wooden pew facing the main altar and said a short prayer for Sean. Fiona held my hand. Her little girl fingers were long, tiny, and soft. She still wore a full-moon scar on her right hand, a souvenir of an IV from the neonatal intensive care unit where she lived her fledgling first weeks.

I said, "God, please take good care of Daddy and let him know we love him and think about him all the time."

"Hey, Mom, check out my new Bakugan!" Finley fried the tender moment like a magnifying glass sizzling a spider in the sun. He wanted me to look at a red plastic ball that opened into a monster. It was just like one I threw from the car in South Africa when Finn kept pestering me from the back seat. I bought him a new Bakugan out of guilt.

We started in the direction of Federation Square, which my *Lonely Planet* guidebook called "a riotous explosion of steel, glass, and abstract geometry." The square was a gathering place for culture and protest and occupied a city block.

But first, I spotted a sign for a beauty school. Yes, they had a pedicure appointment open, and yes, it was essential enough to steal thirty minutes of tourist time in Melbourne. My feet had endured hours of standing, flying, driving, and months of neglect. I deserved a pedicure.

Twenty dollars later, my hoofs were massaged, buffed, and polished. Fiona got a free mini-manicure while Finley performed handstands on the next seat.

Afterward, I threaded rush-hour traffic like a game of

Disneyland bumper cars, minus the fun of bumping. It was stop, start, nudge, wave, mutter, stop, start, nudge, wave, mutter. Repeat ad infinitum. Putter down Elizabeth Street, then onto Lygon. I'd read about the right-turn rule requiring you not to creep into the intersection lest a tram inserts its front section into your car's midsection. I vowed never to drive in Melbourne again.

We putted to the Eastern Freeway, following our hosts' directions to her home near the small town of Wandin. I'd enrolled in an organization called *Servas* before leaving Spokane; it's a group founded on the ideals of peace, dedicated to forging connections between people from around the world. We could stay for free in a travel host's home for two nights at a time, in exchange for stories and maybe a bottle of wine and a trinket from our homeland.

I'd imagined Australia much differently: more wild and open. What I saw during the hour between Melbourne and Wandin was instead strip malls, traffic, BP and Shell gas stations, McDonald's and a fast-food joint called Hungry Jack whose logo looked just like Burger King's. If it weren't for Hungry Jack, we could have been in Spokane.

Except I'd never eaten kangaroo meat, watched Santa roll up to primary school in summer in a fire truck, or watched anyone play a didgeridoo, all of which we did while visiting with our first host family at their farm in Wandin. Kathi, a nurse, and her architect husband, Jack, had four children, and also tended sixty goats, a few sheep, and some cows. Fiona and Finley took turns bottle-feeding a kid. All of us chased the goat who escaped the pasture when one of six children left the gate open.

The Gundels lived in a large, modern, messy house. Clothing and papers exploded from every corner. They were generous with their time and their home, lending us their guest cottage down the driveway. I had enough privacy to color the roots of my hair one evening using a ten-dollar mix I bought in an Aussie supermarket. I set my materials around the edge of the pedestal bathroom sink and focused on the task beneath a single dim bulb. I scrubbed splooshes and swipes of dye that escaped, hoping our hosts wouldn't have a permanent reminder of their American guests.

After bidding farewell to our hosts, we headed to an area of Melbourne called St. Kilda. This is where Sean's brother, Steve, lived. I had seen Steve at Sean's funeral nine months earlier, but we didn't have much time to chat about life and catch up.

I remembered the event as two sets of moving pictures: one fast, one slow; one hazy, one in sharp relief, like a Polaroid picture that starts as a fuzz of nothing and develops to reveal a story. With everything moving so fast, I was still trying to read the emotional temperature of Sean's family after the service. I recall Steve's presence and the way he looked at me as if he wanted to say something more than, "I'm sorry."

Sean had told me about when Steve came to live with him in Grand Rapids. Sean was working as a videographer for the TV station where we'd met. His brother was able to freelance there, and in the process broke a fifty-thousand-dollar camera. Steve was known as "Thor" because of his height and long thick blond hair. One time, Sean said he and Steve went to see the Grateful Dead, where Steve sold someone a half-eaten sausage in the parking lot. I tried to find the family resemblance in Steve's face, but I couldn't. Sean looked nothing like Steve. They had different fathers. Sean was short, with light brown hair, while his younger brother and two sisters were tall and blond. But they all shared an upbringing and a history.

Facebook Post: December 15, 2010 at 7:36 a.m.
Dawn Picken: We stayed with a different Servas host last night in burbs east of Melbourne. Retired couple who've traveled a lot. They were even in Spokane last year! I got a kick out of their pics of the Bloomsday Runners and Davenport hotel. And Anita and Joe have an ideal home for guests: bedrooms in a new separate wing, immaculate bathroom, stocked and available pantry. I could live there. Nice folks, too.

The kids and I helped ourselves to corn flakes, milk, and toast for breakfast, which we ate at Anita and Joe's black granite counter. Fiona swiveled on her barstool and said she wanted to return to the playroom, where our hosts had crates of toys for grandchildren.

"After brekkie, we're going to finish our house," said Fiona. Already the kids were picking up down-under slang, the way Australians abbreviated everything, so that afternoon became arvo and registration became rego. I noted other Aussie phrases in my notebook, like, "Good on ya," "G'daymatehowyagoing?" and the ubiquitous, "No worries, mate!"

Anita was intrepid—she'd backpacked through Southeast Asia

and spent weeks traveling Europe with a grandson. Joe preferred to stay home, though he sometimes traveled with Anita, who appreciated his French language skills. Joe had attended a French school in Egypt growing up.

Our hosts treated us like family members who'd wandered back into the fold after disappearing for several years. They had, in fact, offered up their home for a week if we wanted to stay that long. My breakneck itinerary didn't offer much time in Melbourne, but we enjoyed their place and attention during our two-night stay. Anita wrote a list of contacts she had in New Zealand, did our laundry, and offered to watch Fiona and Finley while I rode to the market at the Caribbean Pavilion in Joe's white convertible MG.

I went to fetch Fiona and Finley from the playroom after our talk. Finley had lined up a menagerie of animals that we had seen on our African safari: giraffes, zebras, rhinoceroses, lions.

He instructed Fiona, "Pretend I'm the daddy, and they have to go with me." Daddy. The kids always wanted to go with daddy. Or be the daddy. They wanted Daddy.

So did I.

We left Anita and Joe's house for a trip into Melbourne, where we met Karlene. She was in her early thirties and had once lived in Spokane. Her husband died of melanoma, leaving her to raise their son, now almost ten. Karlene was quick to laugh and flash her broad smile beneath a wide-brimmed straw hat. Her red hair and freckles meant she, too, was a candidate for skin cancer. She said she was careful to slop on sunscreen for herself and her son, especially since this corner of the world was close to Antarctica and its ozone layer hole, permitting more UV radiation to reach our skin than it would in North America.

We met at Queen Victoria Market, a historic landmark spread over two city blocks, where vendors sold everything from Italian limoncello to Chinese Barbie doll copies with the unfortunate name of *Benign Girl.*

We talked of what life had been like since her husband died.

Karlene said, "It gets easier with time. But each day that passes brings you further from the life you shared together."

I thought about the last ten months—the whirl of widow's duties, travel planning, shopping, sightseeing, child minding…the rare moments when I could stop to think. And cry. The busyness of life is like the Colorado River in spring—its eddies rushing, churning, spuming forward. Only rarely had I allowed our life raft to moor inside a quiet cove. Only inside the cove did I realize Sean's voice was fading, or I'd forgotten which leg first had the disease, or how many skin grafts the doctors had performed. Or took just a moment longer to evoke the hue of his eyes or the pattern of his thinning hair. Time unseated detail and faded my mental pictures. Time was heartache's balm. And memory's thief.

Karlene had returned to university to study public policy and recently started dating. She was the second young widow I had spoken with face-to-face. We shared similar challenges: raising a child alone and navigating the new waters of dating. "What's that like?" I asked.

"It's different than I thought it would be. Getting those first butterflies in your stomach is surprising. And nice. I never thought I'd be giddy again over a guy. It's early, but I'm enjoying it."

I rolled this idea around like a marble in my mind. After waiting until age twenty-nine to marry and then having children with my love, I never expected to jump on the dating wheel again. That was so twenty-something. And I was forty.

Facebook Post:

Dawn Picken: *Drove from Melbourne to the Great Ocean Road. Sounds impressive, till I tell you I zigged when I should've zagged and saw the Great Hay Fields and Forests Road for an extra half hour. Let's say the signage here is confusing. Had hardly any problems navigating South Africa. I was relieved when an Aussie told me, "The signage is really* *bad here. They don't tell you what road you're on unless you're at the beginning or end."*

We overnighted at a holiday park in Lorne, along the Great Ocean Road. At the beach, Fiona and Finley scuttled like sand crabs. Fiona cupped a brown jelly creature in one hand and rushed toward me. Her mouth was open wide, as if laughing and shouting at once. Her missing top two teeth channeled a happy pumpkin expression. Finley charged at me like a five-year-old cheetah. His mouth, too, was wide open, ready to eat the world with shiny milk teeth.

Their energy and vitality stirred pride and sadness. I was the only adult to witness these rushing sprites. My sturdy fairy children. I looked to the side. Only air and ocean. Sean's absence was as palpable as grains of sand beneath my toes, as the space before my lonely lips. I still had conversations with him — in my head. Ours was a one-sided relationship, and mine was the only body at the table. Or in the bed.

Facebook Post:
Dawn Picken: *Drew half a heart in the sand tonight along the Great Ocean Road. That's how I feel many times—half-hearted. I'm always missing something (someone). The picture didn't last long. Fiona came and completed the heart, then drew a big maze in the sand with a path leading to Daddy. Kids and I walked it. Then played freeze tag on the beach.*
JN: *I'm sure you will be able to trace Sean's love throughout your life, all of your life. You're in our thoughts.*

Facebook Post:
Dawn Picken: *Since I last wrote, we drove the Great Ocean Road to Warrnambool to stay with a Servas host, Jenny. She put us up on just a day's notice, fed us dinner, then drove us out to a wildlife reserve where kangaroos, emus, and koalas*

roam free. No koala sightings, but we saw dozens of kangas and a few emus. (Finn said, "I can't remember that name. I'm calling them ostriches.")

Fiona's grief emerged in ways less obvious than mine. One day, somewhere between the Twelve Apostles — rocks that rose above the Southern Ocean — and Port Fairy, Finley chirped from the back seat, "Mom, Fiona's crying!"

"Honey, what's wrong?" I asked.

"I wanted to hold the bunny one more time," she said.

The bunny. The one the kids on the farm had killed at our first host family. That creature would never draw another breath, but my little girl longed to cuddle it again. I searched for some scrap with which to console my six-year-old, while focusing on the road, keeping us safe between a yellow stripe of paint on one side, rocks and crashing ocean on the other.

"Oh honey," I said. "The bunny was dead. You have to let it go."

I knew it wasn't that easy.

We flew to Sydney after that, where I had arranged a month earlier to stay at the home of Sean's old high school classmate. I remembered when, two years earlier, Sean had received an e-mail from Roger saying he'd moved the family from Cleveland, Ohio to Sydney, Australia.

Sean said, "How cool is that? We should do that one day. I'd like to live in Australia or Ireland. Maybe we could try it for a year. I'll ask Roger for more details."

Without benefit of research about how to immigrate to Oz or the Emerald Isle, it sounded doable. Simply box up the house and move to Sydney or Dublin. Kind of like buying a new pair of pants. If we didn't like it, we'd pack ourselves and two kids back into four or eight suitcases and return home. But Sean never made that move. His transition across the great divide had been more permanent.

I bypassed downtown Sydney in a small black rented Hyundai. After driving in Melbourne, I pinky promised not to attempt navigating Sydney traffic after we'd reached our destination.

Roger and Elise and their two kids lived in a four-bedroom home with brick driveway and swimming pool in Gordon, in Sydney's leafy northern burbs. They would be leaving tomorrow on a three-week car trip of Australia. The kids and I would have the run of their house, with its American-sized refrigerator and clothes dryer. I wanted to weep at our good fortune.

We ate pancakes and bacon with our hosts before they drove away in their doll-sized Honda Jazz. Half their luggage sat on the roof; the other half was crammed into the back hatch and smooshed around the kids. They even left us wrapped Christmas presents.

Driving around Gordon, visiting shops in the city and strolling boardwalks at the beach, I saw few Christmas decorations. A garland here, a Santa there. By American standards, it looked like the Grinch had come and stolen Christmas. And the weather was not "Chestnuts roasting on an Open Fire," "White Christmas," or "Walking in a Winter Wonderland." None of the old holiday standards applied to the land of Oz. It felt like a Christmas-free zone. It was eighty degrees outside, sunny—not a boot, scarf, or a mitten anywhere. I was drunk with good fortune, like someone had spiked the eggnog (which would be much too rich for Sydney summer heat). It would be my first Christmas without Sean, and someone had cancelled the occasion. It had been a lucky accident in the lucky country: visit the Southern Hemisphere, where seasons are upside down, and nothing is as it should be for the holidays. If it helped me not miss Sean so much, I'd take it.

Chapter 23

Christmas in Oz

Late December, 2010

My favorite childhood Christmas was the year a blizzard kept us from taking the hour-and-a-half drive to Grandma Picken's along Ohio's North Shore. While I loved going to Grandma's—with all my cousins, aunts, uncles, neighbors and smells of almond cookies, sauerkraut balls, croissants, and honey ham—the year of the blizzard provided a chance to cocoon with our own family. Just the four of us, half a convenience store's worth of snacks, and a fire in the fireplace. We were allowed to open a single gift that night: a Nintendo video game. At about nine and eleven years old, my sister, Heather, and I played Ladybug and Q-bert until our parents told us we had to go to bed or Santa wouldn't come that night. We conked out in our own beds rather than in the car on the way to Ashtabula. Being home made our Christmas that year.

Now I was in Sydney. Only three of us. Missing Sean. Sleeping in strangers' beds in a home filled with travel guides, including books about traveling abroad as a family. My hosts had circled the world, venturing to India and Indonesia and other places I'd only read about. I was glad to be settled in one place as the holidays approached rather than sleeping on the road.

Still, there were things to see and adventures to be had. The kids and I walked the famous Sydney Harbour Bridge. It took about twenty minutes to stroll a mile from one end to the other. Fiona and Finley complained like disgruntled mules. By the time we finished the crossing on this bluebird day in one of the world's shiniest, happiest cities, Fiona was sputtering with unhappiness and fatigue. I took a picture of her, so I could show her later what a tantrum looked like. This wound her up even more: the picture features a little girl, long bangs parsed into strips like damp mop strands, wearing a pink and white striped tunic bought at a Paris flea market. Her flared nostrils and downturned mouth had been cultivated through years of practice. And the eyes — oh, those gray-blue eyes: they looked straight at the camera, an expression of anguish from a little girl who had lost her best dolly. Or friend. Or daddy. One hand reached up as if to block the camera lens.

"You're acting like a baby," taunted Finley. "See? I'm not crying."

"I have the worst family in the world!" Fiona cried. "Nobody's nice to me. I wish I had a different family."

All the posed, smiling pictures from our travels told less than half the story. The times we waited in line, got lost, packed, unpacked, packed again, queued relentlessly at the airport, were hungry or achy, felt blasé, blank, or fatigued, angry or sad — we rarely captured those times on camera. I did take notes, though. Sometimes I shared these moments on Facebook for empathy, suggestions, but mostly, to show our trip was *real*.

Facebook Post:
Dawn Picken: *I can't tell where Finley's manipulation ends and mourning for Sean begins. He's thrown a giant fit tonight*

after a day of being especially naughty. He was saying, "You hate me, you hate me." Then he told me his heart was beating too fast and that he forgot what his dad looked like. He demanded I sleep with him (as usual). I'm not equipped for Finn; maybe I should return to university for a psychology degree.

TS: *Hang in there. This is his way of mourning. He wants to make sure that no matter how bad he is you will never leave him. Discipline like usual, follow with hugs and kisses.*

MK: *Dawn, you are a good mom. Finn is working it out his way, which can be hard on you. The important thing is he's talking about his feelings. Many boys his age don't have a vocabulary to do that yet. I hope tomorrow is a better day for all of you. I miss seeing you and the kids but love hearing about your journey.*

After a self-imposed time-out, I put down my book and returned to the room where Fiona and Finley were sleeping (rather, should be sleeping, but weren't).

I cradled Finley's chubby five-year-old cheeks in my palms and looked into his blinking, baby-man eyes. "Honey," I said, "it's gonna be alright. Your heart is fine. We're still a family."

I pulled a photo collage of Sean from behind my back. A photographer friend, Barb, made it for Sean's memorial, and I had carried extra copies around the world. I showed the kids the pictures, explaining what each one was. "There's Fiona and Daddy on top of the sand dunes on the Oregon Coast"; "That's a picture of all of us in our kitchen in Spokane when you guys were two and four"; "That's Daddy at work with his video camera."

The kids studied the page, eyes widening in recognition.

"Daddy!" said Finley. "I remember!"

"Yes, honey," I said. "You can look at this again in the morning. It's late. Get some sleep, okay?"

December 21, I broke from my tradition of waiting until the last minute in each location we visited to scatter some of Sean's ashes. With a week remaining in Sydney, we caught a ferry from Darling Harbour to Circular Quay. That's where I pinched some of my late husband's gray dust between thumb and forefinger. I glanced to my left, right, behind me to see if anyone was watching before flinging human remains into Sydney's harbor. All clear. Everyone else on the ferry was either snapping pictures or checking phones. We were about to pass before the Opera House as Sean's particles landed on the water. "Look!" said Finley. "I see a Daddy head in the water. It's growing!"

We crashed in front of the TV at Grapevines B&B our first night in Hunter Valley. I wanted to save my strength for the grueling day ahead: sipping, swallowing, spitting. Maybe not spitting. The guesthouse owner brought us a stack of DVDs including *Finding Nemo*. I had forgotten the fish went to Sydney. The kids saw the Harbour Bridge and Opera House and squealed in delight.

"We were there!" yelled Finley. Our travels had been validated by Disney.

I splurged on a horse and carriage ride: for sixty-five dollars per adult and forty dollars per kid, we'd be chauffeured to three of Hunter Valley's wine estates. Fiona and Finley played in the grass near tasting rooms of Mistletoe Wines. With no need to drive anywhere, I was free to sniff and sip Shiraz, Semillon, and Chardonnay. One winery owner from Buffalo, New York told me she didn't miss snowy Christmases.

The tasting room manager at Iron Bark Hill gave the kids orange juice, coloring sheets, and colored pencils. She then told me my half bottle of blended red was on the house. The kids and I ended our day's tour with a visit to the Smelly Cheese Shop, where Fiona and Finley snarfed the most pungent of French blues, Australian wasabi cheddar, and Italian Gorgonzola said to contain "liberal striations of greenish blue mold."

Facebook Post:
Dawn Picken: Not gonna pretend I'm okay with the fact that this is our first Christmas without Sean. He should be here; Fi and Finn should have a father; I should have a husband. However, I can't imagine a better place right now than Australia. The setting, the weather, the differences are comforting. I've found great joy in staying at the home of Sean's old high school friend. And we're there thanks to Sean. He continues to give. It's so like him.
DW: Dawn, THANK YOU for your total honesty, and just always sharing what is on your heart. It gives many of us the realization that—hey, it's okay to express our sadness and pain and release it to those who love and care about us, which

sets us free to help others.

SB: *Yes, all those firsts really, really suck. I love, love, love that you'll meet Vanessa. I, too, cannot think of a better place for you to be.*

Sarah had connected me via e-mail with an Aussie named Vanessa. Sarah and Vanessa met at a conference for the MISS foundation, an organization for families who've experienced the death of a child. Sarah suffered the stillbirth of her daughter, Grace. Vanessa lost a daughter, Layla, at one day old. She used her skills as a video producer and writer to create an award-winning documentary about grief and hope.

Vanessa invited us to join her and her two children Christmas Eve after expressing her thoughts in an e-mail:

I am so sorry for that loss and how much it must have wrenched your life apart as well as the children's. We can bear our own loss, but it must be so hard to see the children cope with their own grief. I love what you are doing.

Facebook Post:
Dawn Picken: *Finally got kids into bed at 10 p.m. last night after arriving back home from the church service. Told them they had to be asleep so Santa could come. Fiona asked me, "Did you ask Santa for anything?" "No, I didn't," I told her. "How about Daddy?" Fi asked. Gulp. "Do I want Santa to bring Daddy back? Yes. Yes, I do want him to bring Daddy back."*

Sean and I had shared twelve Christmases together. Twelve seasons of baking, buying, wrapping, and tree-cutting. We attended Christmas Eve services at St. John's, the scent of pine and incense mingling with memory and music. Tears would well in my eyes while singing "Angels We Have Heard on High," and "Silent Night." All the Christmases I'd ever lived would wander up one arm, down the other, into my core, and down through my feet while standing on the heated tiles inside the Cathedral's enormous sanctuary. Ghosts of holidays past whispered and sang. For a while, each Christmas seemed better than the last.

This Christmas, I woke around 6:30 a.m. to finish wrapping presents. Fiona and Finley appeared an hour later. Fiona wore blue and lavender Dora the Explorer shorty pajamas; Finley had a pj top borrowed from our host family emblazoned with lizards.

Facebook Post:
Dawn Picken: *Merry Christmas (morning) from Australia, mates! Fi and Finn have just finished opening presents. Somehow, Santa found them. He knew, however, that we're traveling light, so he didn't go too crazy. Six presents versus 26. No one noticed.*
SF: *Merry Christmas to all of you. I ushered the four o'clock children's service and just knew that Fi and Finn would have been right up there helping Margaret with her sermon if they had been here.*
LC: *Merry Christmas, Dawn! Shrimp on the barbeque for you for Christmas dinner?*

On the advice of an experienced widow, my original plan had been to keep the day low-key, with just the kids and I together.

But that plan was foiled by Vanessa. She had called and invited me to Christmas Eve mass at her church. "They have a live nativity, and it's very casual," she added.

"Absolutely," I said. "Sounds lovely."

"Oh, and would you like to come to brunch Christmas morning at my mum's place? She lives in the Eastern suburbs with a view of the harbor."

How could I resist?

We met Vanessa and her two kids at mass. We sat in a courtyard between the Catholic school and the parish with hundreds of Aussies, enjoying the remnants of a sunny day, singing Christmas carols (including "Rudolph the Red-Nosed

Reindeer") and watching as a live donkey, two sheep, and a dog were led into the nativity scene. As I sat and took in the service, I thought about the duties I'd relieved myself of this Christmas:

I did not send out seventy-five photo cards with a year-end letter.

I did not sift through four boxes of Christmas ornaments Sean and I had collected for more than ten years.

I did not buy presents for anyone but my two kids.

I did not host or attend pre-Christmas parties.

I had been happy as a traveling spectator. As long as someone told me where to go and when to be there, I would bring the champagne.

Vanessa's mom, Anne, lived in a beautiful condo overlooking Sydney Harbor. The sun sparkled on the water as we ate fruit salad, crepes (slightly burned), and drank champagne. Fiona and Finley played with their new friends, Frankie (Francesca), age five, and Raf (Raphael), age eight. We moved on to Vanessa's sister's home around the corner for more family and more food: tiger prawns, mango salad, rice salad, spinach salad, lettuce salad, asparagus, turkey, roast beef, and pumpkin, followed several hours later by a dense plum pudding that Henry, Vanessa's brother, set on fire.

Before dinner, one of the family remarked they usually set an empty place at Christmas for people who are no longer there, and that we had taken that empty spot. Sean's gift: his spirit continued pulling the kids and me in unfamiliar directions, drawing us into new experiences with new friends.

My favorite Christmas present was from Vanessa, who gave me a typed letter and a bracelet. She wrote: *This bracelet is a symbol of connection. To know what it is to feel grief. To know what it is to feel alone in that grief. That connection can then be passed along to the next person you meet. Happy Christmas, Dawn. I recognize it is a sad one for you and the children also. My wish for you is that these two states can reside together in peace.*

Fiona and Finley played for hours with balls, in the treehouse, on the swing, on the trampoline, with toys I pried from their hands shortly before 8:00 p.m. "I don't wanna go!" said Fiona. "I wanna play with my friends!"

It had been a not-awful Christmas. I hadn't cried. Is that winning? Maybe not, but I'd set the bar for successful holidays at ground level.

Facebook Post:
Dawn Picken: *At a park near Sydney today, the kids and I queued to pat a koala. Its handler said, "This koala's name is Sean. Spelled S-E-A-N."*
"See, kids?" I said. "Daddy's come back as a koala."
I looked into Sean's gray eyes and allowed myself to wonder. He moved one paw slowly, as if trying to exit for his next eucalyptus fix.

Facebook Post: December 31, 2010 at 9:48 a.m.
Dawn Picken: *Planning to jam in around Sydney Harbour with 1.5 million other merry-makers to ring in the New Year tonight. They have a fireworks celebration at 9 p.m. for families. Taking the train, of course. Love the train.*
DS: *Hey, Dawn, are you coming back to Spokane? I hope so.*
Dawn Picken: *That's the plan (back home to Spokane). The renters move out of our house in August, so we'll have a place to live any time after that.*

I dragged the kids from the comforts of the house in the burbs—away from toys, TV, and geckos to ride the train to Sydney for New Year's. We arrived at 2:00 p.m. because I'd read in the paper it could be packed. I wanted a good seat.

We arrived about six hours too early. Fiona and Finley took turns running, coloring, whining, "I'm bored!" and eating the picnic I'd packed, plus five-dollar mystery sausages inside pieces of white bread. I took pictures to pass the time: Finley pretending to sleep in the grass, both kids coloring, Finley and me at the harbor's edge.

I moved our blanket three times in hopes of securing the perfect vantage point—a patch overlooking the six peaks of Sydney's Opera House. In the end, it didn't matter because we stood for the fireworks.

I considered the night a success not because Sydney's fireworks were stunning (they were), but because no one got lost, and the kids fell asleep immediately after their bedtime snack.

Facebook Post: January 1 at 1:47 a.m.
Dawn Picken: Happy New Year, everyone!
LR: We spent New Year's with a mother and son from Australia. They were very interesting and of course the ACCENTS.
Jeffrey Neuberger: Happy New Year, Dawn, from winter wonderland. Saw the Sydney fireworks on TV last night—amazing. Thought I saw you and the kids! I'm sure I did.

I barely stayed awake long enough to read Jeff's comment. We had a long day of travel ahead tomorrow, and I still had to do laundry, pack, and clean. I was sad to leave Sydney. A two-week stint had convinced me I could live there happily, if not for the fact that a two-bedroom house cost around a million dollars. But you never get the real story about a place on holiday, do you? It had been a snapshot in time. A tiny window for a new widow.

Facebook Post: January 1 at 1:57 p.m.
Dawn Picken: We fly to Christchurch tonight. We'll spend 10 days on the South Island before landing in our temporary home on the North Island. New Year, New Zealand.

Chapter 24

Rough Start in New Zealand

January, 2011

At Sydney airport, I couldn't find a luggage cart, so I carried a backpack and wheeled a large suitcase. I asked the kids to roll one small suitcase each. This worked for about ten seconds until Finley got bored. Fiona took up his slack. We arrived at the departure desk, where I didn't see our flight listed. We were three hours early — maybe they hadn't started check-in? I shuffled the kids to a coffee stand, where I nursed a latte and doled out biscuits. I resisted the urge to buy a glass of wine. I needed to be alert to run the airport gauntlet of departure counter, security screening, and flight boarding.

Fiona, Finley, and I queued for five minutes before I realized WE WERE IN THE WRONG LINE. Shit. No problem, we'd just zip over to the other counter. The queue held maybe twenty parties ahead of us, so it shouldn't take long, right? Wrong. Wrong, wrong, wrong. Forty minutes later, I was still standing in line while Finley and Fiona played with kid games mounted on a nearby pillar. What could possibly be taking SO DAMN LONG? Forty bag shuffles and three "Fiona, stand where I can see you!" later, I was face-to-face with the agent empowered to remove the luggage albatross from my neck and send us to the Land of the Long White Cloud, New Zealand.

"Oh, we have a problem," said Julie, the airline employee. I'd heard that phrase before about a third of our flights. One time, the airline failed to assign us seats. Another time, agents became confused by the fact the kids had two middle names. You'd think I'd have learned by then not to panic. But I was not ZEN. I was ZEN's polar opposite, ACK. I could feel my face getting hot and my pulse start to pound any time an airline employee said, "Oh, we have a problem." Our problem this time: lack of an entry visa and an outbound ticket from New Zealand. The country's list of requirements for entry, which I had read and reread online, stated you must have a visa, outbound ticket, *or* proof of means to buy an outbound ticket. Since we were unable to secure visas before leaving the States (I did apply—my application was rejected because I applied too soon, and we couldn't apply while traveling because you must send away your passport), I was going with Option Three. But Julie's airline apparently didn't know about Option Three.

"Oh, no," she said. "Immigration in New Zealand will need to see you've already booked a ticket out of the country." (Note to travelers: Tourism NZ wants you to visit. Government NZ wants to ensure you leave.)

"What about showing proof you can buy the ticket?" I asked, feeling more feverish and jittery with each syncopation of my heart.

"No, you need to have purchased the ticket," insisted Julie. Our flight was due to leave in forty-five minutes, and we might not be on it. Julie said the only way around the situation was for her to sell us a fully refundable ticket.

"How about to Sydney?" she asked.

"Sure, whatever," I replied.

"You can cancel the ticket and get a refund as soon as you leave Immigration in New Zealand."

Nineteen hundred dollars later, we were cleared for take-off. Almost. First, we had do something I'd not had to do before: enter immigration screening to leave Australia after filling out three forms. Card for me. Card for Fiona. Card for Finley. *Where have you been? How much did you buy? Why did you come?*

The Aussie immigration agent was a nice enough bloke. "Hey, yoa missun yoa teeth!" he tells Fiona with a smile. "Yep. I sold them in exchange for two kangaroo hearts and a koala pelt, which I've packed in my suitcase." I didn't say that last part.

"Good on you!" said Aussie Agent. "Have a nice trip."

At the gate, airline employee Julie, the one who'd hastily sold us nearly two thousand dollars of airline tickets, scanned our boarding passes. "They're so cute," she said, looking at Fiona and Finley. Then she asked, "Where's Daddy?"

"Daddy's in heaven. He's dead," Finley replied matter-of-factly.

Julie's face fell as she responded, "Oh, I'm sorry. Well, have a nice trip."

We did, in fact, have a nice trip. I used the last of my Aussie currency to buy sandwiches to silence our rumbling stomachs and wine to dull the buzzing in my head. Two and a half hours after takeoff, we landed in Christchurch, New Zealand. Our Kiwi Adventure awaited.

Not so fast. The agent at immigration demanded the electronic itinerary for our outbound journey. It was the print-out Julie promised we didn't need. "Oh, no," she'd said, after I asked about getting a receipt. "Immigration can see that in their computer. You don't need a copy."

Bullshit. The nice lady at immigration said she couldn't see any such thing. Good ol' Julie had just been trying to get me outta there, because our flight was boarding, and she had to work the gate. And I had been too harried, trying to keep the kids from jumping on the luggage belt, to stomp my feet and insist on a receipt for our two-thousand-dollar tickets.

By the time we sailed to the front of the immigration line (someone waved us through to the family queue), it was midnight, and Fiona and Finley were running the length of a picture mural with scenes of Aotearoa: whales, dolphins, mountains. Finn started beating the whale. "No, Finley, no!"

Meanwhile, Immigration Lady cut us a break, allowing us into New Zealand. "But you really do need the electronic receipt for your ticket," she said. I'd just spent a huge amount of money on tickets I hadn't actually needed.

Next, we queued for customs. Like Australia, New Zealand has rigid standards about which items you can bring from abroad, specifically, food. The safest bet is not to bring anything to eat. But I had learned that was unwise when traveling with Fiona and Finley. After checking online, I learned you can, in fact, BYOF (bring your own food) into NZ. It just can't be anything fresh (fruit, vegetables, meat, cheese). My tactic was to declare everything.

"Look at my bag of snacks," I'd say to anyone wearing a uniform at the Christchurch airport. My Tim-Tams (Australian chocolate sandwich cookies), crackers, jam, chocolate, and my peanut butter passed inspection. No one asked me to explain my African fertility statue (you must declare wood products, too), which I bought for a friend in the States.

We quickly regained custody of our luggage and were off to find a taxi to take us two miles to our motel. I had chosen this particular motel because they advertised a free airport shuttle. Not for us though. Even though the January 1 holiday had passed (it was, after all, past midnight on January second), the shuttle wasn't running. The motel's owners recommended we catch a cab. The kids and I prowled the taxi rank like burglars casing a business.

"How much for a ride to the Airport Lodge Motel?" I asked.

"Oh, that's close. They have their own shuttle," said drivers one and two.

"It would be very expensive," said drivers three and four.

"Can you give me an estimate?" I asked. Nope. Lots of shaking heads. I explained to the kids no one wanted to take us to our motel because it was so close.

"I don't like New Zealand!" said Finley. I couldn't disagree.

I remembered the name of a taxi company, Gold Band, recommended by the motel owner. I approached the driver at the end of the queue.

"Can you take us to the Airport Lodge Motel?"

He eyed me with disgust. "Really? That close? Really? For cryin' out loud! Ugh."

"So, will you or will you not take us there?"

"Ugh," he grunted again. He motioned to grab our luggage, which I interpreted as, "Yes, I'll drive you bloody tourists to the motel." Five minutes and many more grunts later, we were there. The ride cost the equivalent of sixteen US dollars.

After a coma-like slumber at the motel, life in Kiwiland improved. We grabbed our rental car, a 1990s Nissan Sunny with "El Cheapo, loved by Jucy" plastered on the doors. The car had already seen 135,000 kilometers. We visited Christchurch's Botanic Gardens, where we picnicked along the river ("Mom, I'm tired of peanut butter sandwiches," moaned Fiona, who, by that time, had eaten about ninety-nine of them on our world tour). The garden not only featured the equivalent of plant haute couture, but also a kiddie splash pool and playground. Fiona slipped in a mud puddle and fell while running. "MAH-MEE! I'm wet!" No worries. "You're changing into your swimsuit, anyway," I told her.

After a couple of hours, I lured the kids from the water with ice cream. I wanted to see the city center, a fifteen-minute walk. Fiona and Finley stretched that to forty-five minutes. First, they stopped to climb a giant tree. I was exasperated. I just wanted to GET THERE. Why was I always on a schedule? What was the rush? "Come with us, Mom," said the kids.

I relented, scaling the tree just in time to catch the eye of a passing tourist tram operator, who was narrating, "This tree is one of the oldest in Christchurch. Oh, and look, there are a few kids in there. Oh wait, one of them's the mum!"

We did reach the city center, where I bought a SIM card that provided a local number for my phone. My first call in New Zealand was to our hosts for the next two nights, Betty and John. Betty provided directions to their house, saying, "It's pretty easy, really." "Pretty easy" is my directional kiss of death. Way-finding's a cinch when you've lived in a place for years, or even weeks. But when you've just arrived, navigating a crisscross of one-way streets becomes a case of "you can't get there from here." And I was too cheap to pony up the extra eight dollars per day to rent a GPS. I circled Christchurch a couple times, finally finding the magic road (Colombo Street) that would lead us from town to our hosts' home in Governor's Bay. We passed crumbled buildings along the way, remnants of the magnitude seven earthquake that had shaken Christchurch in September 2010. Unlike the quake in Haiti in January 2010, which killed hundreds of thousands of people, no one had died in the 2010 Canterbury quake.

Betty had warned, "When you get to the driveway, don't stop. Just put it in low gear and keep going. It's quite steep."

The driveway pitched at such an extreme angle, the kids' feet pointed skyward as we headed up and up. Not that they noticed. Fiona and Finley were fast asleep. Jenny greeted me with a hug, as if we were old friends. We'd only corresponded via e-mail a couple of times. She and her husband were part of Servas, the same organization we'd used in Australia. They were one of the only hosts able or willing to take in our party of three during the holidays. It was, after all, January 3, when many Kiwis were away on holiday or hosting their own families. Betty helped me lug bags up two flights of stairs to a two-level house perched on a hill, with a stunning view of shimmering water and green-brown bearpaw-shaped hills rimming the bay.

"Do they have toys?" asked Finley. It's his first question when he enters any new house.

"Yes," said Betty. "We have lots of toys we keep for our grandchildren."

In seconds, the kids were entranced with a plastic kitchen set, wooden train, and Legos. There was even a rooftop patio perfect for playtime.

And I got to talk to grown-ups. It would be my first extended adult conversation in several days. I might never shut up. Betty told me her daughter had been an AFS exchange student in Whitefish, Montana. Whitefish was only a few hours from home in Spokane. Sean and I had skied there. And I, too, had been an AFS student (in Luxembourg).

"Our daughter traveled five years, all over the world," said Betty. "I think being an exchange student helped give her the travel bug."

Betty also had a son whose wife was battling breast cancer. The cancer had spread. Cancer knows no geography. In places we've traveled, from France to Ireland to England, Switzerland, Spain, Luxembourg, Africa, Australia and now, New Zealand, I listened to these stories, thinking we're the same fragile humans who love our families, get sick, get our hearts broken. Knowing life is short and fragile, we string together moments like pearls, praying the cord won't fray, sending our treasure skittering across the floor.

The evening was still warm, and Betty had made breaded fish for dinner, plus salad and green beans from her garden. Finley fondled the beans with a fascination normally reserved for chocolates or hard candy. He held one over his plate and squeezed peas from the pod. "Look!" he exclaimed. "They're pooping."

The next morning, over a breakfast of cereal, rhubarb-orange sauce, and Betty's thick homemade white bread toast, Finley said to our host: "You should have your teeth fixed." Oh. My. God.

"What did Finn say?" asked Betty. She hadn't heard.

"He just wants some milk," I responded. "I'll get it." Hadn't I told Finley not to comment on people's appearance?

We left Governor's Bay after a two-night stay to drive four hours to the middle of the South Island. Our destination was Dansey's Pass Holiday Park. It was owned by American expats, friends of Sean's old friends in Maryland. The park lies next to the burbling Maerewhenua River, tucked into the Kakanui Mountains of North Central Otago. Its large, open green lawn is a place the kids could run and play games. There was a playground with a trampoline, flying fox (zipline), and games, plus TV in the lounge for rainy days. It rained the second day we were there, so I took the kids to the pool in Oamaru, forty-five minutes by car.

When it was time to leave the pool, Finley pretended not to hear me. "FIN-LEEEE! IT'S TIME TO COME OUT! FIN-LEEEE! I'M LEAVING WITHOUT YOU!" Would I really leave him behind if he didn't get out of the pool that instant? No. Was I desperate for a simpler life in a land where you only had to say things once? Yes.

I brought both kids into the women's changing room. I didn't

271

want Finley alone with a bunch of strangers in the men's changing area. "Come on, Finn. Help me get you into your shirt." Finley was distracted, looking at ladies coming and going, glancing at the woman nearest us. She shot us a disapproving look and said, "Did you notice there's a family changing room?"

I stammered, "Uh, yeah, but it was taken."

She huffed. "I don't appreciate a wee boy staring at me!"

Cut us a break. He's five, for God's sake. I just kept my mouth shut and hustled out.

That night, I tried to coax the kids into bed at nine thirty. It was twilight, and they were loath to sleep while any light remained in the sky.

"But I'm not tired!" said Finley.

"I am," said Fiona. And later, "MOM-EE! Finley won't let me sleep!" Finn wanted to crawl into bed with Fiona instead of sleeping in his own bunk.

"FINLEY!" I barked. "Why can't you leave your sister alone? Why can't you help us? Help me! Why doesn't anybody help me?"

As soon as I said the words, I gave myself a mental kick. No help? Bullshit. How many people's homes had we stayed in? How many people raised money to ensure I could pay hospital bills? How many people had watched my children, cleaned our house, cooked us meals? I had received so much help it was almost embarrassing.

Still, my throat started to constrict. There was a breakdown, as Boz Scaggs sang, "dead ahead." And I was in way over my head. Sure, I had help around the world, but I felt damn lonely. I couldn't do this on my own anymore. I wanted out. But I *had* gotten out. Way out. Outta Spokane. Outta the States. Outta my job, my church, my friends, my family. I was way out of everything, seven thousand miles from my old life. Did I want to go back to it so I could get some help?

I succumbed to the primal urge to spank Finley, swatting him with an open hand twice on his behind. It was not part of my discipline practice, not only because it demonstrates violence, but also, it doesn't work. The few times I'd lashed out in anger, I felt powerful for several seconds, like I had *handled* the situation. I had shown my kids who was boss. But that feeling always vanished like a firework into the night sky, and I was left holding the memory of a small, savage ember.

"You hate me, you hate me!" cried Finley. "I wish I was dead!"

"No Finn. Honey, don't say that." I was near tears.

"My heart's beating too fast," said Finley. "I forgot what Daddy looks like."

I invoked my Rule of Bereavement, which states none of us are allowed major discussions about Sean when we're tired or hungry. Wait until tomorrow. "I love you, Finley. Let's talk about this after you've had a good sleep and breakfast. I'm going to the kitchen to get something to drink. Go to sleep. Please."

I crossed the wide lawn to the communal kitchen at the holiday park. I would grab my half-full bottle of Pinot Gris from the fridge and pour a healthy glass. A tumbler. At 10:00 p.m., only a few campers were about, playing cards in the back room or washing dishes. One of the owners, Marjie, stood in the front room with a broom. Her hair was pulled into a kerchief. I delayed the wine grab. Might look bad.

"Hi, Marjie. Always working, huh?"

She said, "Well, there's enough of a lull to get some cleaning done."

"I'm glad we found this place," I told her. "It feels so remote. Very peaceful." *It would be if the kids would go to sleep.*

"It's hard being on your own with kids, isn't it?" asked Marjie.

Uh-oh. The lump in my throat started to make a repeat appearance. I could feel the tears trying to escape. *Pathetic. Don't cry, don't cry, don't cry.*

"Yeah, it is tough." I steadied my voice. "They're good kids, but they're a lot of work."

"I know you're only here for a few days," she said. "I wish there were something we could do to help you with Fiona and Finley."

Running. I hadn't run in a couple days, since leaving Christchurch. If I could run, I'd feel much better. "Actually, if you could watch the kids for an hour tomorrow morning, I could go for a run."

"Absolutely," said Margie. "We'd love to. Just name the time."

The run, three miles out of camp and back again, was life-affirming. I felt like me again. That night, we stood around a large campfire with other travelers. We were toasting marshmallows and chatting, when I met Leith, from Te Anau. We talked about how much our kids were enjoying this place, and I filled her in on our travels so far. "We're heading to Milford Sound next," I told her. "We're going to stay at a holiday park near your town."

"Join us for dinner while you're there," said Leith. "I'll give you my number."

I checked out the next day, presenting my credit card to Marjie, who waved it away.

"This one's on us," she said. "I have a feeling you'll be back."

We drove to the bottom of the South Island, staying on a dairy farm in Invercargill with Servas hosts. Finley swung from the multidirectional sign at Bluff, the southernmost town we could drive to before Stewart Island. London and Paris lay about 19,000 kilometers (11,800 miles) away; Sydney is 2,020 kilometers (1,255 miles). Cape Town is 10,500 kilometers (6,500 miles). All those cities in one round-the-world trip. Did I ever believe I would visit all those places? Yes, but not without Sean.

After a stop in Te Anau—including dinner with Leith, husband, Daryl, and two boys (whose dinnertime burping contest sent Fiona, aghast, to sit with the grown-ups)—we cruised the fjords of Milford Sound, raced down the luge track at Queenstown (where Finley told me I was "going too fast") and continued back to Christchurch, where we had just enough time to peek inside the enormous Anglican Cathedral, something we hadn't done during our first visit.

This is where we'd catch our flight to the North Island. The land of back-to-school kids, shorter and fewer trips, a base from which to accumulate bikes, toys, and hopefully, friends. Six months to cool our heels. A place of rest and relief.

Chapter 25

Finding Home

Mid-January, 2011

As I wound through the fern forests of the Karangahake Gorge en route from the Auckland airport, I imagined what this new place would be. I'd seen pictures online of Mount Maunganui, with its extinct volcanic dome sticking out like a lumpy green-banded exclamation point on the end of a skinny peninsula.

Highway Two cut through sister city, Tauranga. A sign proclaimed, "Mt Maunganui, 7 kms." I crossed the harbor bridge to enter Mount city limits. The arrival was underwhelming — to the left sat the port, its container ships flanked by metal silos, rock piles, and mountains of lumber. I smelled the industrial area before I saw it. I tried to discern what they produced: treated wood, petroleum, fertilizer? It didn't look like the seaside resort in the photos. I continued to Maunganui Road and navigated the roundabout at Golf Road, turning left. The house I'd rented was on Oceanbeach Road. After a few false turns, I found our "bach" (Kiwi for beach house). It was across the street from the ocean, which we couldn't see from the house, due to all the other homes crowded along the ocean side.

Despite the fact that it was impossibly small, the bach contained three bedrooms. I'd secured the place for six weeks, until I could find something more long-term. I found the key outside where the owner said she'd placed it, and stepped in. It was tidy, with the kitchen sink barely wide enough to contain a dinner plate and separate taps, one for cold and one for scalding water. Next to the bathroom, a dryer was mounted upside down above the washing machine. My room had a queen-sized bed. And a chest of drawers. And a closet! Finally, I could unpack my things and live like a settled suburban mom instead of a nomad. The kids marveled at having their own rooms in which to place an imaginary collection of new toys I had promised to buy them when we got to our new home.

One thing I didn't find were sheets. How could I make the beds? I called the real estate agent whose name was tacked to a bulletin board. I left a message on her voicemail and tromped to the main house, where the owner told me friends of hers were staying. Maybe they had extra sheets. I explained my predicament to the woman who answered the door. Thankfully, she found sheets.

"Are you alone?" she asked.

"No, I have my two kids with me. Their dad, my husband, died, and we're traveling around the world with a big stop here to rest."

Her eyes softened, and she said, "We're going out to Milano's down the street for dinner. You're quite welcome to join us. It's supposed to be good. Bring the kids."

I wanted to. The prospect of adult conversation was tantalizing. But I was exhausted, the kids were exhausted, and I didn't think we'd be good company. I told the neighbor thank you but not tonight and asked where the supermarket was. She said the cheapest place was Pak 'n' Save, in a place I'd never heard of called

Pāpāmoa. Her husband appeared behind her and provided directions. Or they suggested I try Countdown, which was more expensive, but closer. Countdown, it was.

I'd planned to grab something for dinner and just enough for breakfast the next morning. But I couldn't resist buying a week's worth of food. It felt luxurious to stock up after ten days of traveling the South Island. Not that we got much for $150. The price of milk shocked me: three dollars NZ per two liters, which equated to more than five dollars per gallon US. I could buy organic for that in the States. A two-pound block of cheddar cheese cost ten dollars. Beer was twenty-two dollars for a twelve-pack. I bought wine instead for seven dollars.

Fiona and Finley took turns seeing who could annoy me most, hopping in and out of the shopping trolley (Kiwi for cart), chasing each other down the aisles, and grabbing food from the shelves. Feral children.

Back at the house, the realtor delivered sheets, telling me that most people who rented baches brought their own. I fixed pasta and cheese for dinner. A glass of wine for me. I coaxed the kids to bed at 9:00 and started plotting my escape: I'd enroll the kids in a holiday program a couple days this week so I could get settled and buy a cheap used car. I'd connected with another Servas member, Brian, who lived just down the street. He had put me in touch with Ken, who ran a car auction for the Lions Club.

Facebook Post:
Dawn Picken: *A friend of my Kiwi Samaritan just called: He's found me a used Honda Accord with 60,000 miles for $1200 US. Says he'll buy it back from me when I'm done with it. Left to my own devices, I would have bought something with twice the miles and twice the price.*

Joy over the car evaporated like the sweat on my neck during the first test drive on an eighty-five-degree day. The little Honda's

278

engine sounded fine, but it was circa 1985 and lacked air conditioning. I couldn't even properly hang my arm out the window due to some Plexiglas bubble contraption, designed to reduce wind resistance. I bought the car anyway. At $1500 NZ I figured I could live with it for six months, even if it was a tiny orange two-door with no air bags. ("How many times have you used your air bags?" asked Ken during the test drive). The miracle of my car dilemma was Ken's friend, Brian, who offered to take my rental car back to Auckland, because he was flying out at exactly the same time the rental was due.

I had enrolled the kids at Mount Maunganui Primary School, a series of single-story, weatherboard buildings set among courtyards and a large, grassy sports field. It stood one block from the ocean. I took Fiona and Finley there a couple weeks early to see the school, talk with the principal and pay fees. Because I had no work visa (I didn't think it worthwhile to complete a medical exam and extensive application for a six-month stay), my ticket into the country had been enrolling my kids as international students. It had cost around $8,000 US per child for a year. I'd already wired some of the money from my American credit union, but because I had no Kiwi bank account, I would pay the balance in cash. The secretary's eyes widened as she accepted an envelope stuffed with hundred-dollar bills.

Pricey errand accomplished, we hit the beach, where the kids built sandcastles, then wandered the shoreline. It was a measure of my weariness and feelings of overload that I didn't immediately run after them. "There's a couple of kids down there," said a man with a Kiwi accent.

"Let 'em go. They'll return when they're hungry," was what I wanted to say. I had awoken that morning with a pounding headache, something so unusual for me, I rarely stocked aspirin.

Maybe asking the kids five times to do everything was taking its toll. It had been nearly a year since Sean died, and like so many other single parents, I was doing the work of two people. I was used to tag-teaming tasks with a parent partner. Through kid complaints, minor injuries, head parasites, infant surgery, tantrums, and tears, my husband had remained our anchor — the guy happy to spend most of his time at home. Solo parenting was like trying to move a sofa up a flight of stairs on my own. Every day. With two kids jumping on it.

I regretted telling Finley about my headache when he said, "I hope you're not gonna die." He blinked at me beneath long eyelashes, which nearly swept the top of his freckled cheeks.

Outside our bach, the kids found a mewling cat. "Mommy, we have to feed it!" they cried. "It'll starve!"

I owned a cat once, in Grand Rapids. It clawed my arm bloody during the first (and last) bath I gave it. I had the cat declawed. It meowed as loudly as a dog barks, and my elderly neighbors complained. "You want to buy a muzzle?" asked the pet store employee. "For a cat?" I bought the muzzle.

"I'm not allowed to own a cat again," I fibbed to the kids. "The International Cat Lover's Society will take it away."

"But how will they know where to find you, Mommy?"

"Oh, they'll know," I told them, but I bought the cat food anyway.

The intensity of the sun's rays, accumulation of months of travel, and running after two pint-sized powerhouses had made me sleepy. For the first time in a year, I was going to take a nap. In the middle of the afternoon. I announced my intentions to Fiona and Finley, allowed them to watch TV, shut myself in the bedroom and immediately fell asleep.

I was awakened thirty minutes later by a tearful Fiona, who was screaming just outside my room, "Mommy, Mommy, where are you?"

I bolted upright, flung open the door, and roared like a lion, "I was trying to sleep! I am *so tired*! Fiona, I told you I was taking a nap. I was *right here* the whole time. Why didn't you listen?"

The TV blared. The kids didn't hear me or had already forgotten their terror.

"That's IT! No TV for two weeks. And I'm not doing anything for you tonight except make dinner."

Maybe your daughter's afraid of losing you. The way she lost her daddy.

I was lethargic. And hot. I took my temperature—101.4. No wonder. What if I had another liver infection? The last one, when Finley was five months old, had required large doses of antibiotics, a CT scan, and several doctor visits. I had no health insurance in New Zealand. I didn't know anyone at the Mount. There was no one to watch the kids if I got sick.

The next day, I woke up and checked my temperature. Normal. No headache. I had apparently been suffering from a sunburn. We picnicked at the Mount Main Beach (in the shade) where the kids jumped waves, waded in shallow water, and rubbed their arms and legs into the sand to make angels. We climbed to the top of Mount Drury, a small foothill of the larger Mount Maunganui the town was named for. I struck up a conversation with a fellow runner as the Mount, all 761 feet of her, stretched before us.

"Can you run up the Mount?" I asked.

"Nah," she answered. "I think it's too steep to run up. Lots of people run around the base though."

There was a party across the road that night—loud music, young people traipsing in and out. If I had been young and childless, I would have wandered over. But a forty-year-old widow with two small children doesn't get many impromptu beach party invitations.

"Quite certain I'll never find love again," I told my journal. "Prince Charming may exist for sixteen- or twenty-one-year-olds, but not for me."

Our days consisted of reading street signs and guidebooks,

exploring, making footprints in the sand. Down the street at the beachfront home of the man who helped me buy the Honda, Brian strummed a ukulele while Fiona played with a box of toys left for the grandchildren.

"Should we have lunch here?" Brian asked his wife. "Do we have food in the fridge? What are we doing?" I brightened at the mention of a meal shared with other grown-ups.

They were waiting for their son to arrive from Auckland, and in fact, they didn't have food. Who doesn't stock their kitchen? I pictured my friends and neighbors in Spokane, with overstuffed pantries, fridges, and freezers full of Costco-sized groceries. We bought six-pound bags of frozen (saline-injected) chicken breasts, pizzas three at a time, and tortillas in a forty-count bag. Even with a half-full fridge, we'd still have enough lunch for a soccer team. That went triple for our Mormon neighbors, who stockpiled a year's worth of food for emergencies.

One time, when we were out of maple syrup, I told Fiona to ask the Smiths if we could borrow a little. Fiona returned to our kitchen triumphantly, like a fisherwoman who'd just landed a fifty-pound mackerel. "They said we could keep the whole bottle," Fiona said. "They have six more in the basement."

Back at our bach, Kelsey, a fifteen-year-old whose name I found on the library notice board, arrived to babysit. We had been in Mount Maunganui nearly a week, and I would finally get to climb the Mount.

Kelsey was thin, with strawberry-blonde hair. She wore a blue romper and, shortly after introductions, showed Fiona and Finley how she could insert the tip of her tongue into her nostril. The kids were enamored. Fi hugged Kelsey, clinging to her like a barnacle.

I parked a mile from the Mount, walked to the base, then hiked to the top. The track started as wood-bordered stairs, then progressed to uneven stone steps. By the time I reached the grassy plateau at the top of those stairs, I was panting. It provided an excuse to admire the view. White sand swept out in dual arcs from a rock- and tree-covered peninsula called Leisure Island (Moturiki in Māori). Twin beaches looked like two giant sand breasts. The ocean was cerulean and shimmering, like someone had sprinkled diamonds on top.

I had huffed, puffed, and panted uphill for forty minutes. I hadn't thought to bring water. I was rewarded for my efforts with a postcard panorama: a peninsula stacked with apartments and homes, sprinkled with green space; to my left, the Pacific Ocean rolling to shore; on the right, a multi-tiered cruise ship sat in the harbor. Matakana and Mayor Islands lay behind, like chess pieces on opposite ends of the board. *I get to live here for six months.*

The closest thing I had to a connection in that place was the phone number of a family who lived about an hour away in Whakatane. The Sampsons were related to a couple I met while working at the Spokane Chamber of Commerce. "You should connect with Gary and Alexandra," said my Spokane connection. "They have kids about the same age as your two."

When I returned from the Mount, I called the number and introduced myself to Alexandra (Alex for short), who immediately said the kids and I were welcome to spend the night. I couldn't pack fast enough. "Hey, kids, we get to meet some new friends. Their children are the same ages as you."

"What are their names?" asked Fiona.

"I forgot," I said. "We'll find out when we get there."

We entered the Sampsons' twelve-acre property through a long driveway, passing a small river, which rushed along the drive.

The family greeted us. The kids, blonde-haired and blue-eyed, were Bailey and Clay. They were exactly the same ages as Fiona and Finley, and all four immediately took to each other. Within minutes, they were bouncing on the trampoline and zipping down the flying fox.

Gary worked in the yard, and I sat in the large kitchen at the granite counter while Alexandra sliced strawberries. My mouth started watering as I looked at the plump jewel-toned berries. Alex was in her mid-thirties, with bright blue eyes and blonde hair. We found common ground in running and the fact that she and Gary traveled America for a year before having kids.

"I could live there again," she said, with a wistful smile as she tucked berries into a bowl.

The next morning, we woke to the sound of rain gushing in torrents on the roof. The Sampsons offered the use of their garage treadmill. After my run, I was prepared to face the day: January 23, 2011. It was the first anniversary of Sean's death, which I failed to mention until we were sitting down to dinner. I felt sheepish revisiting death. *Will I upset anyone?*

"Shall we light a candle or something?" asked Alex.

"Yes, that would be nice." I asked the kids if they'd like to say anything.

"Can I do the fire?" asked Finley.

"I miss you, Daddy," said Fiona.

"My friend's grandmother died," said Bailey.

"My friend's cat died," said Clay.

"We miss you, Sean," I said. "We miss you every day, but I'm glad you've brought us to this place."

That night, I composed "crap poetry," trying to corral and organize my feelings.

Un-happy Anniversary, Sweetie
Still Missing You

Sean,

It's been 365 days since you left earth and I'm still missing you.

A whole year without my right arm.

A whole year without the one who could make things right.

A whole year without the one who chose me to be wife and mother.

A whole year without the one who knew me best and loved me anyway.

A whole year. I'm still missing you.

I need you:

Hovering above a heaping bowl of cereal each morning.

Holding our children in your arms.

Retreating to the basement to finish a project.

Telling me how proud you are of me, of us.

Giving our children a bath at night when I'm too tired for the task.

Shoveling snow for an hour, twice a day, when the flakes won't stop.

Laughing at me and with me. Making me laugh.

Pitching our tent trailer.

Raising our son to be a man.

Mowing the grass.

Raising our daughter to be a lady.

Taking pictures to preserve our family's history.

Holding me in your arms, telling me everything will work out fine.

Reminding me I have an anchor in this world.

Reassuring me I'll never be alone.

Sean, I loved you for a decade as your wife. I'll love you decades more as your widow. I'll never stop loving you. We'll never stop loving you.

And we'll never stop missing you.

Chapter 26

Love and Live While You Can

Late January, 2011

I had planned to spend one night at the Sampsons' — we wound up staying three. I told our newfound friends to please visit us at the Mount.

Two days later, the kids and I visited our farmer friends, Joan and Gordon from Invercargill, at their bach in Whangamatā, a beach town on the Coromandel Peninsula. It was the day before Fiona's seventh birthday.

The bach was funky, with a large deck and a living room floor made of shiny, pressed particle board. I presented our hosts with fresh fruit from the Sampson family orchard before dashing to the supermarket to buy Fiona a birthday cake. Thirty dollars got me a small round black forest cake with chocolate frosting and maraschino cherries on top. I bought a cheap Chinese Barbie doll from Sunny's, the variety store down the street. On the box was written, "She make warm gift for client." I planted Faux Barbie, feet first, atop the cake. I also bought the kids their first boogie boards:

Finley's had a smiling, big-toothed shark; Fiona's featured a happy dolphin.

On the beach, the kids hoisted their boards in the air and the wind fluttered them like kites. The estuary turned out to be the place for kids, with its shallow depth and gentle current. Gordon played not only with his own granddaughters, but my kids too. I waded in the estuary up to my waist and discovered something trapped in the crotch of the tank-style maillot I had just bought in town. Shit, it was the liner you're supposed to dispose of before wearing. It was crumpled up down there. I waded even further into the water to surreptitiously hook one finger into the bottom of my suit to fish it out.

Gordon's six-year-old granddaughter, Caitlin, asked me to throw her. "Sure," I said. I struggled; she was around Fiona's age but about twenty-five pounds heavier.

Finley waved to me as he climbed aboard his boogie board. "Hey, Mom, look at this!"

At the bach, Joan and I talked about her bout with breast cancer. I told her my mom, too, had had the disease. Unlike Mom, Joan had a mastectomy, though no chemotherapy or radiation. She also had something in common with my kids: her dad had died when she was seven years old.

"I didn't understand what people meant when they said, 'Oh good, he's gone to heaven.'"

Me either.

Joan said she didn't have the energy anymore to keep up with her granddaughter. I offered to take all four kids into town so she could visit with a friend. Finley whined during the fifteen-minute walk down Achilles Road. "Are we there yet?" he asked.

"Not yet," I said. "Keep going."

I pushed the four-year-old in a stroller. Finley wanted a turn. "No, Finn. You're too crazy."

Finley shouted, "You hate me! You wish I was dead."

Salvation arrived at the playground, where the kids played together for forty minutes. I sought sanctuary in the shade with a book.

Later, on my own, I visited a pottery shop, where I bought a blue and purple stoneware serving bowl, along with two matching mugs as a gift for our hosts. I joked with Joan and Gordon that they could use the mugs for hot water when they shared a single tea bag. Either they both loved weak tea or they were very thrifty.

We feted Fiona's birthday a couple days early with a barbeque of grilled venison, modest presents (an art set from the beach shop), and the black forest cake with cherries and faux Barbie.

"What do you think, Fi?" I asked.

"I think it looks kinda weird," she said.

But it tasted chocolatey and rich. The kids asked for seconds.

We bunked behind the house in a "sleep-out," a garage converted into two bedrooms. At 6:00 the next morning, I heard banging. I was certain there was someone at the door. I got up to check. No one. That instant, I remembered I'd been having a beautiful dream: someone, maybe Sean, maybe Gordon, had appeared and told me everything would be alright.

"Did you knock on my door?" I asked Gordon later that morning, while we ran on the beach at low tide. He said no, he did not.

After a half hour of clean-up, we said our goodbyes. I was wistful, wondering when I would enjoy their company again. A month later, they let us use their bach when my friends, Leanne, Mark, and Jean visited from the States. I e-mailed and sent a card expressing thanks, but I never got a reply.

At the Mount, the kids and I met again with the primary school principal, who showed us to the kids' classrooms. Fiona would be with Mr. P in Room Eight. Finley had Ms. D, a young woman with chin-length brown hair who said, "Oh, Washington! I've always wanted to go and see the Smithsonian."

"Oh, we're from Washington State, on the other side," I corrected her. We got that a lot.

January 27, Fiona's birthday, she spent most of the day at the holiday program in Pāpāmoa. She wanted to bring treats for the kids, all of whom she had only seen twice before. I baked brownies and chocolate muffins, which delighted her. It was the simplest birthday ever.

I took the kids to see the movie *Rapunzel*, to which we were ten minutes late. I cried when Rapunzel sang, "Turn back the hands of time/bring back what once was mine." I wanted to rewind our own clock. Sean was mine. Ours. The months following his death had made him more like *something* I used to possess, rather than *someone* with whom I'd shared a life. We didn't get to keep him, only borrowed him for a time, like checking out a library book.

We visited the Anglican church down the street for the first time. Round the world, we'd done the same — popped into Anglican venues in Paris, London, South Africa. I sought familiar rituals of prayer and communion. Mostly, I sought community.

The small modern parish in Mount Maunganui had a projector screen from which we recited prayers and hymns. The kids and I were welcomed as newcomers and the congregation sang "Happy Birthday" to Fiona while she beamed beside me.

At morning tea, I met a woman named Maggie who told me she had a twelve-year-old daughter.

"Maybe she could babysit sometime," I said.

"Oh," said Maggie, "you're not allowed to sit until you're fourteen here. And kids can't be left alone until they're fourteen."

I flashed back to my law-breaking half-hour run in Te Anau. I had been so desperate for exercise, I'd told the kids the night before I that would run early the next day.

"If you wake up, just turn on the TV," I said. "Don't go outside or answer the door."

They slept through my run. Small mercies.

I took Fiona and Finley to a runner's group called the Hash House Harriers, which billed itself as "drinkers with a running problem." I'd hashed in Spokane, running with at least two hundred other people. Just a few dozen people, mostly walkers, showed up at a house in Tauranga for "the Hash." People with nicknames like "Two Humps," "Hash Pimp," and "Blue Virgin" chugged beer beforehand and sang raunchy songs afterward. They nicknamed Finley "Raspy" because of his Demi Moore-sounding voice. Fiona was dubbed "Toothless," thanks to her missing front teeth. I walked with the kids, telling them they'd get a dollar apiece for each kilometer. I decided later I'd revisit the Hash without kids.

I packed lunches for the first day of school: salami and cheese sandwiches with crusts cut off. Not thinking they needed swimsuits (referred to in New Zealand as "togs"), I left them out.

"Mommy!" said Fiona. "We swim after lunch!" Fiona explained the order of the school day: "We have morning tea (snack) at ten and have to eat for ten minutes at lunch before we play." An hour and twenty minutes of each day was usually spent outside.

Fiona said, "Everyone gets a buddy in my class. My buddy is Teegan."

I wished I had a buddy.

Except for the loneliness, I was having a blast. My Aunt Leslie, when I called her from Sydney, asked, "Has it been worth it so far?"

"Well," I said, "yes. All the people we've met, the places we've seen, the new thoughts I've had — those experiences are priceless. So far, I'm glad we left. I'm glad we're here."

Facebook Post:
Dawn Picken: *When you have one of those moments where you're so happy, you can feel your heart expanding, you must take a mental/soul picture to preserve the memory. Remind yourself you deserve this moment. Soak in the joy, because it won't last forever.*

SF: Certainly soak in the moment and memorize it. That is how you preserve them. Then, on the bleaker days, pull out that memory and see it again. Maybe even share it around. Then it is even more preserved. You deserve those moments.
KF: Between those great moments, take time to vacuum all the little micro-moments, like seeing a lovely flower, greeting the salesperson in the store with a smile, your children holding your hand. They are morsels of joy to carry us through. Roll them through your mind for the rest of the day like fine chocolate truffles.

Traveling and living abroad meant higher highs and lower lows. Until I settled somewhere (and we weren't settled yet), I would feel everything more intensely. Lack of home base left me restless, hyperaware, self-conscious. I was expanding my circle of friends and my vocabulary, learning a quirky version of English. Flips-flops were jandals; "supposed to" was expressed as "meant to"; "stroller" was "pushchair"; "popsicle" was "ice block"; "lots" was "heaps". It was a fine and tenuous existence, though I felt the walls of our tiny bach closing in after one month.

Facebook Post:
Dawn Picken: For the moment, I live in a tiny bach (holiday home) and drive a tiny car. I have a tiny wardrobe and a tiny pile of stuff. Sometimes, you must downsize your trappings to supersize your life.
JJ: It is amazing how much stuff we accumulate, but do we really need it?

In search of companionship, I joined a group called "Socially Single" at the Anglican Church in Tauranga. Their service with its rock band and theater seating was too modern and fundamentalist for me, but the congregation was large enough to house a decent-sized crowd of adults younger than sixty.

The singles group set off to the Te Waihou walkway, a path 4.7

kilometers along the upper Waihou River, whose waters ran clear and blue. I rode with Kaitlyn, who had been widowed ten years before. She told me her late husband had been two decades her senior, that he drained their savings before getting stomach cancer. Kaitlyn said she had dated but had yet to find "the one." Or would that be "the second one?"

After a walk through bush and a fern forest to an icy cold spring, I chatted over a sack lunch with Lee, a sixty-year-old whose wife had died from pancreatic cancer two years earlier.

"We had eighteen months after her diagnosis, and it was the most amazing eighteen months of my life," he said, leaning in, his light-brown eyebrows forming a straight line. He bit into his ham and cheese panini before continuing, "We really lived. I would stay with her in bed instead of getting up to check the rugby scores like I used to. I was present for her. With her. I wish we would've had that scare forty years sooner."

I wouldn't be hearing these stories if Sean hadn't died. My loss has opened the door to another world—one of heartache, longing, connection, compassion. I was compelled to listen and learn. And I'd give it all back for another day with Sean.

I took the kids to Rotorua one day, to Kuirau Park, to watch mud bubble and gurgle from the ground. Fiona insisted I ask a woman at the information center why there was so much geothermal activity around Rotorua.

"Because this is where the fire gods put it," she said.

Māori legend said a beautiful young woman named Kuiarau was bathing in the water when a taniwha (legendary creature) dragged her to his lair below the lake. This angered the gods above and made the lake boil to destroy the taniwha forever. After that, the bubbling lake and steaming land have been known by the lost woman's name (although the spelling has changed).

We sat inside a gazebo to soak our feet in hot, bubbling mineral water. Next to us was a large man whose brown skin and tattoos marked him as Māori. After revealing we were on a year-long trip following the death of my husband, he told us he was sorry.

"In my culture," he said, "we keep the body in the house four days, go to church each day, and have a hangi [meal steamed in the ground]."

I was fascinated by this custom. Before burial, it was common for the coffin to be left open so mourners could touch, kiss, hug, and cry over the tupapaku (corpse) to express grief. Māori believed the tupapaku should never be left alone. People traveled great distances for a tangi (funeral), and if it was at a marae (Māori communal area), speeches were made as if mourners were talking directly to the dead. Māori believed the body's spirit remained with the corpse until the time of burial.

In American culture, we hold a hasty memorial service and dispose of the body by cremating it or encasing it in a pricey casket made of polished wood or even steel, lined with satin. Around the time we arrived in New Zealand, the US death care industry contributed about $20 billion each year to the economy. The average American funeral cost $8,000 and lasted just a couple hours. We overspend. And under-grieve.

We stopped at Fat Dog Café for dinner on our way out of Rotorua. I ordered the kids chicken and fries. I got the backpacker special called "Only the Lonely," which includes a glass of wine and dessert.

Finley wanted to test his new scooter after dinner at Volcanic Park Playground overlooking Lake Rotorua. I watched floatplanes and black swans while Finn wobbled the scooter back and forth to gain momentum. The party ended when Fiona kicked Finley.

Life had improved since the kids started school. I joined groups like Mount Joggers and started making more friends. I met a runner named Lee who was also a writer and had lived in Wisconsin for four years. She reminded me of one of my Spokane friends — both were women who had one parent of Asian decent (Lee's mum was

Chinese), and like my friend Marti, Lee also looked about ten years younger than her age. We ran halfway around the base track, until a sign proclaimed it was "closed due to slips" from last month's heavy rains. We crossed the beach, ran to the tip of Leisure Island, then back to the main road, up the green slopes of Mount Drury. I wasn't used to running hills. It was torture. *Maybe I should join the beginner's group?*

Free grief counseling was advertised in a local paper. It had been a year since Sean died. And I was considering starting to date. Maybe there were loose ends to tie. At first, I was told I must wait three weeks for an opening. Ten minutes after my call, the receptionist phoned.

"We just had a cancellation," she said. "Can you be here at one thirty today?"

I met with Janet, telling her I wanted to use our six months in New Zealand to honor Sean's memory. "Maybe I'll find love again." Tears interrupted my sentence. This expression of hope reopened an unhealed wound.

Janet gave me a newspaper clipping about another local woman who lost her husband and started a group of widows with kids.

I listened to more tales of love and loss during dinner with Socially Singles. Jane's nonsmoking mother had died of lung cancer at age sixty. She told me she gave her mother a fatal dose of morphine. It was the first time we'd met.

"I felt like I'd murdered her afterward," she said, voice quivering. "But she was in so much pain. She had eleven tumors on her brain."

I prayed someone would give me a deathly dose if I were ever in such pain. Bearing witness to Sean's pain had shattered my faith in Western medicine's ability to comfort. It weakened the foundations of my hospice training, with its emphasis on pain management and symptom relief. I'd known Sean had felt pain, excruciating, unrelenting pain. I knew because he told me so.

"Why can't you make him more comfortable?" I had asked his surgeon.

"We can," said Doctor B. "But then we'd have to put him back on the ventilator, because we'd relax him to the point where he'd stop breathing on his own." Everything has a side effect.

Jane also told me about a friend who had died after her car rolled downhill onto her — she tried to stop it and was electrocuted on a fence. Her children, ages three, six and eight, found her.

What was the point of these sad stories? So our dead could shout from the grave, "Love and live while you can!" Even when the kids cried and complained. Even when your head hurt. Even when you had untangled yourself from friends, committees, projects, and the relentless struggle of life, then found more threads to weave into a new community.

And our old community still connected with us, virtually and face-to-face. In late February, we got three visitors from the States: "Grandma" Jean, who had babysat the kids from the time Fiona was around two, and Leanne, who used to work with me at WOOD-TV (where Sean and I met), with her husband, Mark. Jean unloaded a suitcase of presents for the kids and showered me with lunches out, plus paid-for groceries.

"You don't have to do that," I said.

"Now, honey," she said in her slightly raspy seventy-seven-year-old voice, "it's my money, and I can do what I want with it."

Chapter 27

The Last of Sean's Ashes

February, 2011

Jean watched the kids while I flew to Wellington to meet Leanne and Mark. We learned about another earthquake in Christchurch shortly after their arrival. It was much worse than the first one; the announcer on television at Discovery Lodge, where we overnighted before hiking the Tongariro Crossing, said sixty-five people were confirmed dead so far. The Cathedral's tower had toppled with tourists inside.

I called our travel host and new friend, Betty, in Christchurch to make sure she was okay. She told me the wall of the room where we had slept was cracked, a bookcase had crashed to the floor, and the stove was smashed, but they were fine.

Leanne, Mark, and I woke at 5:00 the next morning to catch the bus to the trailhead. We would hike the Tongariro Crossing, billed as the best one-day trek in New Zealand, with its lava rock moonscape, brilliant blue and green lakes, and tree canopy near the finish. Our twenty-two-kilometer (nearly fourteen-mile) route

296

included summiting Mount Tongariro, an active volcano. We descended into the crater and were halfway to the summit when my phone beeped. It was a text message from Amanda in Wellington, who'd also recently moved to New Zealand from Spokane.

"People r worried about u," she texted. "U should c yr Facebook wall."

I asked her to post on my wall I'm okay. I hadn't considered most people wouldn't have a clue I was on the North Island, hundreds of miles from quakes on the South Island.

Facebook Post: February 22, 2011
Amanda Fitch, posting for Dawn Picken:
Dawn is FINE! She is on a little vacation down in Wellington: she and I and her friends Mark and Leanne had lunch together yesterday and learned of the earthquake at the same time on the news. She is camping now and away from internet. Her kids are farther north, too, and wouldn't have been affected by the quake. We didn't even feel it, and she's off having fun unaware of your comments. No doubt she'll tell you when she gets back to her house!
JF: *Thank you so much—I figured she was away from the internet.*
LC: *Thank you, Amanda! I'm so glad I introduced you two! A big sigh of relief.*
Susan Picken: *Thanks so much for your post. I was certainly worried about my daughter and grandkids!*

I enjoyed not being in the driver's seat for once. I was a back-seater while Mark drove. At a Backpacker's in Taupo called Rainbow's End, we shared a meal of chicken, corn, salad, and bread and talked about blessings and obligations.

"You know, I left Spokane so soon after Sean died," I said. "It's not like I had time to repay the community, to even start repaying…" I trailed off, spearing a chunk of chicken.

"It's not about repayment," said Leanne. "Your friends don't expect that."

I believed most people gave generously, from their hearts, not expecting anything but "thank you" in return. When I gave, I wanted to know the gift was received: did you get the flowers? The check? Did it arrive okay? Thank you helped, though I didn't expect anything more. Isn't that what it means to give a gift? If we were truly generous, wouldn't most (if not all) of our giving be anonymous?

On the other end of the spectrum sat scorekeepers. Not only did they require a thank-you note, they secretly or openly felt they owned a piece of you after the fact. Whether it was your time and company or public recognition of their good deed or a favor, they expected this from you, because you *owed* them. In times of need, you couldn't immediately spot the scorekeepers though. It was like trying to find the pigeon in a flock of doves. Who had the time and energy?

"My theory," I told Leanne and Mark, "is you can't possibly pay everyone back, even if you retrace your steps. But I do believe in paying it forward. When the time comes, I'll know what to do and how to do it, because it had been done for me."

Leanne, Mark, and I drove back to Mount Maunganui, where we had one night at home before the next mini-adventure.

The six of us — my friends, plus Jean and the kids — headed to the Coromandel for a weekend. We visited Hahei, where Mark scooped up Finley and swung him around in the waves. Finley laughed, and even though I couldn't hear him over the crash of the waves, I could see his happiness. He got to play with a man. One thing I couldn't be for Finley was male. I was grateful for Mark's presence while still thinking, *It should be Sean.*

That night, we scattered the last of Sean's ashes (the last of what I'd brought; most of Sean's embers lived at Steph's house in Olympia) on the beach. The wind quickly changed direction, and Sean's remains blew back onto me. I didn't recoil, thinking of a young widow in Spokane who'd intentionally swallowed some of her late husband's ashes to have him inside her. But I didn't eat Sean.

We traveled the winding, narrow road from the Coromandel back to the Mount, where I farewelled my American friends with hugs and tears.

Throughout all our trips and connections made, I had been looking for a new rental house, which was proving more difficult than I'd imagined. Then I had the good fortune of being introduced to Amy by the woman who answered the phone at her work. "Where in North America are you from?" she asked, in the casual way of many Kiwis, so as not to offend Canadians or Americans. When I told her I was American, she said, "You have to meet our CEO. She's from the States."

Amy and I met for coffee at Starbucks, then took the kids to the beach, including her five-year-old daughter, Blythe. Amy was forty-six, with an MBA and a string of career successes. She was looking for a flatmate to help with bills on her new four-bedroom house in Pāpāmoa. We decided to try an experiment in communal living for two months.

We called Amy's house the "American Embassy." With double-glazed windows and three heat pumps, it was everything most Kiwi homes were not, namely warm in winter. Even though it never snowed at the beach, Amy warned it could still get cold, down to freezing. "And New Zealand homes don't have central heating," she said. "You could freeze in a bach during winter."

The arrangement worked better than expected. Amy was gone during the day, leaving me to write or do errands. I had dinner ready for all of us each night. We joked she was the husband arriving after a long day at the office. "Honey, I'm home!" she'd say. One of us cleaned the dishes while the other bathed the kids. I could even pop out to the grocery store at night while Amy was home. She could vent about the difficulties of having a Kiwi ex-partner and about her desire to return to the States; I could ponder my single status and whether it was time to re-enter the dating pool.

I'd met with the young widows' group one day at a Tauranga café. Seeing three of them gathered, hearing their stories, opened another universe for me. These women were six years, eight years past the deaths of their husbands and they were happily entangled in new relationships. One was even engaged.

"Where did you meet your partners?" I asked.

"Find Someone," said Andrea.

"Find Someone," said Denise.

"Find Someone," said Jo.

"What's Find Someone?" I asked.

"It's a dating website," said Andrea. "Really the best one out there. The other one's kind of sleazy; it has married men looking to fool around."

Having taken myself on two dinner dates and a couple singles' outings, I could see finding a companion would require a better strategy than walking around town. I signed up for the website. While most people spit-shine their profiles and downplay their baggage (i.e., fact they've had a life, which, face it, you do if you're over thirty), I laid out my situation, bulky emotional suitcases and all:

> I'm extroverted and adventurous. I enjoy running, writing, and relaxing in a cafe with a nice cup of coffee. I'm in NZ as part of a world tour with my children following the death in January 2010 of my husband (their father). I love to travel, although pushing, pulling, and dragging 2 small fries (ages 5 & 7) around the globe has its challenges. I'm an American from Spokane, Washington. I've lived in Europe and speak French and Luxembourgish. I write (sometimes) a blog: http://www.pickendawn.blogspot.com
> Sense of humor is key. You must be able to laugh at yourself

and along with me, too. Also, must love travel and be fit. I'd like to find someone who enjoys good food and wine and has seen some of the world. Must have a kind heart—are you the neighbor who helps others?

Buoyed by the fact my time in New Zealand was short, shrouded in a cloak of anonymity, I put myself out there to see what might happen. My confidence about the opposite sex after being widowed and traveling the world was about as high as ready-to-eat feijoa fruit (feijoas fall to the ground when they're ripe). I was forty, with two small children and a decade of memories as someone else's spouse. Who wanted that? Apparently, plenty of Kiwi men, because within two weeks of creating a profile on FSO, I had more than 100 "smiles" (a way of telling someone you like their picture, profile, or both) and dozens of messages. Some were stuffed with lazy prose and innuendo:

Porpoise 456:" Hi I like your profile if you are interested in finding out more about me please get back to me."

Uh, no. Thanks.

Some, like "Fiasco's" were plain odd, including multiple choice like we were in middle school:

"So, what about your ideal bloke then?
a) meek and mild
b) willing to throw you over his shoulder on the odd occasion
c) ready to put you over his knee should the need ever arise what a great smile you have!!!! Lovely"

Uh, no. Thanks.

This was from "Grasscutter":

"Hi i sent you a smile I see you have done tv I work on flim set if you are keen would like to get to no you."

301

Yeah, he could "no" me, alright. Why did I feel like everyone's English teacher?

Other would-be suitors took time to read my profile or better yet, read my blog to learn more about this person they wanted to chat up, feel up, or both.

"Come with Me" wrote:

"Good on you. I've enjoyed reading and laughing at the challenges you encounter and relate through your blog. I can so readily empathise with your experiences. I'm a widower with two daughters, my wife passed away four years ago from breast cancer. Just to let you know that things do get easier, as your children grow up. But it is great to treasure the moments while they are young and think that you are the greatest person in their world."

"Your Dream Man" wrote:

"Hi and welcome to New Zealand
I do hope you are enjoying the country and the people whom I am sure you will find very friendly I took the liberty of taking a look at your blog - tragic that you lost Sean so early in your and your children's lives together and if I can encourage you in anything at all, it is that while Sean was with you all he would surely have experienced what real love was and he obviously accepted and responded to that in an wonderful unconditional way...
Wud you like to talk??"

He sounded nice. But he lived in Auckland. Too far. Sorry.

I only met with four guys from FSO in person: two Scotts, one Dirk, and one Craig. The first three had potential. The last guy was the only bona fide ass-hat. Craig wanted to meet while he was in town from Auckland. I was fifteen minutes late to the pub. He sent the following string of texts in advance of our visit:

Wot r u wearing? Meet u outside. R u far away?
I thort we said 7:30
Shake yr booty then, as i look like a spare prick at wedding
waitn outside a pub
Eta?
B rite ther

I should have gone with my gut and said, "No way, José," but curiosity got the best of me. Mr. "Spare Prick" seemed — surprise — uptight. He had the neat, groomed appearance of a metrosexual, someone who probably spent more time in front of a mirror than me. I never heard from him after our first meeting. I would survive.

In each case, before a rendezvous, I felt I was interviewing for a job. Hair? Check. Makeup? Check. Resume? It was like I had fallen off the career ladder and was seeking to re-enter the workforce.

My references? Um, they're a bit dated, unlike myself, which has not been dated for a long, long time. Past experience? Yes, ten years of fidelity as a spouse. I can be a pain in the ass though. I'm impatient. Compulsively neat. Have been known to yell at my kids. Like to be alone. Maybe not as much as I thought.

Wading into the dating pool at age forty due to widowhood is not unlike getting canned from a job at the same age. You're "out there," but not by choice. On the plus side, I was more comfortable in my own skin after four decades of living than I was at age twenty. I had already done the marriage thing. The mommy thing. It was time to do the dating thing. The just-for-kicks thing. The thing that might result in someone's hands on me besides my five- and seven-year-old children.

That was why I briefly exchanged messages with a twenty-seven-year-old ("McDreamy"). I told my Aunt Leslie I was flirting online with a young'un, and she said, "Dawn, he's the same age as your cousin!" Yes, but I wasn't trying to channel a relative. McDreamy's picture was hot. His writing, however, was not. When

303

I asked if he'd like to meet for coffee, he replied:

> "Something has gone in my car and i had bn having a little trouble with it.i took it to my garrage and they plughed in the computer into a plug to see what was going on and the part is dying so i have to replace it as i use it every day.its a common thing and im upset to a extent to a degree. but it did sound good thou. give me bout to weeks or so to get this bill out of the way."

My flatmate, Amy, pointed out I wouldn't be dating him for his brains; this youngster couldn't string together a sentence. Or figure out how to meet for coffee while his vehicle was garaged. Another case of unfulfilled curiosity. I didn't need to meet a hot, dense toy boy (they reverse "boy toy" in NZ) just to confirm he was cute as a puppy but dumb as a brick.

So I shelved online dating. Because one of those dates — the one that felt least like a job interview and more like the rekindling of an old friendship — had blossomed into something wonderful.

Chapter 28

Chasing Rainbows With Dirk'66

I didn't expect to find love in New Zealand. At best, I thought I could have a few dates with someone who, unlike Finley, would not kick me under the table at lunch or dinner.

The Find Someone friend I kept going back to called himself "Dirk'66" (he was born in 1966). For a week before meeting face-to-face, we exchanged messages online. I told him I was about to take the kids to see Lionel Richie in New Plymouth.

> **Dirk'66 1:55 p.m. Mon 14 Mar:**
> *I would love to go to that concert, he has such good music. I even remember the Commodores where he started. (Showing my age haha.) I grew up in New Plymouth and go back there every couple of months at least. Went down to the Simply Red concert not so long ago, which was good. I have a few things on this week, but maybe you would like to have coffee at the Mount sometime?*

I would've loved to have seen Simply Red! Takes me back to the 80's. I'd love to meet for coffee. Your schedule must be tighter than mine, so pick times between 9-3 (except tomorrow and Friday, when I run with the Joggers in the mornings) and we'll try to find a time to connect.

It was St. Patrick's Day when I drove to Sidetrack Cafe, across from the Mount Main Beach, to meet Dirk'66. I parked my little orange Honda and quickly checked my hair and lipstick. I was about five minutes early and didn't want to appear too eager, so I stared out across the beach for a few minutes, watching the spindrift come off the waves, spray blowing from the surf. A man wearing a red t-shirt emblazoned with white waves and a surfer stood on the boardwalk. He was not much taller than me, with thick light-brown hair and a rounded gut. I wondered if he was my coffee date? I had hoped for an athlete.

I crossed the street, exactly on time. The guy in the red t-shirt was sitting at a sidewalk table. He saw me and gave a little wave.

"How you going?" he smiled. "I thought I saw you across the way. I'm Dirk." With his accent, it almost sounded like his name was Day-rk.

He asked me what I would like to drink. I told him I'd love a long black with steamed trim milk on the side (so American, ordering things on the side). He disappeared for a few minutes, leaving me to people watch and contemplate the meeting.

He seems nice. Friendly. Even if there's no love connection, I bet he'd make a great friend.

Dirk returned with a number on a skinny metal stand: 17. He removed his Ray-Bans, uncovering deep-set almond-shaped brown eyes. He looked squinty without glasses.

"So, how long have you been in New Zealand?" he asked.

"Just a couple of months," I said. He looked at me as if he was really interested. I told him about Sean, our world tour, about the fact that the kids and I were only staying six more months. I flung all the baggage onto the table, then tried to lighten my heavy history by explaining my plans were short-term.

"I really just wanted to find someone to hang out with while I'm here," I said. "I have a home and a life back in Spokane, so this is really just a break—a time-out."

Dirk said, "I can understand that. I'm kind of looking for the same. No pressure. It's nice to have someone to take walks with on the beach or have a coffee."

For an hour we sat talking about our former careers (he had been in sales but gave it up to train as a pilot), families (he had a brother in Ireland and a sister in New Plymouth), and our childhoods. I got goose bumps when he told me his father had died when he was six years old, the same age as Fiona when Sean died. His mum brought the family from their home in Ireland to New Zealand when Dirk was eight. Already, he and I had something in common besides coffee.

I registered for a workshop called "Relating Well in New Zealand." It was designed to help new migrants adapt to Kiwi culture. Even though I was only staying a short time, I would learn something valuable, meet new people, and gather more material for my blog.

The facilitators asked us to envision our own dreams by using markers and crayons on a large sheet of paper divided in 3 sections: #1 was "Where am I?" #2: "Where do I want to be?" #3: What's stopping me from living my dream? Initially, it seemed like a kindergarten assignment, but it forced us to tap our brains in a different way. When you're a chronic list-maker, creating a drawing (even one that looks like your five-year-old's artwork) can be clarifying. [My crude drawing features squiggly blue and green lines representing the ocean and a brown peak depicting a mountain. Two stick-figure children are jumping in the waves. In the foreground, I've drawn the back of my head and the back of a man's head.]

I invited Dirk to Quiz Night at a pub on Tauranga's Strand.

He agreed to come along and suggested bringing his friend Stuart, a fellow pilot.

I sat in a booth next to Dirk, who was wearing a blue and white checkered shirt. He smelled like aftershave and soap. He was clean-shaven and smiling.

"Hi, Dawn. Good to see you," he said. "You look lovely."

I was wearing a red top with a scoop-neck white insert I'd bought at the local Kmart, and the large round silver necklace with koru design I wore nearly every day. I had slapped on makeup and straightened my hair for the night. "Thanks. You're not so bad yourself," I said with a smile.

He bought me a cider, and I introduced him to my Hash House Harrier friends, whose real names escaped me because I never used them. "This is Bin Garden and Blue Virgin."

Dirk and Stuart laughed. They spent much of the night joshing with each other. My leg sometimes brushed against my date's, generating a tiny charge of electricity.

I was no student of Kiwi trivia, but I could be a scholar of Dirk'66. I didn't want the night to end. And I wanted time alone with this bloke.

I texted him the next day.
Last nite was fun. How 'bout a real date some time?

His response:
That b cool. How 'bout Amphora at the Mount 2moro nite?

Facebook Post: April 12, 2011 at 5:15 p.m.
Dawn Picken: If it's Tuesday, it must be "Two date Tuesday." Had a lunch date already. Have a dinner date tonight.
MA: I have been seeing someone. Very surreal experience. You will learn a lot more about yourself than you realized.

Enjoy yourself.

Dawn Picken: *OMG! Good on you! Yeah, this could be an interesting ride.*

KG: *All I can say is those are two lucky guys.*

I drove from Amy's house to meet Dirk for dinner. The Mount was busy for an off-season weeknight, so I parked my little Honda on Victoria Road, one block back from the restaurant. When I arrived at Amphora, my guy was waiting, dressed in jeans and a button-down light blue shirt. The maître d' showed us to a table at the front.

Over a meal of salmon (me) and steak (him), we talked more about our families, career goals (which I had shelved at the moment to look after the kids, plus I had no work visa), places we'd traveled.

Dirk's only trip to the States had consisted of nine hours in Santa Monica. "I met some rich woman with a convertible Porsche who showed me around. We saw Angelina Jolie. You kind of look like her," he said earnestly.

Dirk had also lived abroad for six or seven years, most of the time in London. "I got tired of the traffic and the two-hour commute to and from work each day."

"I loved South Africa," I told him. "I know it can be dangerous, but I never felt threatened on the tourist track. I'll go back someday."

He said, "I visited Cape Town with a mate for a month once. We had a great time. Drove the coast to Knysna, partied in the clubs."

"I did that too," I replied. "Except for the partying in the clubs. I was mostly traveling alone with the kids."

"You're a brave lady." The way he said "lady" sounded like a compliment, not like "old lady," but rather someone of stature.

We laughed about online dating. I told Dirk about the

metrosexual who messaged me that he felt like a *"spare prick at wedding waiting outside a pub."*

"He's a fool," said Dirk. "I wouldn't say or text that. Where do these guys get off?"

He had met a couple of young women, one of whom had turned into a friend. "She was too young," he explained. "I guess I wanted someone closer to my own age."

I described my single forays into town, how I got dressed up, hired a babysitter, and took myself out to dinner just to get away from the kids. "I can't imagine meeting someone that way though," I said. "Everyone who's out is with friends, or they're already coupled."

Dirk lowered his fork with its piece of medium-rare scotch fillet (rib eye, in America), looked into my eyes, and said, "It's upsetting to think of you going out by yourself. I would've loved to have been with you."

I told him being alone didn't bother me. Then why was I there, enjoying being with him so much?

For three hours, conversation flowed like sand through my fingers. Dirk listened — it was evident in the way he responded to me. I heard him, too, though my mind started to wander. My eyes moved from his eyes to his patrician nose, with its straight, slim lines, to his mouth. I start wondering what it would be like to kiss him.

He looks good. He smells good. He's funny. Those lips.

We ordered the apple and feijoa crumble with vanilla ice cream. I was more interested in lingering than continuing to eat, but when the dessert arrived, it was piping hot and fragrant. Steam mingled with vapors from the ice cream. The combination of sweet feijoa and tart apple danced in my mouth. It tasted like love.

We finished our dessert but were still talking at ten p.m. when the staff started vacuuming.

"They're cleaning up," said Dirk. "I'll pay the bill and we can go."

He walked me to my car. We stood face-to-face in the cool night air under a star-dappled sky. "Don't let me forget," he said. "I made you a CD—all those songs you wrote about on your blog. Thanks for having dinner with me. I hope I didn't burn your ears off."

Then, he said, "I'm kinda shy." A beat later, "Do you mind if I kiss you?"

"No, I don't mind." I leaned in.

He smelled like aftershave and apple feijoa crumble. His lips were just as strong and soft as I'd imagined. I stifled a whimper, feeling for a secure place to land, like *I* was the pilot seeking a safe patch to touch down. The sensation of the kiss reminded me of my first TV newsroom live shot: it was as if the top of my head were separating from the rest of me, allowing sparks to fly.

I could have kissed him a long, long time. But we were on a public street. And it was late.

"I didn't know how you felt about me," he said when he pulled away. "I thought maybe you wanted to be mates who met for coffee."

"I was wondering if we might kiss. I had a really nice time," I said, an understated way of explaining I felt sunshine and rainbows and electricity and warmth and home.

"Yeah, me too," he said. "Drive safely. And text so I know you got home okay."

I popped a cassette tape of Mariah Carey's *Music Box* into the Honda's ancient radio. She sang, "Anytime You Need a Friend." I cried two tablespoons of tears during the twelve-kilometer drive to Pāpāmoa. The rendezvous had left me conflicted. *How could I kiss another man? He wasn't Sean. What did that mean for Sean? He wasn't coming back, whether I kissed another man or not.*

I was still snuffling when I walked through the door of Amy's house.

"How was it?" she asked, rounding the corner. She spotted my red, watery eyes and stopped. "Oh, honey, what's wrong?"

"He kissed me," I sniffed. "And it was warm and wonderful." I was sobbing again.

Amy bent her five foot, eleven-inch frame to hug me. "It's okay. Don't feel guilty. You're still alive. Sean would want you to live your life. Don't overthink it. Enjoy this."

I knew she was right, though it felt like spitting on Sean's ashes to have had my lips locked with another man's. I was closing the door on my marriage, even though the door had already slammed when Sean died. *The union is over because he's dead. You're allowed to find another man.*

I woke the next morning with butterflies still dancing in my tummy. I nearly walked into a wall daydreaming about Dirk. I couldn't wait to see him again.

My friend Frankie was visiting from Spokane with her Kiwi boyfriend. I invited them and Dirk to Amy's for dinner. We chatted like old friends and watched Finley perform a series of steps he had learned at school called the Haka (Māori war dance that involves projecting your tongue, which Finn was really good at).

Dirk sat next to me at dinner, wearing jeans and a smooth white shirt. He was even more handsome than I remembered, with his strong jaw and thick carpet of hair I wanted to comb my fingers through. This time, I brushed his leg intentionally. It still felt electric. As much as I was enjoying our guests, I couldn't wait until they left so Dirk and I could be alone.

Frankie and her friend went at around 10 p.m. Amy was on a work trip to Wellington. The kids were in bed. Dirk and I were *alone*, sitting at the kitchen table together. I played a CD of techno Aboriginal music I had bought in Sydney. It's funky and entrancing. Dirk and I debriefed the night.

"I really like your friends," he said. "I got to chat to Walt for a while. Seems like a good Kiwi bloke."

"Yeah, I feel lucky to have had someone from Spokane join us for dinner. Glad they could meet you."

I told him the kiss the night before had taken me aback. "It would be like you not flying for a year and a half, and then suddenly, you're up in the air. Discovering you can still do it, that you still love it—that's mind-blowing. You've made me feel seventeen again."

He leaned in, the scent of cologne infusing his skin. I was drunk sniffing his neck. I nearly laughed, remembering a joke from the movie *Anchorman*. *What's that smell? Sex Panther. Works sixty percent of the time, all the time.*

The haunting beats and melodies of Aboriginal techno played as we made out. Suddenly, it was more than the goodbye kiss we had shared before. Desire took off like the Helios Probe at 154,000 miles per hour. *Whoa. Wow. This guy can kiss.* Hairs on my forearms stood at attention. My body tingled into a heightened state of alert. *Cells, we've gone Defcon Five. More friendly fire ahead.*

We kissed like that for a half hour but managed to resist the urge to move to the sofa.

"I better go," he said. "Before we…"

"I get it," I interrupted. "I don't want you to go, but you're right."

The next day, Finley was practicing his writing skills. He wanted to write to Daddy like I did on Facebook and my blog.

Facebook Post: April 18, 2011 at 10:32 p.m.
Dawn Picken: *I love Dad He plas with me We love you Hope yrer haven fun in the hivin Yrer in my hrt Yrer with me — Finley, age 5, all by himself. Finley wrote this along with a note to me and stuffed it into an envelope.*
LC: *Oh wow. What a Mom moment. Finn is too busy to give you a lot of "deep thought" windows into his soul, but look at that. Hope you're havin fun in heaven—that is so sweet.*

I took the kids to the South Island over the April school holidays. I had already planned a visit to see friends and explore places we hadn't yet been, like Nelson, Golden Bay, and Abel Tasman National Park.

The evening before we left, Dirk came for dinner. Amy watched the kids afterward so he and I could walk the beach. We made it as far as the dunes before stretching out in an alcove away from prying eyes. Dirk ran a finger along my side, from my shoulder, along my waist, down the side of my thigh. I felt the current running beneath my clothes.

"I'd like to kiss you all over," he said. I might have fainted, if I hadn't already been lying down.

Is he trying to say he wants to sleep with me? Don't be dense. Of course he wants to sleep with you. He's male. You've kissed.

During the South Island trip, I was mooning over the bloke. He, too, was traveling, visiting Wellington with family. We exchanged rapid-fire volleys of text messages. I pulled over to the side of the road when I heard my Nokia strumming its Gran Vals.

I can't wait to hold you again. And I think we need to make a play date.

"Mommy, why are you laughing?" asked Fiona. "What's so funny?"

"Nothing, honey. Dirk just sent me a joke."

"Can you tell us the joke?" asked Finley.

My heart was beating the conga as our plane touched down in Tauranga. We were home. Dirk was coming to get us. I grabbed the kids and trotted from tarmac to terminal.

"Hey, kids. Hi, Dawn," he said, grinning.

What? No kiss?

Dirk brought the kids tin lunch boxes—pink Barbie for Fiona and blue *Toy Story* for Finley, both filled with candy. He was scoring points.

At Amy's house, I told Dirk to make himself comfortable on the couch while I put the kids to bed. They had nearly been asleep during the ten-minute ride home. I was hoping they would conk out quickly. Neither grumbled as I tucked them in bed.

Dirk was sitting on Amy's brown sofa in front of the TV, wearing his navy-blue Abercrombie t-shirt and jeans.

"Can I get you something? Some tea?" I asked.

"Sure, that'd be nice." He flicked off the TV and turned on the stereo.

I made tea, brought it back to the sofa, and sat down.

"I'm so happy to see you again," I said.

"Me too," said Dirk. "I wanted to kiss you so badly at the airport, but I didn't want to frighten the kids."

He leaned in and kissed me. Soon, we had moved from upright to horizontal. And forgotten the tea. Who needed tea when we had those lips, those arms, that undeniable excitement between us? The way I was breathing, I might as well have been running up the Mount. My head started to spin.

"Oh," said Dirk. "Wow. This could really go somewhere. Do you want it to go somewhere?"

We'd been texting for two weeks about where we wanted this to go. I'd even talked to Amy about it before we had left. I wasn't someone to rush sex — I'd slept with three other guys in my life.

"What are you gonna wait for?" asked Amy. "You're only here for six months. Are you going to wait until two weeks before you leave to sleep with him? You're both grown adults. You're allowed to do this."

She had a point.

"Yes. Absolutely," I told Dirk. "Let's have a play date."

"When?" he asked.

"How 'bout tomorrow?" I said, smiling. I leaned over and kissed him. Hard.

Because we both had flatmates, we had to plan our encounter. It would happen at Amy's, during the day, while the kids were in school. I told Dirk to come over at eleven the next day.

"What should I bring?"

"How about a bottle of bubbles," I said. "No way I'm gonna do this stone cold sober."

On the day, I was nervous as hell. I texted Amy to warn her not to come home for lunch. She texted back a smiley face.

I dropped the kids at school, hit the gym for a quick workout, then showered at home. I'd nearly forgotten about condoms. Hopefully, Dirk would remember, but I couldn't take the chance. I remembered where I might have stashed one — in the garage, in the large green suitcase. I'd bought an Oprah magazine in Africa that had included a free condom as part of an AIDS prevention promotion. The suitcase nearly knocked me in the head as I eased it down. Back home, I used a cervical cap. But I hadn't brought it with me because I was certain I wouldn't be having sex for a very long time.

Dirk arrived at 11:00 with a bottle and a gift certificate to the Polynesian Spa in Rotorua. The bubbles needed chilling, so we stashed them in the freezer and drank red wine in the interim. We started making out.

"Let's move to the bedroom," I suggested.

Once there, he removed my jean leggings, long-sleeved shirt, and lacy turquoise bra. I was in disbelief over the weirdness of our morning tryst. I felt like a virgin again. This would be the first time I had been with a man since Sean died. I had drawn the heavy curtains in the bedroom, but there was enough daylight for both of us to see each other. No hiding in the dark, or even under the covers.

"You are so beautiful," said Dirk. I could feel the crimson rush from head to toe.

He whipped off his shirt, then his pants and boxer shorts. I was lying on the bed as he planted one knee beside me, saying, "Pretend I'm Brad Pitt."

Actually, I don't want to pretend. You're you, and I'm attracted to you and I don't want you to be anyone other than who you are. But I didn't say it, instead trembling beneath my new lover's touch, feeling the warmth of his skin, his round, slightly hairy tummy pressed against mine.

I took another look at this man in my bed. He had broad shoulders, a V sunburned into his chest, and a large tattoo on his upper right bicep.

Oh my God. I had no idea Dirk had a tattoo anywhere. I'm going to have sex with him, and I didn't know about the tattoo. What else don't I know?

"How long have you had the tattoo?" I asked.

"I got it for my fortieth birthday," he said. "I designed it myself."

The tattoo was a flaming circle of red, black, and green with a yin-yang symbol, and the koru, a spiral shape based on a new, unfurling silver fern frond that symbolizes growth and new life. I'd adopted the koru as my own symbol of new life after Sean's death and had recently bought a koru picture for my room. The room we were in.

"What's your middle name?" I asked, suddenly realizing I needed this piece of information before we proceeded.

"I don't have one."

I looked at him and grinned wickedly. "Let's say it's Leroy."

We kissed again and the fire — flames not unlike those of Dirk's tattoo — started raging.

I had no idea I possessed that depth of desire. I thought my sex drive had died with Sean. Once, a member of the young widow's group had said, "You'll find sex is still really important. It can even be more exciting. You know who you are, and you're more comfortable in your own skin." I hadn't believed her until that

317

moment.

That first time meant discovery of each other's bodies and a rediscovery of my own longing. It was passionate and awkward. There was the fumbling with condoms, the nervousness. Yet I would've cried with relief had I not been so completely satisfied and happy. We lay together afterward for more than an hour before I realized it was 2:45. Time to get the kids from school.

> **Facebook Post: May 3, 2011 at 3:55 p.m.**
> **Dawn Picken**: Have stopped bracing for bad to better embrace what's good.
> **SF:** Embracing is good!
> **Dawn Picken:** Have been embracing a fair amount lately.

Sex became part of the glue that bound us. If I had thought I was falling for Dirk before sleeping with him, now he really had me. I could think of little else.

Two months into the relationship, we were seeing each other every day. I started including the kids. We spent a day together in Omokoroa, where we picnicked at the water's edge and played at the playground. Dirk straddled a seesaw with Fiona and Finley on the other side. They squealed with delight when he bumped them up into the air.

Later that day, at McLaren Falls, Fiona caught us stealing a kiss. "Are you gonna marry Dirk?" she asked.

"No, honey. We've only known each other a couple months, and you have to go out with someone at least a year to really know them before you can consider getting married." I dispensed my philosophies about dating, sex, and marriage to my kids as if it was gospel. *No sex until you're an adult, as in, over eighteen. No marriage before the age of twenty-five. Or thirty. You can't have a baby until you're married.*

It's funny how much your faith in old ideas can change through the years. Looking back, I see someone whose idealism about marriage colored her view of relationships. Sean had provided the foundation for how I thought about love and commitment. His love had given me confidence and trust that would flow to new people in my life, regardless of whether they deserved it or not.

One day, Finley reported, "Jaden says his mum had him when she was nineteen. How is that even possible? You can't get married at nineteen!"

I might have to reword my lectures.

Another day, while driving the kids home from school, they asked how babies were made.

"You remember, I told you before. The man puts his sperm into the woman's egg."

"Yeah, I know," said Fiona. "But how does she get the sperm in there? Does she swallow it?"

I narrowly avoided swerving off the road and tried not to laugh too hard. I repeated the conversation to Dirk, who quickly responded to "Does she swallow it?" with, "Only if he's lucky."

Perhaps what struck me most about him initially was the uncanny, almost unnerving sense that I'd met him before. *"Don't I know you already?"* I thought. *"Wait a minute. Don't tell me. I know your type. Not to get weird on you, but I'm getting a real kindness vibe. A guy-who'd-give-the-shirt-off-his-back vibe. An easy-like-Sunday-morning vibe."*

Despite my intention to stall using the "L" word, the fact was there were way too many "I really, really like you's" being thrown around. They started feeling like old chewing gum against the roof of my mouth. I didn't want to keep chewing gum when I was hungry for a real meal. So I said it. And I confessed to Dirk that before him, fifty percent of the men I'd loved had died.

"How many men is that?" he asked.

"Just one," I told him. "I was only ever in love with two other men in my life." Statistically, it was not a large sample, but shouldn't fifty percent serve as a cautionary tale? Tangle with me, and your odds are grim.

Dirk must have enjoyed living dangerously, because he stuck around. We took our first road trip together, driving the hour and a half to the Coromandel Peninsula. We stayed in Whangamatā for forty-eight hours of child-free bliss. Amy, who will forever have my loyalty, watched the kids that weekend.

I booked a converted garage someone had turned into a wee holiday retreat. We had sunshine and rain, walks on the beaches of Whangamatā, Onemana, Tairua. We chased rainbows and ate Thai food, lemon-sized feijoas, and s'mores with genuine American graham crackers. We watched *The Simpsons* and *So I Married an Axe Murderer*. Listened to Earth, Wind & Fire's "September," "Got to Get You into My Life," Level 42's "Something About You," and the Commodores, "Easy Like Sunday Morning."

I was searching for ways to explain what felt like seventeen-year-old behavior. I found a 2008 *Time* magazine article called "The Science of Romance: Why We Love" that sought to outline why — biologically and psychologically — anyone, even a forty-year-old globe-trotting widowed mum with two small fries would succumb to love's charms:

> *"There's the transcendent sense of tenderness you feel toward a person who sparks your interest. There's the sublime feeling of relief and reward when that interest is returned. There are the flowers you buy and the poetry you write and the impulsive trip you make to the other side of the world, just so you can spend 48 hours in the presence of a lover who's far away."*
>
> *...Helen Fisher, an anthropologist at Rutgers University and something of the Queen Mum of romance research [said people:] "...live for love, die for love, kill for love. It can be stronger than the drive to stay alive."*

I had read that we love people not so much for who they are, but for how they make us feel about ourselves. If your partner (if you have one) makes you feel like the cleverest, most beautiful, funniest person on the planet, you're lucky. I started to think maybe after a run of bad luck — of witnessing suffering, keeping vigil at the hospital, navigating death, and the brokenness of a grieving heart — that I had gotten lucky, too.

My best friend from high school, Shelly, told me shortly after Sean's memorial service over coffee at Lindaman's in Spokane that I would, indeed, find love again. "When it's time," she said, "Sean will bring that to you." I wanted to believe Shelly was right. I knew Dirk was not Sean, and I didn't want him to be (there was the Kiwi accent and the tattoo). I refused to inhabit the past. I was not confused. Just bemused. And relieved to be in Dirk's presence. It was like a rush of oxygen entered the room when he entered. I threw my arms around him and silently prayed, "It's you. It's you. Thank God, it's you."

Not Sean.

Dirk'66.

I didn't expect to flip, or fall, for anyone. I wrote on Facebook in September 2009, when Sean was in the hospital in the Intensive Care Unit that I was "falling" into the ICU's abyss. It had been my seventh circle of hell.

A year and a half later, I was falling, floating, unsubtly and unmistakably in love. My seventh heaven.

After so many months as a Party of Three, I got a rush when I stepped outside myself and watched our Party of Four. The laughter, the playing, even the scolding (mine) assumed a different tone. Even if it was just for the occasional afternoon, those moments were precious — snapshots of a time when someone I loved was enjoying my children with me.

I didn't yet have the full story about our relationship. I couldn't write the ending. We were still at the start — a step-by-step-by-

321

kissing-by-storytelling-by-embracing start. I would let time do its sorting, peeling back each half of our love, His and Hers. Time would decide whether it was... substantial. Did we have a short-term slice of Kiwi nirvana or something to cling to for a lifetime?

A part of me was afraid. Those three little words, "I love you," were a gateway phrase: first, comes "I love you," then comes ICU and brushing your person's teeth. For some, love conjures images of wine, kisses, and chocolate cake. For me, love brings back memories of IV drips, the smell of rubbing alcohol, the feel of weak hand squeezes. Love had led to consent forms, decisions, ultimate responsibility, and ultimate heartache.

Was I going for Relationship, Round Two? Despite my fears, yes. I had tasted the impermanence of life, the bitter and the sweet. The allure of love was beckoning me to forge a new path. Evidence that life was short appeared every day: it looked like a Sean-sized hole. If my stint on earth were as brief as his, I would have just eight more years to live and love (though hopefully, I'll have many more than eight). I wanted to fill those years with companionship and joy.

I could not read, imagine or reason my way to love; I would have to get my hands dirty — get my heart dirty — to experience what it meant to love and be loved again.

Epilogue

I can't believe we're still here. The year-long stint away from America has turned into an eleven-year hiatus. My children have spent nearly their entire school careers in Aotearoa. I still dabble in journalism, writing a regular column for a regional publication while teaching business studies at the equivalent of a community college. I still miss TV reporting, though I have not explored the possibility of doing it here because getting to the studios requires a three-hour road trip. I have focused instead on parenting and maintaining a circle of friends, including my wonderful running and writing buddies, plus other awesome girlfriends.

I know what you're wondering: what about Dirk? Did you end up with the Kiwi bloke?

Yes and no. We did, in fact, continue to date, even when I returned to Spokane for four months to reacquaint with friends and to try to sell my house. I boomeranged back to New Zealand and married Dirk (not his real name, because you know where this story is headed) in 2014. We had two weddings—one in New Zealand and another in Spokane.

What has transpired in the decade between meeting Dirk and today could fill a couple more books. I won't bore you with details, but I will say he and I were vastly different people with less in common than I believed when we met. I have never regretted starting a new life in this beautiful country, but I would not make the same relationship choices today that I did in those tender early years after Sean died.

The silver lining is that the marriage, which at one time was a love match, also afforded our family New Zealand citizenship. For that, I will be forever grateful to my adopted home.

My children are healthy and thriving. I am happy with my work and with my community, though I am starting to get itchy feet now that the nestlings are about to fly.

Thank you for coming along on this journey. I hope our family's story has provided you a few moments for reflection and some laughs, too.

Acknowledgements

This book would not have happened without early encouragement from my former flatmate, Amy Thaler, and writer's retreats with Lee Murray, Jan Goldie and Piper Mejia. You all listened to me and believed in this project even when it was truly a shitty first draft.

Beta readers Becky Aud-Jennison, Leanne Suter, Cheryl Branz, Katarina Sörstedt, James Tubbs, Chelsea Dannen Maguire and Kate Mathias are among those who took time to read through later versions to help improve the manuscript. Doctor Debra Gore helped ensure the text was medically accurate. Dan Strawn provided a healthy kick in my metaphorical ass to finally publish, as he read an early draft of this book and was inspired to publish his own memoir. Kudos to him for beating me to it, and thanks, Dan.

New Zealand Society of Authors mentor Rae McGregor was instrumental in helping to polish what I had already written and nudging me to keep going.

Thanks and appreciation to the medical staff in Spokane and North Idaho who looked after Sean during his four-and-a-half-month hospitalization. Your compassion and dedication gave us precious extra months with him, even though the outcome was not what anyone had imagined.

Huge admiration and thanks to our Spokane family of friends, who showed what a caring community looks like. You know that people are selfless when not only do they pitch in during a crisis, but they also help you leave after the dust has settled. Our hearts will always live in the foothills of those mountains and they will always flutter watching the thundering Spokane Falls or driving I-90 over the ridge from the airport, where the city rises to greet us.

I am humbled and pleased at the outpouring of support our family has received from our Kiwi community. We have dived into the diaspora and will be forever grateful to have been embraced by so many people in Aotearoa. A special thanks to my mates at Mount Maunganui Runners and Walkers who have sustained me through runs glorious and ugly as well as several life crises.

Thanks to my mom, Susan, and my dad, Tom, for raising me to be independent. Lessons encoded early on have led me to this expat life, but we relish our long visits with you. I am forever grateful for the love you have shown me and your grandchildren.

I am heartbroken that Sean's sister, Stephanie died in 2015. She was my rock during Sean's illness and the world has lost another beautiful soul. Thank you, Steph, for injecting humor and light into a very dark time.

To Fiona and Finley, my greatest loves. You are my heartbeats. Thanks for making me a mom.

To Sean. Thanks for the life we shared. I miss you today and forever.

About The Author

Dawn Picken is an American expat living in the Bay of Plenty, New Zealand. She has spent more than two decades in journalism, first as a radio reporter for NPR affiliates in Oxford, Ohio and Springfield, Illinois, before moving onto television reporting and anchoring in Springfield, Grand Rapids, Michigan and Spokane, Washington. She has won numerous journalism awards for general and consumer reporting, along with fellowships from Investigative Reporters and Editors (IRE) and the Poytner Institute for Media Studies. She has written for publications including NZME, owner of the New Zealand Herald and Bay of Plenty Times as well as the Spokesman-Review and for commercial clients in North America and New Zealand. She teaches business and marketing and founded a storytelling event called Tell Me Tauranga/Kōrerohia Mai that connects locals with the art of true tales and with each other.

🐦@dpicken
Dawnpicken.com

CPSIA information can be obtained
at www.ICGtesting.com
Printed in the USA
LVHW041540271222
736006LV00004B/90